KNACK®
MAKE IT EASY

WINE
BASICS

KNACK®

WINE
BASICS

A Complete Illustrated Guide to Understanding, Selecting & Enjoying Wine

ALAN BOEHMER

Principal photography by Renée Comet

KNACK®
MAKE IT EASY

Guilford, Connecticut
An imprint of Globe Pequot Press

Copyright © 2009 by Morris Book Publishing, LLC

ALL RIGHTS RESERVED. No part of this book may be reproduced or transmitted in any form by any means, electronic or mechanical, including photocopying and recording, or by any information storage and retrieval system, except as may be expressly permitted in writing from the publisher. Requests for permission should be addressed to Globe Pequot Press, Attn: Rights and Permissions Department, P.O. Box 480, Guilford, CT 06437.

Knack is a registered trademark of Morris Publishing Group, LLC, and is used with express permission.

Editor-in-Chief: Maureen Graney
Editor: Katie Benoit
Cover Design: Paul Beatrice, Bret Kerr
Text Design: Paul Beatrice
Layout: Kim Burdick
Cover photos (left to right): Renée Comet, © Tom Higgins/shutterstock, Renée Comet, © shutterstock
Back cover photo by Renée Comet
Additional Photo Research by Anna Adesanya
Interior Photos by Renée Comet with the exception of those on p. 235
Maps by Melissa Baker © Morris Book Publishing, LLC

Library of Congress Cataloging-in-Publication Data

Boehmer, Alan.
  Knack wine basics : a complete illustrated guide to understanding, selecting & enjoying wine / Alan Boehmer ; principal photography by Renée Comet.
      p. cm.
  Includes index.
  ISBN 978-1-59921-540-2
  1. Wine and wine making--Amateurs' manuals. I. Comet, Renée, 1957- II. Title. III. Title: Wine basics.
  TP548.2.B64 2009
  641.2'2--dc22
                           2009024022

The information in this book is true and complete to the best of our knowledge. All recommendations are made without guarantee on the part of the author or Globe Pequot Press. The author and Globe Pequot Press disclaim any liability in connection with the use of this information.

Printed in China

10 9 8 7 6 5 4 3 2 1

Dedication:

To Brian McClintic, Sommelier and Chevalier du Crachoir

Acknowledgments:

The information contained in this book would not have been possible without the assistance of the St. Stephen's Wine Study Group of San Luis Obispo, California, whose monthly tastings over the past decade have uncovered a wealth of valuable knowledge.

Photographer Acknowledgments

A special thank you to Wide World of Wines, Pearson's Wine, and Total Wine for generously lending bottles of wine. To Steve Borko, who was willing to open some very old wines from his collection to be photographed. To the people at Sur La Table, who are always so helpful and generous. —Renée Comet

An additional thank you goes to:

Wide World of Wines
2201 Wisconsin Ave. NW
Washington, DC 20007
202.333.7500
www.wideworldofwines.com
Elliott Staren
Hugo Linares
Amy Neal

Pearson's Wine
2436 Wisconsin Ave. NW
Washington, DC 20007
202.333.6666
www.pearsonswine.com
Steve Silver

See additional photo credits on page 234.

CONTENTS

INTRODUCTION

If your home library contains only a single book on wine, this book would be an excellent choice. If a picture is still worth a thousand words, consider the lavish use of photographs and captions in this book that allow you to learn a maximum amount of useful information with a minimum of effort. The text here provides you with the most useful information in the most succinct fashion.

The scope of *Knack Wine Basics* is broad, encompassing the distinctions of each grape variety and major wine-producing region in the world. You will receive advice on every facet of wine enjoyment, from wine openers, glassware, and decanters to pairing wine with food, cooking with wine, and ordering wine in a restaurant. Recommendations are given throughout this book to guide you in finding the best wines at the right price point. Our Resources section links you to the top wine Web sites for education and wine sales on the Internet.

Wine and Culture

While wine has been associated with food and culture for thousands of years, the past century has seen a growing evolution both in quality winemaking and in its role as a complement to foods. Because we are paying closer attention to the quality of our foods and wines than past generations, we need better information on a wide spectrum of food and wine issues. Past generations paid little attention to such matters as glassware, optimum food and wine pairing, wine storage, and cooking with wine. A common mantra of the past has been "red wine with meat, white wine with chicken and fish." Today we are confronted by dozens of food and wine pairing possibilities. It's not enough to simply know that Chardonnay goes well with grilled chicken. We need to know which type of Chardonnay makes the best pairing—a lean, crisp Chablis? an unwooded Australian Chardonnay? or a full malolactic heavily-oaked American one?

Value Wines

There was a time in the lives of many people reading this book when all wines were affordable. Fifty years ago the great Première Grand Cru wines of Bordeaux could be purchased for under $20. Local wine shops in major cities stocked the finest wines of Burgundy—all at affordable prices because the demand was low. Today those wines cost hundreds of dollars or pounds and are affordable only by the very wealthy.

That said, there has never before been the plethora of quality, inexpensive wines that we now see on the market. Winemakers who attend to the value-oriented spectrum are highly trained and are making wines to exacting standards to fill that ever-expanding market niche.

Wines priced under $5 are flooding the market from Chile, Italy, and Spain. Many are perfectly sound, flawless wines and extremely good values for everyday consumption. The trick: overcropped vines, mechanical harvesting, and tank fermenting. These procedures lead to decent, if somewhat monodimensional wines without noticeable flaws. No need to turn up your nose because the wine costs $2 or $3. It may well be perfectly sound, just not very aromatic or complex.

Older Wines

It's commonly believed that older wines are better. That's true of certain wines, but not most. Wines made with the requisite structure for extended cellaring will undergo a transformation of aroma and taste over time. Many red wines will improve over a few years following bottling. Five to ten years on a typical New World Cabernet Sauvignon usually hits the optimum point. Most red varieties usually peak a few years after bottling and few dry white wines improve at all with age. White wines made in a leaner style fare better in the cellar than fat, oaky ones. Sweet white wines can last for many years. The key factor that influences wine longevity is balance. That refers to an optimum ratio of fruit and acid, plus tannins in red wines. If a red wine is deliciously fruit-driven but lacks sufficient acids or tannins, it should be drunk soon after its release. It will become flaccid and dull over time.

Wine, like all other living things, has a lifespan and a peak of excellence. Most wines worldwide are made in a style that drinks well soon after release; but many will improve over time—like people.

Older red wines carry a very different flavor and aroma profile. Over time the fresh fruit evolves into aromas and flavors of dried fruit and sometimes coffee, tobacco, leather, earth, dust, forest floor, and truffles. White wines may develop flavors of butterscotch and tropical fruit. These characteristics are prized by wine connoisseurs, but are frequently offputting for the casual wine drinker.

Paying Attention

Enjoying wine is like listening to classical music. There's a spectrum; some of it is light and easy, other pieces are more complex and more demanding of the listener or consumer. If you are in a social situation busy with conversation, the complexities of a fine wine are likely to be lost. Even a mid-grade wine may not fare better than a good value wine. Fine wines, like classical music, require focused attention. If your guests are going to be more focused on conversation, let the conversation be the dominant event.

Enjoying a fine wine is very much like attending a concert. You sit quietly and listen to every detail in the music you paid good money to hear. You try to catch as many details and nuances as you can. And the more you notice, the greater your enjoyment of the music. Fine wine demands the same level of attention.

The same advice holds for the dinner table. Dinner conversation can easily overwhelm the food/wine marriage you have tried so hard to achieve. The key is accurately assessing the proclivities of your guests. Known wine lovers will always pay close attention; casual wine drinkers may not.

Finding the Wine You Like

Looking at a wine display, consumers can be easily frustrated by the bewildering choice of varieties and obscure labels. Many people fall back on known varieties and miss out on lesser known wines that might be more to their taste or even less expensive. This book will provide a valuable resource for understanding the differences between wine varieties and regions of origin. You will learn how to interpret foreign labels that can lead you to an enhanced wine

experience. You will be armed with all the necessary information to make wise and cogent wine buying decisions.

Wine Pricing

Because wine prices fluctuate from vintage to vintage we use symbols to suggest approximate price ranges for the wines we recommend in this book.

$	Under US$20
$$	$20–30
$$$	$30–40
$$$$	$40–50
$$$$$	over $50

Since this book is intended to be a resource beyond the current year we have not listed vintage specifics in our wine recommendations. It's more useful to know that a certain producer is a reliable source of a certain type of wine year after year.

Welcome, Reader

And now on to the wonderful journey into the fascinating world of wine! The knowledge contained in the pages before you represents a lifetime of experience with wine. Much has changed over the years and continues to change at an ever more rapid pace. Wine laws and appellation designations are in constant flux and may have already moved

ahead by this time. Newly trained, talented winemakers are transforming the wine industry worldwide. It's an exciting time to be pursuing the pleasures of wine and it is our hope that this book will open up new vistas of wine appreciation for you.

Alan Boehmer
newworldwine.suite101.com

POPULAR CORKSCREWS
Which one is right for you?

Most fine wines are finished with cork or synthetic closures that require the use of a corkscrew. The lead capsule covering the cork helps keep oxygen from entering the wine. It is normally removed by cutting around the top of the capsule, exposing the cork. The corkscrew is placed in the center of the cork and driven all the way to the bottom of the cork. If the cork should break, try to remove the remaining cork by reinserting the corkscrew. If the cork refuses to be extracted, push the remaining cork into the bottle and decant the wine using a fine filter or tea strainer.

The simple bartender's corkscrew, also known as the "waiter's friend," is the most widely used. It comes in one- and two-stage models. The two-stage model has a hinge that allows you to extract corks in two stages. It is generally preferred.

Simple Corkscrew

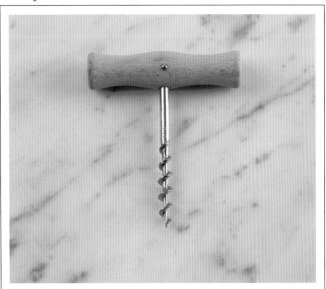

- The traditional corkscrew employs a simple design and is inexpensive.

- The screw portion is called the "worm." Be sure to insert it all the way to the bottom of the cork. Pull the cork out using a twisting motion.

- The simple corkscrew is difficult to use with many synthetic corks whose fit is tighter and more uniform than real cork.

- Simple corkscrews are awkward to use and have largely been replaced by more efficient designs.

The Waiter's Friend Corkscrew

- Its small design and ease of use make the waiter's friend the most widely used corkscrew design.

- Most waiter's friend designs include a small folding knife in the handle for cutting through the lead capsule.

- The notched end fits over the rim of the bottle, providing leverage.

- The waiter's friend gets its name from the folding design that allows a server to keep it in his pocket without damaging his clothes.

The butler's friend is operated by rocking the prongs back and forth between the cork and the inside wall of the bottle. You then twist and pull out the cork. This corkscrew leaves the cork whole and undamaged so a bottle can be securely recorked. It's also the opener of choice for soft or damaged corks.

The more expensive and bulky Rabbit corkscrew will remove a cork from both bottle and corkscrew with one down-and-up motion.

The Butler's Friend Corkscrew

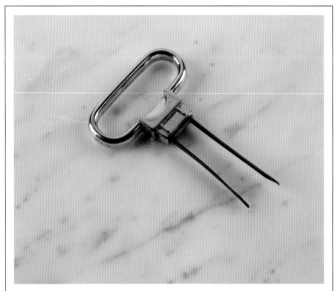

- The butler's friend is also known as the "ah-so."

- Slide the longer prong between the cork and bottle, and then insert the shorter prong in the opposite side. Drive the prongs down the bottle wall by rocking back and forth. Twist and pull out the cork.

- This is the only wine opener that will remove the cork without damaging it.

- Its name reflects the notion that a butler can recork the bottle for service at a future time.

The Rabbit

- Its elaborate construction makes this corkscrew more expensive than other designs.

- Less-expensive models feature fragile worms and tend to break easily. They also take up more storage space than other designs.

- The Rabbit removes the cork from both the bottle and worm with a single down-and-up motion.

- It's a good choice for those who need to open many bottles at the same time—for example, at a party or wine-tasting event.

GLASSWARE
Learn which glass to use and why it's important

The glass you choose for your wine is supremely important. Choosing the wrong glass is like watching a movie with the room lights on. The right glass frames your wine and allows its qualities to shine.

Most of the crystal companies of Europe and America offer a line of *functional stemware*. These glasses attempt to showcase wine in the best possible way. The first of these companies was the French firm Baccarat, which in concert with the winemakers of Bordeaux offered the Perfection wine glass back in the 1950s. This was an 8-ounce straight-sided tulip, offered at a time when most wine was drunk from tumblers or water glasses.

More recently, glassware companies have introduced stemware to showcase specific varietals. If cost is no object, you

Burgundy Glass

- Red wine glasses typically are larger than white wine glasses. The glass pictured here holds a full 750-milliliter bottle, or 26 ounces.

- A proper red wine glass should hold a minimum of 16 ounces. Large glasses offer a large *headspace* so the wine can be fully aerated when swirled.

- The glass shape is bulbous with an inward-curving top to allow vigorous swirling.

- The largest glasses are used for big, full-bodied, aromatic red wines such as red Bordeaux and Cabernet Sauvignon.

Sauvignon Blanc Glass

- White wine glasses are smaller and less bulbous than those used for red wine. The high stem reflects an elegant design rather than a function.

- White wines can be served in red wine glasses, but they don't need as much headspace as do reds.

- Fine red wines should not be served in white wine glasses because they require more aeration to release their aromas.

- Full-bodied white wines benefit from larger glasses; lighter white wines perform well in smaller glasses of around 12 ounces.

might invest in a stemware arsenal, but many wine lovers question whether a few shapes and sizes will fill the bill just as well.

Shape and volume are extremely important. For any still wine, the glass should hold at least 12 ounces and for red wines, much more. The sides must curve inward at the top to allow swirling. A stem allows you to observe the beauty of the wine and to keep your hands from warming the wine. To enjoy your fine wines to the fullest, you will need different glasses for red, white, sparkling, and dessert wine.

YELLOW LIGHT

A Note about Crystal:
Crystal glassware is made using lead. The higher the lead content, the clearer the glass—and the softer! High-lead crystal glasses scratch easily and may lose their clarity over time if washed in a dishwasher. Lead-free crystal glassware is becoming increasingly available. High quality polycarbonate glassware is beginning to appear, but lacks the heft and appeal of fine crystal.

Riedel "O" Glass

- The "O" glasses are typically large capacity—usually around 20 ounces—and designed primarily for red wines. The missing stem prevents the wine from expressing itself visually when you are holding it in your hand.

- The main rationale for the "O" glass is its sleek and attractive design.

- The lack of a stem gives this glass a lower center of gravity and makes it less likely to spill if bumped.

- Slightly smaller versions of the "O" glass are offered for white wine.

Colored and Cut Crystal Glasses

- Colored wine glasses should never be used for fine wine because the glass obscures the color and texture of the wine.

- There is a tradition in Germany and eastern Europe of serving white wines in high-stemmed, colored crystal.

- Fine wine is typically served in thin, often hand-blown glassware that emphasizes wine rather than the glass.

- Heavy, cut crystal stemware obscures the beauty of wine and is usually improperly shaped. Exceptions are made for sparkling wine and dessert wine glasses.

THE ALL-PURPOSE WINE GLASS
Can one glass really serve the needs of every wine?

Because of increasing pressure from the restaurant industry, wine glass producers have developed multifunctional glassware designs. There have always been wine glasses that had no particular focus. And the notion that each varietal wine should be matched to specific shapes and sizes of glassware is a recent one that, above all, promotes the sale of expensive glassware. Most wine professionals would agree that

Sauvignon Blanc and Viognier, for example, do not need glassware of slightly different shape and size, yet some crystal houses offer them. (The Viognier glass is slightly more bulbous.) The rationale is that more aromatic wines need more headspace for aromas to be most expressive. At professional wine tastings where multiple varieties are evaluated, it is rare to be presented with more than a single wine glass type.

Ravenscroft All-purpose Tasting Glass

- This glass design features a generous bowl size.

- It has rounded sides and is inward slanting at the top. This design allows the user to swirl the wine to release its aromatics.

- The high profile keeps

- wine inside the glass when swirled.

- This glass is 6.25 inches high, is dishwasher safe, and has a capacity of 12 ounces.

- It can be used for any still wine, red, pink, or white.

Spiegelau One4All White and Red

- This glassware set distinguishes between glasses designed for red and for white wines. Pink wines should be served in the white wine glass.

- This glass features a universal, all-purpose design. It comes in two sizes—larger for reds, smaller for whites.

- It is made from lead-free crystal and is dishwasher safe. This is the design often used in wine industry tastings.

- This glassware costs less than dedicated crystal designs and is functional for all dry white and red wines.

The old-fashioned, all-purpose wine glass will not show any wine in its best light due to its inadequate capacity. But, new designs from houses such as Ravenscroft and Spiegelau work very well over a broad range of wines. They are offered in red and white sizes. The shapes for red wine and white wine are almost identical. So if you must restrict yourself to one or two glass types, choose those.

Assortment of Riedel Glasses

- This is the glassware of choice if you regularly enjoy a spectrum of wines and desire the optimum design for each wine type.

- The Riedel glassware comes in several collection series at a range of quality levels and price points. The shape of the glass is more impor-

tant than the manufacture.

- The top-quality Sommelier series is very thin and should be handwashed. The middle-grade Vinum series is the most popular. These glasses are easily obtained or replaced throughout the United States and Canada.

Recommended Basic Glassware

- Bordeaux glass: 26 ounces

- Chardonnay glass: 16 ounces

- Champagne flute: 6-8 ounces

- Dessert wine glass: 4 ounces

DECANTERS

When should you decant your wine, and what are the best decanters?

Decanting, or pouring a bottle of wine into another vessel, is not just a nicety for formal dinner parties. There are many good reasons to decant, so you should have at least one decanter on hand if you expect to encounter any of these circumstances: very old red wines, unfiltered and unfined red wines, old vintage Port wines, or wines with broken corks. Broken corks are a common occurrence when a wine has

soaked through most of the cork, as is often the case with older wines.

Most red wines will throw sediment as they age. The purpose of the indentation in the bottom of wine bottles, known as a "punt," is to help contain those sediments when you pour. The shape of a Bordeaux bottle, also most New World Cabernet Sauvignons, features sharply angled shoulders in

Traditional Method of Decanting

- Outdated, this method, using a candle, adjusts the bottle angle to keep the sediment in the shoulder of the bottle. When sediment is passed through the neck of the bottle, the angle of the bottle is adjusted down to encourage the sediment to fall into the shoulder.

- If the wine is heavily sedimented, this method may result in wasted wine.

- It works only with bottles with angular shoulders, such as Bordeaux and Cabernet Sauvignon bottles.

Captain's Decanter

- This is the most popular traditional decanter shape. Its primary disadvantage is that its narrow neck makes it difficult to clean.

- The very low center of gravity discourages tipping over.

- Use in conjunction with

a tea filter. Very fine silver filters are available and are said to contribute no metallic taste to the wine, but inexpensive fine tea filters work just as well.

- Unlike wine glasses, cut crystal decanters can showcase the visual beauty of a wine.

which sediments collect towards the end of the pour.

But when there is too much sediment or broken cork in the bottle, you will need to decant. Decanting also aerates the wine in a way that just removing the cork and letting it stand upright will not do. The older the red wine, the longer it will take to recover from its long sleep inside the bottle. Many old red wines actually take many hours or even overnight to fully open up. Decanting shortens the awakening time substantially.

In general, white wines need not be decanted unless you see visible sediment. Sediment in white wines is usually a precipitation of harmless tartrate crystals. Vintage Ports almost always throw sediment over time. Some of these are called "crusted Ports" because of their tendency to do so.

Wines younger than ten years rarely will require decanting, but all wines benefit from the procedure. A crystal decanter of wine lends an element of elegance to a formal table.

Utilitarian Decanter

- This straightforward decanter is traditional and features a no-nonsense design.

- It's practical and functions just as well as any other shape. Traditional decanters are used for brandy and other spirits as well as for wine.

- Some come prepackaged with funnel and silver-plated filter.

- It's much easier to clean than exotic-shaped decanters.

Art Decanter

- Its exotic, visually appealing and elegant design makes it an art piece as well as a practical wine decanter.

- Art decanters add elegance to a formal table.

- Some models are expensive. Fine crystal art decant-ers typically cost over $100 and often much more.

- They must be handwashed and may be very difficult to maintain in a sparkling, spotless condition.

HOW TO TASTE WINE

Learn to maximize the pleasure that wine offers through a disciplined tasting procedure

Enjoying wine to the fullest need not be ritualized, but there are a few particulars that will greatly enhance your wine-tasting experience: *color*—young red wines will be a bluish red. As they age, the color warms to ruby, then garnet, and finally brick red. In old red wines, the pigment may coalesce, leaving a clear edge that can be seen when the glass is tilted. Unfiltered wines may not be crystal clear but may have a richer flavor. *Texture*—swirl the wine and see if it descends in sheets or "tears" or "legs" on the inside of the glass. *Smell*—much of the expressiveness of a wine is in its aroma. All wines should exhibit strong fruit aromas such as citrus, plum, cherry, or blackberry. But many other aromas

Swirling the Wine

![The Three S's of Wine Tasting notepad]

The Three S's of Wine Tasting

· Swirl

· Smell

· Sip

· In formal or informal wine-tasting events, a fourth S is added: spit.

- Swirling reveals the visual beauty of the wine.

- Swirling opens up the wine by introducing oxygen and releasing the wine's aromatics.

- Wines should be swirled often between sips.

- Swirling allows you to see the wine's texture or viscosity as it returns to the bottom of the bowl. Older wines and those high in sugar or alcohol will form "legs" on the inside of the glass. This shows viscosity and is always a desirable characteristic.

Older Wines Show Special Characteristics

- The color of red wines changes from a bluish red to an orange-red. The older the wine, the more orange and transparent the color.

- Older white wines will assume a golden color. Eventually they will turn brown and become undrinkable. Those wines

- are said to be "maderized."

- The pigments have consolidated, leaving a clear edge. Older wines, when swirled, can suggest abstract paintings when backlit. Older wines take time to open up and release their aromatics. They should always be decanted.

may be present, too, such as herbs, flowers, minerals, earth, and spice. *Flavor*—the flavor of a wine usually follows the aromas, but not always. Some wines will exhibit differences between aromas and flavors. German Rieslings, for example, often exhibit a petrol or burnt rubber aroma, which usually does not appear in the flavor. If you experience a dryness, or puckeriness, in a red wine, there are unresolved tannins. These will soften over time. *Finish*—notice how the taste of the wine lingers on your palate.

Texture

- Fine wine will almost always show visual texture.

- Texture takes the form of "tears" or "legs" as they drip down the inside of the glass. Young wines and wines low in alcohol form sheets rather than legs.

- Tears reflect the viscosity of the wine and are influenced not only by the wine's richness but also by the level of alcohol and sugar.

- Sweet wines and wines higher in alcohol have a greater viscosity than dry wines.

How Oak Affects the Taste of Wine

- Oak barrels are to the winemaker what the spice rack is to the chef. Fermenting or maturing a wine in oak barrels imparts a secondary layer of flavor and aroma to the wine.

- Oak barrels may be toasted over a fire to promote certain specific characteristics. Typical oak enhancements are impressions of vanilla, spice, roasted nuts, and meaty flavors.

- New oak barrels lose their influence after 3-5 years and are said to be "neutral."

A HOME WINE-TASTING PARTY

Learn, celebrate, party, and entertain by discovering wine with your friends

You can learn a great deal about wine by hosting a *wine-tasting party*. These fun-filled events can be informal occasions or structured, formal events. Invite friends to come with a favorite wine. The host or hostess provides appetizers. This offers a chance to experience a range of wines at one time. Discoveries are bound to occur.

Another interesting and informative event is the *wine dinner.* The host establishes the menu, and each guest brings a food course and a bottle of wine chosen to complement the course. Or the host can invite a local authority (wine merchant, educator, winemaker, or knowledgeable amateur) who provides all the wines, and guests chip in to cover costs.

A Formal Tasting

- This is a typical setup for comparing similar wines directly. Multiple identical glasses are needed.

- Wines to be compared are poured at the same time. Tasting commences after all wines are poured. This is called "flight." Tastings may consist of multiple flights.

- Compare color and clarity, aromatics, taste, and finish. Neutral crackers are often used to cleanse the palate between tastes. Other foods are not served because they can interfere with the impression of the wine.

- Retaste each wine several times.

A Varietal Tasting

- Two identical glasses are useful so that comparisons may be made. The wines are poured in pairs.

- All wines are of the same variety. A varietal tasting can feature a range of qualities and prices. The cost of the wine is shared by the group, making it possible to include wines normally outside individual budgets.

- Wines may be compared side by side either blind or not blind. Tastings can be of a single variety or multiple varieties from a single region.

A 750-milliliter bottle will provide six 4-ounce pours or a dozen 2-ounce tastes. In any case, plan on one bottle of wine per person. Leftover wine might be left for the host.

The host should provide two wine glasses per person if both red and white wines are to be served. If only a single glass per person is available, the host should provide a pitcher of water for rinsing and a dump bucket to receive wine that a guest might choose not to drink.

Wine study groups can be found in many American cities. These groups may be based on formal wine-tasting events or may consist simply of small groups of wine lovers who meet regularly in homes. Belonging to such a group can lead to a more comprehensive wine education than can be easily achieved otherwise. Local wine merchants are usually aware of wine study groups operating in their area.

Where no group exists, anyone willing to host such events could easily gain the cooperation of a wine merchant, who might supply not only wine for the events but also customers who would enjoy participating.

A Comparative Tasting

- Comparative tastings allow guests to observe how different winemakers approach the same grape variety.

- Choose varieties that show strong regional differences: Sauvignon Blanc from New Zealand versus California; Oregon Pinot Gris versus Alsatian Pinot Gris;

California Pinot Noir versus red Burgundy, for example. Your wine merchant will be able to offer advice.

- Comparative tastings require two identical wine glasses. Appropriate food items may be included, along with a pitcher of water and a dump bucket.

A Wine Dinner

- Sparkling wines make superb apéritif wines for home events and wine dinners. The foamy head is called the "*mousse*." Be sure to underpour at first to prevent the *mousse* from spilling over the glass.

- Many restaurants and wineries offer expensive wine

dinners that pair appropriate wines with food courses. Such events are easily duplicated at home with much less expense.

- Typically, a single wine is served with each course. The main point is to explore food and wine complements.

11

CLOSURES

What's right or wrong with cork? And what's the best alternative?

Natural cork is the traditional closure for wine bottles. It's made from the bark of living cork oaks that will renew their bark ten to twelve years after being stripped. Natural cork is still the closure of choice because of its unique qualities. Because it is semipermeable, cork closures allow a subtle micro-oxygenation to take place, without which a wine can develop funky or sulfurous aromas and flavors. Wines with

cork closures need to be stored on their sides to keep the bottom of the cork moist and expanded. Dried-out corks invite seepage, excess oxygen, and brittleness. Corks that are moist throughout show that they have not protected the wine from the ingress of oxygen, and the wine is probably ruined.

Although still the closure of choice, natural cork has a dark side. Around 5 percent of all natural corks contain traces of

Traditional Cork Closure

- Cork is available in a range of qualities and lengths. Italian corks are short and narrow; Bordeaux corks are longer and wider.

- Natural cork is the closure of choice for all fine dry wines to be held over a period of years.

- Store cork-finished wines on their sides if they are not to be consumed within a few weeks.

- Cork closures are difficult to reseal. To reseal a cork-finished bottle, insert the dry end first.

Synthetic Cork Closure

- Made from fine-celled poly-olefin foam, synthetic corks are available in a range of colors.

- Synthetic corks are much less expensive than natural cork.

- Synthetic corks are sometimes difficult to open

because of their tight purchase on the bottle neck and difficult to reinsert because they expand upon removal.

- Around 10 percent of modern wines are sealed with synthetic closures.

the chemical TCA (2,4,6-trichloroanisole), which will utterly destroy a wine. Such wines lack aroma or smell of wet newspaper. Flavors are unpleasantly affected. This is the primary rationale for the presentation of cork and sample in restaurant wine service.

Cork-finished bottles are usually overlain with a lead capsule that is cut open with a knife to expose the cork. Some cork-finished wines are sealed with wax, PVC foil, or polylaminated foil.

A host of cork substitutes has become available, each one with its own set of disadvantages. Presently a European company has developed a taint-free natural cork closure, but it's not been on the market long enough for a proper evaluation.

Screwcaps are now used on many wines in the low to medium price range. These are appropriate for wines to be enjoyed in the short term and are much more convenient than traditional cork closures. Wines to be held for more than a year should not be sealed with screwcaps because of the absence of micro-oxygenation.

ZORK Alternative Closure

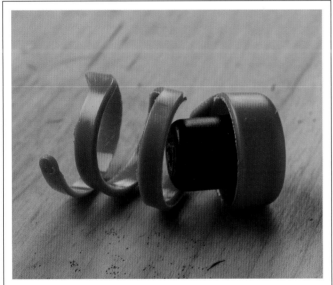

- ZORK is a polyethylene closure in three parts: cap, foil (aluminum), and plunger.

- No opener is needed. The ZORK closure is unpeeled, removed by hand, and re-inserted.

- The ZORK is an ideal closure for wines consumed in the short term. Test results over twenty-four months compare with those of the best screwcap closures.

- This innovative closure is designed primarily for mid-priced wines not intended for long-term storage.

Stelvin Screwcap

- The Stelvin is a high-end screwcap designed specifically for wine.

- No opener is needed. Wines can be securely resealed with a twist.

- Stelvin screwcaps are offered with a range of liners, including natural cork.

- Screwcaps are designed primarily for mid-priced wines not intended for long-term storage, but different liners ensure various levels of permeability, so even expensive wines are sometimes offered with Stelvin screwcaps.

RESTAURANT WINE SERVICE

Here is all you need to know about ordering wine in a restaurant

Most restaurants offer wine options by the glass, a carafe of house wine, or a half or full bottle from a wine list. House wines may be the least expensive option but usually offer the poorest value. Older wines may offer the best value because their prices reflect the markup at the time the restaurant purchased the wine. The longer the restaurant has held the wine, the better the value. Typical markups range from 100 to

200 percent of retail price in the case of bottles, much more in the case of house wines. To determine markup, search the wine list for a wine whose retail price you know. That markup reflects the restaurant's pricing policy. Wines by the glass are often based on 25 percent of the bottle's asking price. Order by the glass if you intend to drink only one glass. Two people ordering the same wine might consider ordering a bottle.

The Sommelier or Wine Steward

- Sommeliers and wine stewards are eager to share their considerable knowledge and experience. They can usually direct you to the best food and wine pairings possible.

- A sommelier will usually ask for a price category. Generally, the more you are

- willing to spend on a bottle of wine, the greater the options and the better the pairing will be.

- Be careful not to overvalue the advice of servers who have not been trained in wine service.

A Restaurant Wine List

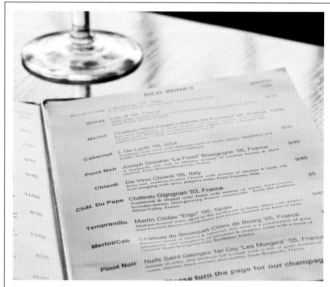

- Wine lists are organized either by foreign/domestic wines or by variety.

- If there's a knowledgeable steward, don't hesitate to ask for advice. He may possess personal knowledge of all the wines on the list and be able to make specific recommendations.

- Popular varieties such as Chardonnay, Pinot Noir, and Cabernet Sauvignon are usually more expensive. Less-favored wines such as Sauvignon Blanc, Riesling, Barbera, Norton, and Zinfandel may present better value.

If you need help, ask to speak with the person in charge of the restaurant's wine cellar, not the server unless you know him to be knowledgeable. If the restaurant employs a sommelier, he will ask whether you seek wine advice. If you do, be sure to tip him.

If your party orders a variety of foods, order by the glass or order a versatile wine that is enjoyable with a range of foods. Such wines might include a sparkling wine, dry rosé, or a light-bodied red.

ZOOM

The Sommelier: A *sommelier* is a wine steward devoted to serving wine. Sommeliers are highly trained students of wine. There are four levels that lead to the certification of master sommelier. Students pursuing certification are tested in technical knowledge of every aspect of wine and must pass blind sensory evaluations. He will be informed about the restaurant's wine offerings. Restaurants without sommeliers depend on their regular wait staff to take wine orders. Sommeliers should be tipped separately if you ask for their help.

Presentation of the Cork

- The cork is set on the table beside the person who ordered the wine. The customer may pick it up and smell it for cork taint if he chooses.

- A small pour is offered for tasting. Tasting is optional because any serious defect will be revealed upon smelling the swirled wine.

- Customer nods to indicate acceptance or returns wine if defective. Returned wines are likely to be retasted behind the scenes.

- Server pours the guests' glasses first, then serves the person who ordered.

The Sample Pour

- A sample pour is offered only to assure the wine's integrity, not to seek the buyer's personal approval.

- Wine must not be returned because it's not what was expected.

- Look for a darker than normal color in white wines, which may indicate oxidation. If it smells funky or metallic, return it.

- Wines finished with screwcaps are less likely to display signs of damage than cork-finished wines.

CORKAGE

When is it wise to bring your own bottle to the restaurant?

Corkage is the term used for the fee charged by a restaurant when you opt to bring your own bottle of wine and receive the waiter's assistance in serving it. It can run from zero to $50 or more per bottle. Average corkage is presently $10–15 (US dollars) per bottle.

If you have a wine cellar loaded with old high-quality wines, paying the corkage charge makes a lot of sense. But if you are thinking of bringing a $10 bottle, forget it unless the charge is minimal. The same wine may be offered by the restaurant at $20. Paying the corkage for inexpensive wines may make them even more expensive than ordering off the wine list.

Smaller restaurants with minimal or no wine cellar will offer corkage at little or no charge. Upscale restaurants with expansive wine offerings will charge more, but they will offer

The Wine Is Presented

Standard Corkage Service

- Glassware

- Ice bucket, if requested

- Opening of the wine by the server

- Presentation of the wine according to the restaurant's standard procedure

- Refilling of glasses as appropriate

- The label is displayed. Be sure it's the wine you ordered. Check the vintage date.

- The cork is presented for evaluation. Be sure it's moist only on one end. If it's wet completely through, the wine may be oxidized. You need not smell the cork. Smell the wine instead.

- A sample pour is offered. Check for appropriate color. Swirl vigorously and smell.

- You may want to take a sip, but the aroma of the wine really shows whether the wine is sound.

Wine List with High Markup

- Restaurants with extensive wine cellars typically charge more for corkage to encourage their customers to purchase from the wine list.

- Markups can be as high as 300% retail price and are typically double the retail price.

- Unreasonable markups are a relic of former times when wine was considered a luxury for the wealthy rather than a standard dinner accompaniment.

- Bring your own wine and pay corkage when markups rise above double retail price.

a higher quality of service. For example, they will provide an ice bucket for white wine and more appropriate glassware.

Many restaurants are allowed to permit you to bring your own wine and take home any leftover wine that you have brought or purchased.

Corkage is charged per bottle, not per event, regardless of the number of people being served.

Wine List with Reasonable Markup

- Double retail markup provides a substantial profit margin for the restaurant, but the restaurant must provide proper storage for the wine.

- The markup is usually established at the time of purchase and many wines improve with proper cellaring, while retaining its original markup.

- Wines that a restaurant has cellared for years may cost little more than its current retail price.

- When wines are offered at double retail or less it can be wise and convenient to order from the wine list.

Wines by the Glass

- In a fine restaurant, all wines are tasted by the wine buyer and selected to complement the restaurant's food offerings.

- The quality of the wines is chosen to complement the food quality. Casual restaurants have short wine lists; luxury restaurants may have more than a thousand wines.

- Wine by the glass is an attractive option for those intending to drink only a single glass.

- Wine is considered a food item when calculating tip.

WHEN TO RETURN A WINE

How often are restaurant wines returned, and what are acceptable reasons?

It is rare for patrons to return wine, even though it is known that around 5 percent of all cork-finished wines will be contaminated. Most consumers incorrectly assume that odd aromas and flavors are a part of the wine's profile.

Modern wineries employ fastidious techniques to ensure that their wines will be sound. These techniques include rinsing the empty bottle, expelling all oxygen by sparging with nitrogen, filling, and applying the closure of choice. The wines may have undergone egg white fining, which removes gross particulates, or sterile filtration, which removes *all* particulates, including yeast cells.

Wines finished with quality screwcaps such as Stelvin are

The Evaluation

- Examine the cork, but there is no need to smell it. If the wine has soaked all the way through the cork, the wine is probably oxidized to some degree.

- Observe the color of the wine to see whether oxidation is in evidence. Oxygen turns all wines brown to some degree.

- Swirl and smell to detect any inappropriate aromas that might suggest cork taint or Brett.

- Nod for acceptance or return the wine if it is defective.

Tartrates

- Tartrates show as white crystals on the underside of the cork and inside the neck of the bottle.

- The presence of tartrates is not a defect.

- Tartrates are precipitates of tartaric acid, the component that gives brightness to the wine. It is also a source of Cream of Tartar, used in cooking.

- Tartrates are most commonly found in white wines that have not undergone harsh filtration.

dependably sound, and quality screwcaps are appearing more frequently on high-quality wines. Dry white or pink wines are almost always intended for early consumption and if finished with a screwcap or alternative closure may be poured with confidence. Wines are returned most often for cork taint (TCA) and oxidation. Cork-tainted wines either suffer a loss of aroma and flavor or smell of wet newspaper. An oxidized wine announces its presence by a darkening or browning of the color. Oxidized white wines may have an earthy, metallic or Sherry-like smell rather than the expected fresh fruit and spice. Oxidized reds are harder to identify.

Wines subjected to excessive levels of heat lose much of their complexity and may exhibit a "cooked fruit" flavor. Red wines are occasionally infected with a rogue strain of yeast known as "Brett" (*brettanomyces*). Even when these wines undergo sterile filtration, yeast has already affected the taste and aroma. Such wines may smell of the barnyard. Pinot Noir is especially vulnerable. A tiny amount of Brett influence may add to a red wine's complexity, so unless excessive, such wines are not necessarily to be considered defective.

Sediment

- Bottle deposit adheres to the sides of the bottle in older red wines. These wines should be decanted.

- Sediment consisting of precipitated tannins, tartrates, and proteins collects at the bottom of the bottle. Pouring the wine through a fine tea strainer will remove most sediment.

- The presence of sediment is most often found in high-quality older red wines.

- The presence of sediment is not a defect but may require that the wine be decanted.

Reasons to Return a Wine

- Cork taint (TCA)

- Oxidation (white wines too dark and smell odd)

- Excessive level of Brett

- "Cooked" flavor resulting from excessive temperature in transport or storage

COMMON WINE DEFECTS
Learn how to tell when a wine is bad

So many things can go wrong in the winemaking process. It's a miracle that these problems so rarely show up in finished wine. The main question is often one of degree. A little of this or that fault might pass notice by the consumer and usually does, particularly if the consumer doesn't know what to look for.

Here are the most commonly encountered wine defects:

Oxidation because of cork saturation: Fill level in bottles may be low in older wines. Check before opening. If cork is saturated and wine smells funky, it's probably oxidized.

Volatile acidity: The wine smells of vinegar.

Ethyl acetate: The wine smells of nail polish remover. This is very common but only a defect when excessive.

Hydrogen sulfide: Smells of rotten eggs. This can be the

Saturated Cork

- Wine has migrated to the top of the cork.

- The cork is wet and fragile. It may disintegrate upon removal.

- The wine is probably oxidized but may be sound. Swirl, smell, and taste.

- This is an issue particular to very old wines. Such wines need considerable aeration before evaluating.

- The presentation of the cork in restaurant wine service assures the customer of a sound cork.

Chardonnay with Normal Color

- Normal Chardonnay color is light to medium straw.

- Unwooded or unoaked Chardonnays are usually lighter.

- Many Chardonnays may be slightly deeper in color

because of more extended skin contact or prefermentation cold soaking.

- The aroma should be fresh and vibrant. It should smell of fruit, flowers, herbs, and vanilla if oaked.

result of a red wine that has been oxygen deprived.

Cork taint: Smells of wet newspaper or not at all. Flavor is absent. Wine is ruined.

Heat damage: This is the most common wine defect. Wine has been subjected to excessive temperature in transport or storage. Wine tastes flat and cooked.

Maderization because of age: All wines discolor over time. Whites gradually turn brown (the color of Madeira). Dry wines lose their fresh character. Sweet wines can benefit if not too excessive.

Brett (brettanomyces): Very common in small amounts. Wine smells of barnyard, sweaty saddle, or cheese.

Refermentation: When wine is bottled without filtration, yeast cells may referment, producing a slight fizziness, which the French call pétulance. Some wines are made to encourage it because it adds an interesting texture to certain wines Some of these faults do not harm wine when present in acceptable levels. Others do. Cork taint ruins a wine, as does heat damage. All others have acceptable levels that can contribute to the character of a wine.

Chardonnay with Oxidized Color

- Oxygen in excess turns wines brown. As white wines are affected by oxygen, they turn a deep golden color. This color should raise a red flag.

- Unusual and unpleasant non-fruity aromas such as metal are hallmarks of an oxidized white wine.

- Oxidation is usually caused by exposure to high temperature in young wines or by cork failure in older wines.

- Oxidized wines are useless for drinking or cooking. Discard them.

The Big Four Common Defects

- Oxidation
- Cork taint
- Heat damage
- Maderization

SAUVIGNON BLANC/SÉMILLON

Try these crisp and refreshing dry whites and luscious dessert wines

Sauvignon Blanc, also called "Sauvignon" and "Fumé Blanc," is one of the oldest of the so-called noble grapes and a parent of Cabernet Sauvignon. Its homeland is in the vineyards of Bordeaux and the Loire Valley, but it is grown successfully worldwide. Very expressive Sauvignon Blanc wines are made in Italy and New Zealand.

Made without oak influence, dry Sauvignon Blanc shows a crisp acidity and a gooseberry, grassy, and herbaceous character. When it is barrel-fermented in oak, its racy brightness is slightly muted and may exhibit hints of tropical fruits.

Sauvignon Blanc makes an excellent apéritif wine and partners well with a wide range of foods, especially fish and

Styles of Sauvignon Blanc

- Sancerre (France): bright, racy, clean

- Bordeaux (France): elegant, dry, light

- New Zealand: intense gooseberry, racy

- California: ripe, often oaked

Sauvignon Blanc Cluster

- Sauvignon is the fourth-most-widely planted grape variety in France.

- A very vigorous growth pattern leads to intensely herbaceous wines if growth is not tightly controlled.

- It is most successfully grown in moderately warm climates such as the Loire Valley in France and the Santa Ynez Valley in California.

- It is most successfully grown in France, Chile, New Zealand, and California.

poultry dishes. It is the wine of choice for goat cheeses.

In partnership with Sémillon, it makes one of the world's greatest dessert wines, Sauternes. Sauternes is made from grapes that are harvested late and subjected to botrytis, the "noble rot." Botrytis mold occurs naturally on grapes grown in wet conditions followed by dry. Sauvignon Blanc also makes an excellent late harvest dessert wine with intense flavors of papaya, melon, quince, ginger, and toffee along with this variety's characteristic acidity. Superb, inexpensive examples are made in Chile and California.

Glass of Sauvignon Blanc

Botrytised Sauvignon Grapes

- Dry versions should be light straw in color.

- New World examples are made to be drunk young, soon after bottling.

- Oak-influenced Sauvignons should be held for at least a year before drinking. They will be rounder, fruitier, and less aggressive.

- White Bordeaux (Sauvignon) ages gracefully for up to fifteen years. New World Sauvignons should be consumed within three years after release.

- Noble rot desiccates the grape berries, concentrating their flavors and sugars.

- Botrytis occurs in temperate climates where morning mists are followed by dry afternoons.

- Botrytised vineyards require several pickings because the mold affects clusters or individual grapes at different rates.

- Botrytis adds a secondary palate of honeyed, rich flavors. These wines are always very sweet and complex. The world's most expensive dessert wines are all botrytis affected.

WHITE WINE

CHARDONNAY
This is America's most widely planted wine grape

The Chardonnay grape is responsible for the world's greatest dry white wines. Native to the Burgundy region of France, it reaches its supreme expression in the great wines of Le Montrachet and surrounding vineyards. It is grown worldwide and comprises around 40 percent of the entire grape crop in California.

When made in a straightforward style with no oak influence, Chardonnay can be a refreshing wine with aromas and flavors of apples, pears, and lemon, but when fermented and aged in oak barrels it takes on a new spectrum of complementary characteristics, such as vanilla and tropical fruits.

No other variety shows the winemaker's characteristic style better than Chardonnay because it lends itself to a wide range of manipulations. The most common of these is to

Major Chardonnay Regions

• Burgundy: classic, balanced, elegant, very dry

• Chablis (France): steely, minerally, very dry

• California: ripe, round, flavorful, complex

• New Zealand: restrained, stylish, assertive

A Mechanical Harvester

• Vineyards must be planted and trellised to facilitate mechanical harvesting.

• Machine harvesting does in hours what a picking crew would need days to do.

• Mechanical harvesting is employed only on level or nearly level vineyard sites.

• Mechanical harvesters remove grape clusters by shaking the trunk of the vine.

• Mechanical harvesting helps keep costs of production down, making lower priced wines economical without sacrificing grape quality.

induce secondary, or malolactic, fermentation. This process converts the harder malic acid into softer lactic acid and imparts a texture that many describe as "buttery."

The combination of oak barrels and secondary fermentation creates the style of Chardonnay most familiar to us. The finest New World Chardonnays invariably subject the wine to new oak barrels, usually French. These 55-gallon barrels are called *barriques* and cost around $1,000 each and are used for three years before being replaced. This is a principal factor that drives up the cost of these wines.

Glass of Chardonnay

- This is America's favorite white wine.

- Chardonnay is made in a variety of styles ranging from bone dry to moderately sweet.

- Unoaked or unwooded Chardonnay is fermented and aged in stainless steel tanks to preserve the fresh fruit character. Unoaked Chardonnay is becoming increasingly popular.

- Chardonnays may undergo a secondary fermentation that converts harsh malic acid into rounder lactic acid, resulting in a mouthfeel often called buttery.

What Different Bottle Shapes Can Tell Us

Sloping shoulder

Angled shoulder

- Most bottle shapes are variations of the Bordeaux and Burgundy bottles.

- Because red Bordeaux wines require years of bottle age, the Bordeaux bottle has sharply angled shoulders to help catch sediment when the wine is poured. White Bordeaux wines use the same bottle shape out of tradition.

- Burgundy bottles are fatter and have gently sloping shoulders, reflecting the fact that the wines of Burgundy, which include Pinot Noir and Chardonnay, do not require extensive bottle aging.

CHENIN BLANC
A wonderful Chardonnay alternative

Chenin Blanc, the great variety from France's Loire Valley, was once the mainstay of major California wineries such as Charles Krug and Wente. The rise of California Chardonnay eclipsed the popularity of Chenin Blanc, and many of the best Chenin Blanc vineyards were budded over to other varieties.

But California wineries never gave up on Chenin. Today there's more Chenin in California vineyards than in all of France. There's also more in South Africa, where it's widely known as "Steen" and occupies around 30 percent of all the country's vineyard area. In California Chenin was largely relegated to the hot Central Valley vineyards and used to prop up less-acidic varieties such as Thompson Seedless and French Colombard for use in cheap jug wines. We estimate that as much as 95 percent of California Chenin is cropped at around

Major Chenin Blanc Regions

- Loire Valley, France: full range from bone dry to very sweet. Loire Valley Chenins display a minerality rarely found in New World examples.

- South Africa: Chenin Blanc has always been South Africa's most popular white variety, but most examples lack the complexity found either in France or California.

- California: especially the Clarksburg appellation near Sacramento, which is gaining notoriety as an ideal location for Chenin Blanc

Hand Harvesting

- Hand harvesting is needed whenever a grapevine ripens its fruit unevenly.

- Hand harvesting is the method of choice for all premium wines and is the only option on steeply inclined vineyards.

- Workers typically make several passes through a vineyard over a period of several days to ensure that no unripe fruit is included.

- Grapes for very expensive dessert wines such as Sauternes, Tokaji, and Ice Wine are sometimes picked by single berries rather than whole clusters.

10 tons per acre, compared with the 1–3 tons per acre associated with fine wine.

In France, Chenin Blanc is made in a range of styles from crisply acidic Savennieres to luscious, honeyed Quarts de Chaume. The most popular examples are from Vouvray and Montlouis.

New World Chenin Blanc is likely to be rounder and slightly sweet. Because it is less expensive to produce than many Chardonnays, California Chenin Blanc often offers exceptional value.

········· GREEN ● LIGHT ·········

Outstanding California Chenin Blancs come from Santa Barbara County (Lucas & Lewellyn), Clarksburg (Ehrhardt), and Napa Valley (Casa Nuestra).

Chenin Blanc

- New World Chenin Blanc exhibits a round, fruity flavor.

- It's usually made in an off-dry style with a sweetness profile similar to that of many New World Chardonnays.

- Chenin Blanc is best served around 50° F, so remove from your refrigerator around thirty minutes before serving. Overchilling will mute the flavors.

- New World Chenin Blanc offers excellent value, with fine California examples priced as low as $12.

A Superb Dessert Wine

- Quarts de Chaume and Bonnezeau, made from Chenin Blanc in France's Loire Valley, are among the world's most esteemed dessert wines. Similar flavors are found in much lighter-styled wines of neighboring Coteaux du Layon.

- Similar wines include Sauternes, Hungary's Tokaji Aszú, and Germany's Trockenbeerenauslese.

- They are best served only moderately chilled and with a moderate pour because these wines are sweet and rich. Quarts de Chaume is an excellent choice to enjoy with liver-based dishes.

WHITE WINE

27

PINOT GRIS/PINOT GRIGIO
America's second-most popular white wine

Pinot Gris, known in Italy as "Pinot Grigio," is a mutation of Pinot Noir and when grown under the right conditions renders a superb, medium-bodied white wine. The northern Italian examples tend to be fairly simple, pleasant wines. The Oregon and California examples are more likely to display gently perfumed aromas of melon, almond, peach, fennel, and orange peel.

The grape gets its name from the bluish-pink color of its skin. It is one of two important Pinot Noir mutations, the other being Pinot Blanc.

In Burgundy it has been allowed to be included in the must of red Burgundy, and it is thought to add a softening influence to wines that are widely thought to consist of 100 percent Pinot Noir.

Major Pinot Gris/Grigio Regions

- Italy: Trentino–Alto Adige and Friuli

- Alsace

- Oregon: Willamette Valley

- Canada: Okanagan Valley, British Columbia

- California: Sacramento Valley (Clarksburg), Santa Barbara County, Napa Valley

Pinot Gris

- Pinot Gris is a lighter, more-delicate wine than Chardonnay and is considered to be a wine of medium weight.

- It features soft, round flavors in New World examples, with more complexity than comparably priced Chardonnays.

- It's an easy drinking wine, an excellent choice when you aren't sure of your guests' wine preferences.

- Avoid the least-expensive bottlings. They are poorly made. The best is obtained for a few dollars more. California and Oregon Pinot Gris are more dependable.

Pinot Gris, like its ancestor Pinot Noir, strongly reflects its *terroir,* or vineyard site. In Alsace it makes some of the most highly prized wines of the region, where it used to be known as "Tokay Pinot Gris." Some of these splendid sweet wines rival Hungarian Tokaji, whereas others are dry and complex. In California, Pinot Grigio, as it is most often called, tends to be made to satisfy consumers looking for a gentle, off-dry wine with layers of flavor. It has a strong appeal to those who are tired of oaky Chardonnay but are offput by the crisp acidity of many Sauvignon Blancs.

Pinot Gris/Grigio, unlike Chardonnay, is made in stainless steel tanks and never sees new oak barrels. This gives the wine a freshness that many New World Chardonnays lack. A few producers age their Pinot Grigio in older, neutral oak to promote a rounder mouthfeel.

New World Pinot Gris reaches its finest expression in Oregon's Willamette Valley. These very affordable wines represent Pinot Gris at its best with good body and a layered flavor profile.

Stainless Steel Fermenters

- Pinot Gris is almost always fermented in stainless steel rather than oak barrels to preserve the fresh fruit character.

- Stainless steel fermenters have water jackets that allow precise temperature control. Pinot Gris is best when cold fermented.

- The use of stainless steel versus oak barrels keeps the cost of production down. This means that a quality Pinot Gris will be a much better value than oak-finished wines of similar quality.

Some Effective Pinot Gris Pairings

- Use as an apéritif, chilled.

- Use as a party wine with an assortment of nuts and finger foods.

- Try it with lightly dressed salads.

- Enjoy it with light food courses, such as sautéed fish or seafood pasta in cream sauces.

- It pairs very well with delicate soft-ripened cheeses and alpine Tomme-style cheeses such as Appenzeller and Emmenthaler.

VIOGNIER/ROUSSANNE
White Rhône varieties are becoming increasingly fashionable

Exotic, sensual, and highly aromatic, Viognier is America's most expensive white grape crop, costing almost as much as Cabernet Sauvignon. Twenty years ago Viognier was not in commercial production anywhere in the New World, and the variety was known only to wine industry professionals. In 1989 John Alban introduced Viognier to San Luis Obispo County, California, after test plantings in five other locations.

The result was nothing short of astonishing, and Viognier is now grown throughout northern California.

California's acreage planted to Viognier now far surpasses France's, where it is relegated to two distinguished vineyards in the northern Rhône Valley: Condrieu and Chateau Grillet. France's most expensive Syrahs blend up to 5 percent Viognier to add an expressive note and round out the tannins.

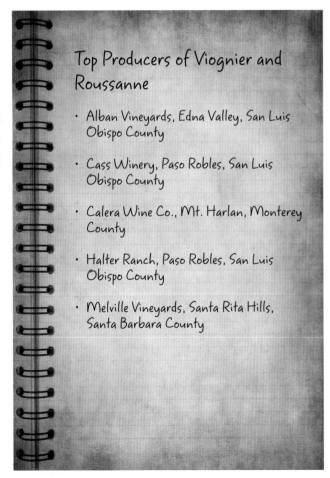

Top Producers of Viognier and Roussanne

- Alban Vineyards, Edna Valley, San Luis Obispo County

- Cass Winery, Paso Robles, San Luis Obispo County

- Calera Wine Co., Mt. Harlan, Monterey County

- Halter Ranch, Paso Robles, San Luis Obispo County

- Melville Vineyards, Santa Rita Hills, Santa Barbara County

Viognier Grape Cluster

- Viognier is one of the most difficult of all white grape varieties to grow and ripen.

- Viognier is reluctant to bear fruit.

- It's very susceptible to diseases such as powdery mildew.

- It offers very low fruit yields.

- Viognier cannot be successfully grown over a wide range of vineyard sites. It's very particular.

In the southern Rhône Valley, Roussanne reaches its greatest expression. Like Viognier in the north, Roussanne is used in red wine blends as well as used as a stand-alone wine of considerable distinction. It's softer and less complex than Viognier but displays very attractive round flavors of peach, lychee, ginger, and honeysuckle with good acidity. The third partner in the white Rhône trio is Marsanne, grown mostly in southern France, California, and Australia. Marsanne is somewhat fat and is best suited for use as a blending wine to take the edge off more-assertive varieties.

•••••••••••••• GREEN ● LIGHT ••••••••••••••

The best examples of Viognier and Roussanne come from France and California's Central Coast, especially San Luis Obispo County's Edna Valley and Santa Barbara County's Santa Ynez Valley.

Viognier

- When grown in the best sites, Viognier yields highly aromatic wines redolent of peach, apricot, and orange blossom. This wine should always be drunk young.

- French examples are traditionally made bone dry. Most New World examples will be off-dry.

- Viognier is traditionally made in stainless steel or neutral oak, but oaked versions are beginning to appear.

- This variety provides a splendid accompaniment to many Oriental foods, particularly Japanese dishes, including sushi.

Condrieu—the Archetype of Viognier

- The tiny Condrieu vineyard in the northern Rhône Valley, along with its neighbor, Chateau Grillet, until recently was the only source of Viognier in the world.

- Condrieu is regarded as the world's best example of this exotic wine, but the best Viogniers from California are rapidly catching up.

- Medium-light in body and very dry, Condrieu makes an excellent and very fashionable apéritif wine.

WHITE WINE

31

RIESLING/GEWÜRZTRAMINER
It's the most versatile white wine in the world

Riesling is unique among the white wine grape varieties. It can be successfully grown in climates too cold for most other varieties and yields a wine with a characteristic flavor profile unlike any other, often described as "intensely floral with subtle notes of petrol."

Riesling reaches its finest expression in the German Rhineland and Mosel River Valley, where alcohol levels are commonly as low as 9 percent. New World Rieslings are usually much higher in alcohol and rarely achieve the near-perfect acid-sweetness balance found in their German counterparts.

The spectrum of wines made from the Riesling grape ranges from very dry to sticky sweet. In its native Germany, several harvesting passes are usually made a week or two apart to

Major Riesling Regions

- Rhine River Valley (Germany)
- Mosel-Saar-Ruwer (Germany)
- Alsace
- Washington State
- New York State: Finger Lakes region
- Canada: Okanagan Valley, Niagara Peninsula
- California: Monterey County

Gewürztraminer Grape Cluster

- Despite its pinkish skin color, Gewürztraminer renders a white wine.

- Both Riesling and Gewürztraminer are bottled as single varietal wines because the wines possess a highly characteristic flavor profile that would be diminished by blending.

- Late harvest Riesling grapes render some of the most highly prized dessert wines in the world, such as Germany's Trockenbeerenauslese and New World late harvest Riesling, usually sold in half bottles. Riesling is the preferred grape variety for making German Eiswein.

provide grapes of different ripeness levels—the earlier harvest yields fruit for the drier style such as Kabinett; later harvests yield grapes with increasing sugar levels. The sweeter the wine, the more complex the flavor and aroma because of increasing ripeness of the fruit. But leaving the fruit on the vine after the first pass carries the risk of losing the entire remaining harvest to inclement weather. This is a common problem in northern Europe. With this risk comes an increase in the price of the finished wine. So the sweeter the Riesling, the more expensive it will be.

Riesling in a Traditional Glass

- Wines made from the Riesling grape often display a subtle smell of burnt rubber or petrol that is a defining characteristic of this grape.

- Riesling wines can accompany a broad spectrum of foods. Off-dry and sweeter examples are excellent with fruit and cheese courses.

- German Rieslings are usually very low in alcohol. Alsatian and New World examples possess normal alcohol levels.

- Riesling is often served in a hock, or high-stemmed wine glass. The glass shape reflects tradition rather than functionality.

Gewürztraminer (spelled without the umlaut in Alsace) is simply a mutation of Traminer. Originally an Italian grape, Gewürztraminer has found a happy home in Germany, New Zealand, the Pacific Northwest, and British Columbia, but it reaches its greatest expression in Alsace.

Gewürztraminer features a dark pink skin and offers exotic aromas and flavors of lychee and heavily perfumed roses. Its opulent and heady aromas and flavors make it a good match with Oriental cuisines, particularly those of Southeast Asia.

German Riesling Styles

- Trocken: dry

- Qualitätswein mit Prädikat: Quality wine with government-controlled descriptions. The descriptions reflect sweetness levels.

- Kabinett: off-dry, suitable for light meat and vegetable food courses

- Spätlese: somewhat sweet. Good with meat courses with fruit sauces, such as duck à l'orange.

- Auslese: late harvest, sweet. Enjoy by itself or with cheese courses.

- Beerenauslese: Grape berries are picked individually at a very late stage of ripeness. A dessert wine.

- Trockenbeerenauslese: literally, dried individual grape berries. These grapes yield about a drop of liquid per berry, and the resulting wine is extremely sweet and very expensive.

CABERNET SAUVIGNON
Powerful, complex, masculine red wine

A relative late-comer to the world's pantheon of wine grape varieties, Cabernet Sauvignon is the result of a unintended field cross between Cabernet Franc (red) and Sauvignon Blanc (white) that is thought to have occurred in the eighteenth century. So an accident of nature produced the world's most honored red wine grape.

Cabernet Sauvignon has many unique and distinguishing characteristics, including a high ratio of skin to pulp, leading to a deep red color; large seeds, or pips, as they are called, which provide a higher level of tannin, which in turn leads to wines of great longevity; and a tolerance for different climates. Although the best Cabernet Sauvignon grapes come from moderately warm climates with marine influence, the grape is successfully grown in regions as different as Russia,

KNACK WINE BASICS

Château Lafite-Rothschild

- The Lafite-Rothschild vineyard was planted in the late seventeenth century.

- The varieties used are not listed on the label, but this wine is predominately Cabernet Sauvignon.

- The term *Mis en bouteilles au château* tells us that the wine was bottled at the château. The New World equivalent is *Estate Bottled*.

- Bordeaux bottles rarely feature back labels that provide additional descriptions of the wine. Alcohol content is listed and is usually lower than that of New World Cabernet Sauvignons.

Beringer Private Reserve Cabernet Sauvignon

- The grape variety is usually listed, but rarely will the blending grapes appear. U.S. law allows up to 25 percent blending grapes to be added to 75 percent base wine when the main variety is listed.

- The term *Produced and Bottled* is the equivalent of the term *Estate Bottled*. Wine must be made at the listed winery from fruit grown in the winery's own vineyard.

- The alcohol content will always be listed. New World Cabernets are usually higher in alcohol than their European counterparts.

Argentina, southern France, and the Pacific Northwest.

The flavors and aromas of Cabernet Sauvignon remind us of blackberries and black currants. But its unusual parentage displays itself in layers of other flavors such as chocolate and coffee. The greatest Cabernet Sauvignons come from Bordeaux and the Médoc in particular. These wines feature *proprietary* labels, such as Château Lafite-Rothschild. Widely considered the equal of Bordeaux's best are the great Cabernet Sauvignons from California's Napa Valley. These usually carry *varietal* labels such as Napa Valley Cabernet Sauvignon.

ZOOM

The Bordeaux Blend/U.S. Meritage: Most great Cabernets include small amounts of certain allowed grapes. These are Merlot, Cabernet Franc, Petite Verdot, and Malbec. California wines using this blending formula may be labeled "Meritage" (rhymes with *heritage*). The blending grapes add lightness, color, and perfume.

Cabernet Sauvignon

- Cabernet Sauvignon is rich and full bodied, often with "brooding" aromatics that reveal themselves in time.

- French Cabernets (red Bordeaux from the Médoc) are drier and leaner and carry tobacco or cedar notes.

- New World Cabernets are fruitier, richer, and mouth-filling. Aromas and flavors suggest blackberries, black currants, and ripe plums.

- Midrange priced Cabernets are suitable for immediate drinking. Expensive bottlings from well-respected producers should be laid down for five to ten years.

Wine Ratings

- There are four widely used rating systems:

- Up to three wine glasses (biccieri)—used in Italy

- Up to five stars—used universally

- The 100-point scale—Wine Spectator, Wine Advocate, Robert Parker, and others

- Levels of recommendation: recommended, highly recommended, etc.

- Wine judges do not always agree on the quality of a wine. Choose a source whose ratings most closely resemble your own preferences.

MERLOT
Meet Cabernet Sauvignon's softer, more voluptuous cousin

Wines made from the Merlot grape are among the world's most expensive, with current release prices for the most coveted examples as high as $2,000 per bottle. But typical New World Merlots are priced substantially lower than comparable Cabernet Sauvignon.

Merlot is the most widely planted red grape in Bordeaux and finds its most agreeable location in the vineyards on the north bank of the Dordogne River in the regions of St. Emilon and Pomerol.

Merlot is easier to grow than Cabernet Sauvignon, which it most closely resembles, but, unlike Cabernet Sauvignon, will perform well only in certain terroirs. So high-quality Merlot, either from Europe or the Americas, is restricted to just a few locations. These locations are still in the process of discovery.

Recommended Merlots

- Twomey Napa Valley Merlot $$
- Beringer Merlot Bancroft Ranch $$
- Pahlmeyer Napa Valley Merlot $$
- Duckhorn Three Palms Merlot $$
- Leonetti Columbia Merlot $$
- Château Clinet, Pomerol $$
- Shafer Napa Merlot $
- Château Le Castelet, Pomerol $
- L'École No. 41 Columbia Valley Merlot $

Merlot Cluster

- Merlot grapes feature a thin skin that leads to lighter color and softer tannins.

- Merlot prefers a slightly damp soil and ripens earlier than Cabernet Sauvignon, making it less susceptible to fickle fall weather.

- Like Pinot Noir, Merlot produces average quality wines unless grown in ideal locations. Inexpensive Merlots are often disappointing.

- Increasing acreage worldwide is being budded over to Merlot, Canada's Okanagan Valley and Niagara Peninsula, South Africa, and eastern Europe.

Merlot's great distinction is its texture. Unlike Cabernet Sauvignon or Cabernet Franc, which are typically high in mouth-puckering tannins, Merlot is soft and smooth on the palate. Because its flavor profile parallels that of Cabernet Sauvignon, it has earned the moniker "Cabernet without the pain."

The most-sought-after Merlot is Château Pétrus in Pomerol. Unlike the other red wines of the region, which are heavily blended, Château Pétrus is 100 percent Merlot. It has no real competition because the geology of the vineyard—known as the *"Pétrus Boutonnière"*—is unique and very old.

Whereas the Merlot-based wines of St. Emilon and Pomerol often display an herbal character that some New World wine lovers find unattractive, New World Merlots are rich with ripe fruit flavors. Excellent Merlots are coming from northeastern Italy, Israel, Napa Valley, Sonoma County, Long Island (New York), and especially Washington State.

The quality of California Merlot has risen dramatically in recent years and will continue to improve as more suitable locations are identified.

Glass of Merlot

- It is lighter in color than Cabernet Sauvignon unless blended with Cabernet Franc, which is common both in France and the New World.

- Merlot does not need extensive cellaring, as does Cabernet Sauvignon. Merlots from St. Emilon and Pomerol can be very long-lived. New World examples are luscious upon release.

- Merlot pairs well with many of the same foods as Cabernet Sauvignon. Exceptions are rich, hearty stews, barbecued steaks, and chocolate.

Chateau Pétrus

- This is typically a pure Merlot from the world's most acclaimed Merlot vineyard. It's fermented in lined concrete vats.

- Its value increases sharply with age, making older bottles worth thousands of dollars.

- Like all Merlot-based wines of St. Emilon and Pomerol, Château Pétrus should not be drunk upon release. The wines age extremely well.

- The geology of the Château Pétrus vineyard more closely resembles that of Burgundy than the rest of Bordeaux.

PINOT NOIR
This classic, ancient variety offers luxurious, complex, and fruity wines that are sure to please

For centuries the red wines of Burgundy made from Pinot Noir grapes have been among the most loved and esteemed red wines in the world. The Pinot Noir grape not only is native to Burgundy but also has mutated there into many of the world's most-admired white grapes—Pinot Blanc, Pinot Gris/Grigio, Pinot Meunier, Aligoté, and even Gamay Noir, the grape of Beaujolais. It is believed by some ampelographers (scholars of the grape) that the name Pinot derives from the pine cone shape of its clusters. Until the twentieth century Pinot Noir was restricted to Burgundy and Alsace. From there it migrated to Germany under the name Spätburgunder.

Attempts to replicate great red wines of Burgundy in the

Major Pinot Noir Regions

- Burgundy: Côtes de Nuits: richer wines

- Burgundy: Côte de Beaune: lighter, fruitier wines

- Alsace: lean, minerally wines

- Willamette Valley, Oregon: rich, sumptuous, deeply flavored wines

- Santa Rita Hills, California: very deep, complex wines with strong terroir identification

- Russian River Valley, California: clean, solid, fruity wines

- Otago, New Zealand: rich and complex wines

Pinot Noir Cluster

- Pinot Noir is one of the oldest known wine grape varieties. Its native home is in Burgundy, France.

- Highly mutable, Pinot Noir has nearly a hundred different clonal varieties, with more on the way.

- Terroir is a critical factor in successful growing of Pinot Noir. It requires specific conditions of soil, climate.

- Thin-skinned grapes lead to wines light in color and low in astringency. They may be enjoyed immediately upon release, but some examples, especially French, benefit from cellaring.

New World were unsuccessful until the 1980s, when clonal selection proved to be key in growing Pinot Noir in California and Oregon. Because Pinot Noir is the most mutable wine grape in the world, it's not surprising that there are dozens of sports, some of which adapt to terroirs different from Burgundy. When such a sport is discovered, it is cloned for planting in a suitable location. Clonal development took root in Dijon, Burgundy's capital city, and the resultant clones are known as "Dijon clones." Clones are widely planted in California and Oregon and have led to wines of great distinction.

Pinot Noir

- A light ruby color is typical, but some Pinot Noir is made using longer skin contact, which results in a darker, richer wine.

- Pinot Noir is aromatic, with flavors of cherry, plum, violet, and pomegranate. Perhaps no other wine variety expresses the specifics of its location more than Pinot Noir, so appellation is an important factor. Older Pinot Noirs often develop strong earthy dimensions, such as truffles, forest floor, and mushrooms.

- Pinot Noir, especially red Burgundy, is one of the world's great food wines.

Unique Conditions Needed for This Difficult Varietal

- Pinot Noir requires cool, often fog-prone growing conditions and marine sediment or volcanic soils. The soils of Burgundy consist of Jurassic limestone formations that form very stony topsoils on gentle slopes. The world's greatest Pinot Noirs hail from this region.

- Next to the great Grand Cru Burgundies, such as Romanée-Conti, Eschezeau, Musigny, Chambertin, and Clos Vougeot, the finest examples of great Pinot Noir come from Oregon's cool Willamette Valley. The soils here are basaltic.

SYRAH

The great grape of the Rhône Valley finds a very agreeable home in Australia

Syrah is an ancient grape, believed to have originated in Iran. It was brought to France's Rhône Valley by the Romans in the first century AD. It is now grown worldwide under a range of soil types and climates.

The best and most expensive Syrah wines come from the northern Rhône region, south of the city of Lyon. The great

Syrahs of Côte Rôtie can cost hundreds of dollars. Slightly less expensive are the single-vineyard Syrahs of Hermitage, just downriver.

New World Syrahs have enjoyed spectacular success, particularly in Australia, where they are known as "Shiraz," and in California's Central Coast region.

Value-oriented Syrahs

- When price is not a major consideration, winemakers use an arsenal of labor-intensive techniques, including biodynamic farming, expensive new oak barrels, and meticulous "élevage," or cellar methods. Value-oriented wines are likely to be the product of mechanical harvesting and closed-tank stainless steel fermentation.

- Value-oriented wines can be expected to be less aromatic, less complex, and less varietally distinctive.

- Although the great Syrahs from France and Australia are always very expensive, moderately priced examples from California and Washington State offer excellent wines at much more attractive prices.

Open-top Fermenter

- Traditional fermentation vessels are large, wooden vats, but lined-cement and stainless steel are also widely used.

- The open top allows the "cap" or solid matter to be stirred or punched down at intervals. This leads to greater extraction of color and flavor components in the grape skins.

- In the case of great, artisanal wines, the cap may be punched down every few hours, even through the night. Such wines will achieve a richness and body beyond those fermented in large stainless steel tanks.

Syrah is best grown in warm climates. When grown in the best locations, New World Syrah offers a jammy mouthful of ripe blackberry, prune, leather, and meaty overtones. It's a big wine and can be fairly tannic, although not as astringent as Cabernet Sauvignons of similar quality. The French-style Syrah is drier, leaner, and very complex in the finest examples. Its superior structure—the exquisite balance of acid, tannin, and fruit—makes these wines very long-lived. They can be successfully cellared for more than a decade. New World Syrah is best drunk within ten years of the vintage.

A Glass of Syrah

- Syrah is characteristically a very dark, dense wine, often opaque unless strongly back lit.

- Syrah resembles Cabernet Sauvignon in depth and complexity but offers a flavor profile that suggests meaty flavors rather than cedar and tobacco.

- The tannins in Syrah are usually abundant in fine examples but less asser-tive than in Cabernet Sauvignon.

- Serve Syrah (or Shiraz) with richly flavored meat courses such as roast beef, grilled steaks, and lamb.

Penfold's Grange Shiraz

- Penfold's Grange is Austra-lia's most collectible wine and considered by many to be the finest example of Syrah (Shiraz) in the New World.

- Grange is not the product of a single vineyard or even a single appellation. It carries the general "South Australia" appellation.

- Although Grange is the most-honored and expen-sive New World Syrah, other Australian Shirazes that are almost as fine can be found at much lower prices. Top producers are Henschke, Torbeck, and Yalumba.

RED WINE

ZINFANDEL
Try California's unique wine grape

Zinfandel is unique among the world's major wine grapes. First of all, we didn't even know what it was until very recently when DNA fingerprinting positively identified it as a clone of the Italian Primitivo grape. In post-Prohibition years it became the most widely planted red grape in California and remained so until American tastes turned to more "distinguished" varieties.

Zinfandel, believed to have made its New World debut in a New York nursery in 1816, made its way west and quickly became the preferred red grape variety. Because its ancient origins were from south Italy, it is most comfortable in warm climates and was planted in California's Central Valley, Sierra Foothills, and in California's Central Coast. It became the flagship red grape of the Paso Robles region.

The Three R's of Zinfandel

- Unlike wines from quality-oriented wineries that maintain estate vineyards, many of California's top Zinfandels are products of wineries that specialize in this variety and source their fruit from different regions.

- The big names in California Zinfandel are Ridge, Ravenswood, and Rosenblum. All these wineries offer vineyard-designated wines from the best fruit sources at moderate prices.

Zinfandel Cluster

- Zinfandel is a heavy bearing variety, requiring "green harvests" where juvenile clusters are removed to focus the vine's strength in the remaining berries.

- Zinfandel is subject to bunch rot because of its tight clusters that do not promote air circulation.

- There are just a few clonal selections of Zinfandel. They exist in three "lines": Croatian (ancient), Italian Primitivo (1800), and California (1850). Many California Zinfandel vineyards are planted with vineyard selections rather than registered clones.

Central Valley Zinfandel has historically served as a base wine for inexpensive generic red wines, such as those California wines called "Burgundy."

With the progress of viticulture and winemaking in the 1960s, serious efforts were made to bring this variety into the forefront of quality domestic wines. Early examples were heavily overextracted tannic "monsters," and after a brief enthusiasm the American market turned against all varietally labeled red Zinfandel. Today's Zinfandels are polished, very fruit-driven, moderately low-tannin wines.

Zinfandel

- Zinfandel usually displays a purplish rather than reddish color because it is released earlier than those red varieties that require longer cellar time to soften tannin and let the wine "come together."

- Zinfandel is often harvested late, which raises the sugar and alcohol levels.

- Zinfandel is often the most alcoholic of all dry red table wines. Alcohol levels average nearly 15 percent and can rise as high as 17 percent. These wines possess such a strong fruit component that they appear somewhat sweet.

Head-pruned Zinfandel Vine

- The term head-pruning refers to a non-trellised vine training method by which the vine is allowed to develop a central trunk from which the fruit hangs down. The French call this method "gobelet" because its shape resembles a wine glass.

- Most New World wine grapes are trellised to provide easy access to the fruit and, in some cases, mechanical harvesting.

- Zinfandel was planted throughout California in the nineteenth century before the introduction of trellising.

RED WINE

PETITE SIRAH

Rich, dark, and dense, Petite Sirah complements savory stews or grilled steaks

Petite Sirah (note spelling), along with Zinfandel, is one of California's historic grapes and is often found planted in the same vineyard. Its growing conditions are similar, but the varieties are distinctly different.

It was originally developed in the nineteenth century by crossing true Syrah grapes with Peloursin, a southern French grape, and growers hoped that the result would be resistant to powdery mildew. The new hybrid was named after its introducer, Durif. Occasionally we see this variety labeled as "Durif," but it is usually called "Petite Sirah."

Petite Sirah renders an extremely dark, sometimes opaque wine and is the blending wine of choice for Zinfandel and

Organic vs. Biodynamic Farming

Three movements towards eco-friendly viticulture are coming into prominence, spearheaded by Burgundian grape growers:

- Sustainable Farming. Grapes are grown in a manner that protects the soil from depleted nutrients, salinity, and erosion.

- Organic Farming. No herbicides, pesticides, or chemical fertilizers are allowed.

- Biodynamic Farming. Organic farming extended to include specific procedures such as the use of fermented herbal and mineral preparations and deference to the astrological calendar.

Wine Barrel Undergoing the Toasting Process

- Oak wine barrels are formed and shaped over an open flame to facilitate bending of the staves.

- The time the wood is heated by the flame determines the degree of "toast."

- Barrels are custom ordered by wineries in three degrees

of toast: Light, Medium, and Heavy.

- Each degree of toast promotes a different range of flavors and aromas to wine, but this effect fades over time.

other red wines that need propping up. Petite Sirah has found a happy home in the warmer parts of California, Argentina, Israel, and Australia. It outperforms the Durif of southern France, just as California Zinfandel generally outperforms its European Zinfandel counterparts.

The best regions for Petite Sirah are the Russian River drainage of Sonoma County, Paso Robles, and Mendocino. Notable producers are Concannon, Ridge, Guenoc, Rosenblum, and Stags' Leap. The densest, most concentrated Petite Sirah is made by Turley Wine Cellars under the title "Aida."

Petite Sirah

- Most modern viticulturists believe Petite Sirah to be identical to the Durif grape from southern France.

- Widely planted in California in the early twentieth century, Petite Sirah was used as a base wine for generic red wines such as "Burgundy."

- Petite Sirah is the densest and most full-bodied of all popular red wine grapes grown in the U.S.

- Petite Sirah lacks the complexity of Zinfandel, which it closely resembles, and is more tannic because of its small berry size.

Recommended Food Pairings for Petite Sirah

- Grilled Steaks
- Hearty Beef Stews
- Game Dishes
- Spicy Chili
- Indian Curries
- Barbecued Meats

THE WHITE ZINFANDEL CRAZE

A manufacturing mistake changed American wine preferences

Varietally labeled red Zinfandel reached its zenith in the 1960s and 1970s when Santa Cruz Mountain wineries such as David Bruce and Ridge offered thick, rich, and very tannic single-vineyard versions. The market quickly embraced these "monster" wines but eventually tired of the style. At that time, Zinfandel was the most widely planted red grape in California, and sales were rapidly diminishing.

Then an astonishing turn of events occurred. Bob Trinchero of Sutter Home Winery in Napa Valley experienced a "stuck fermentation" while attempting to ferment Zinfandel. The fermentation stopped before dryness was achieved, and the resulting wine was sweet, low in alcohol—and pink! It was offered at a bargain price to tasting-room visitors, who loaded up their trunks with cases of this anomaly. Thus was

A Casual Approach to Wine

- White Zinfandel largely replaced the older proprietary wines (Ripple, Thunderbird, and so forth) designed for people discovering wine or graduating from soda pop.

- No "wine snob" amenities, such as stemware, were needed. White Zinfandel was happily consumed in the most casual fashion.

- White Zinfandel's main appeal was to those unaccustomed to wine and those who embraced "wine coolers." It has always been considered a recreational wine, not a wine to complement foods.

Sutter Home White Zinfandel

- This is the wine that started the White Zinfandel craze. It was the first commercial success and continues to the present day.

- White Zinfandel elevated the Sutter Home Winery from a small family operated business to a major large-scale winery.

- Sutter Home offers a traditional Zinfandel made from fruit grown in Lodi and the Sierra foothills. Sutter Home is the third-largest family-owned winery in the United States after E & J Gallo and Kendall-Jackson.

born White Zinfandel, a wine that had great appeal to the soda-pop crowd and provided a market for all the red Zinfandel fruit that was languishing for buyers.

Red Zinfandel all but disappeared from supermarket shelves, which had taken on a distinctly pink color. It would take more than a decade before true Zinfandel wines would begin to regain their appeal.

White Zinfandel is not made in the manner associated with other rosé wines. It is made in the least-expensive way, usually from machine-harvested fruit partially fermented in large stainless steel tanks. This keeps the cost and quality of these wines low.

They are too sweet for most successful food pairings, although there are exceptions. And they are monodimensional. There just isn't much interest or complexity in the wine. They are wines for quaffing if one doesn't mind the sweetness.

Supermarket shelves have now returned to their red and white coloration, thanks to the return of high-quality Zinfandel, the appearance of quality rosé wines, and an increasing sophistication in the marketplace.

A Glass of White Zinfandel

- White Zinfandel is a result of arrested development. While pretty in the glass, it lacks any sense of varietal character and is said to be monodimensional.

- Primary characteristics of White Zinfandel are low alcohol, no tannins, low acid, and sweetness. To achieve a modicum of complexity, White Zinfandel is sometimes blended with a highly aromatic white wine such as Muscat. White Zinfandel is known only in the United States. No other country produces it in commercial quantities. Higher-quality varietal rosé wines are largely replacing it.

Fruit Compote with White Zinfandel

- White Zinfandel can be used as a simple dessert wine with foods that have some acidity, such as fresh fruit.

- It can be used as a base wine for wine punches.

- It makes a pleasant picnic wine, but should be served ice cold.

- White Zinfandel does not pair well with many savory foods, but can work with foods such as a chicken salad sandwich. Avoid pairing it with cheeses.

TRADITIONAL FRENCH ROSÉ WINES

Chilled European-styled dry rosé wines add elegance to light foods and picnics

European rosé wines have never achieved the popularity of red and white wines, and in France they may be made only in a few delimited areas of the Loire Valley and southern Rhône.

The best-known rosé from the Loire region is Rosé d'Anjou, a pleasant off-dry rosé that was popular in America in the 1970s but that has since fallen out of favor. It is still imported to America under the "Barton & Guestier" label.

Typical French rosé wines are bone dry with racy acidity, making them very attractive to pair with simple foods. The historic vineyards of Tavel and Lirac, across the Rhône River from famed Châteauneuf-du-Pape, provided carefully crafted

Vineyard in Tavel

- Tavel was the first AC in France to be designated strictly for rosé wines. Nearby Lirac produces both rosé and light red wine.

- The Tavel AC largely shares the same geologic substrate as Châteauneuf-du-Pape across the river. Large, polished limestone pebbles dominate the surface.

- Cinsault is king in Tavel. The famous wines of this region are Cinsault-based, with Grenache and sometimes Mourvedre blended in.

- Rosé wines of Tavel and Lirac are deeper and more fully flavored.

The Famous Tavel Rosé

- Tavel Rosé has long been considered the world's best pink wine, but modern efforts from California give Tavel stiff competition.

- Tavel Rosé is made by leaving the juice on the skins briefly to extract color and flavor; then the juice is "bled" or separated from the skins without pressing. A small portion of the skins, or "must," is returned to the free-run juice for additional color and flavor extraction.

- The potential alcohol level of Tavel rosé is high, but government regulations disallow alcohol to exceed 13.5 percent.

48

dry rosé wines for the Sun King, Louis XIV. These wines have been considered the quality standard for rosé wines for centuries. The entire "Tavel" and "Lirac" appellations are mandated for rosé wines only and are the only French ACs (appellation controlée) devoted strictly to rosé wine. These traditional rosé wineries of the southern Rhône Valley have recently been joined by other wineries whose appellation allows rosé production in addition to red and white wine. Notable is the winery of Domaine d'Hortus in the Languedoc region. Rosé wines from Provence appear in the American market as well.

ZOOM

Other European rosé wines that are imported to America include the rosato wines of Italy, the Montepulciano Cerasuolo from Abruzzo, and Spanish rosados from 100 percent Garnacha. All of these wines are dry.

A Bordeaux Rosé

- Bergerac lies east of St. Emilon and enjoys the same soil type—limestone with fossilized starfish, known as "Calcaire d'Asteries."

- Rosé wines of Bergerac use the Bordeaux varieties: Cabernet Sauvignon, Cabernet Franc, and Merlot.

- Bergerac rosés are known for their fruity elegance and are much lower in alcohol than their southern Rhône counterparts.

- French rosé wines made from Bordeaux varieties more closely resemble New World rosés but are lighter in body.

Three Styles of Rosé Wine

- Finished red and white wines are blended together: This is the method used to produce most value-oriented rosé wines. But it is allowed in French AOC regions and is sometimes used in the production of fine wine.

- "Saignée" or "free-run juice": In this method the grapes are not pressed, and the juice that bleeds off as a result of the weight of the grapes is drained off. It carries some of the color and flavor of the grapes. The grapes are subsequently pressed to produce a standard red wine.

- Skin contact: The grapes are pressed, and the juice is left in contact with the skins for two or three days, then separated.

NEW WORLD ROSÉ WINES
This favorite turns a corner and becomes serious

American rosé wines became popular in the 1950s with large-scale commercial wineries attempting to try pink wines instead of the popular fortified wines of that time. It was an early attempt to marry wine with dining. An early effort by E & J Gallo to grow Grenache in California's hot Central Valley resulted in blanched skins that rendered pink wine. The result was marketed widely as Grenache Rosé and was very successful.

Another large California winery picked up the cue and televised the slogan "Put a rose in your glass." Rosé wine from California became the most popular table wine of the period. They were all lightly sweet.

Decades passed before California winemakers began to address rosé wines seriously. Then came an onslaught of varietal rosé wines from Syrah, Grenache, Cabernet Sauvignon,

Common Varieties Used for New World Rosé Wines

- Grenache
- Cinsault
- Syrah
- Cabernet Sauvignon
- Sangiovese
- Pinot Noir (see Vin Gris)
- Blended Rhône Varieties

L'Aventure Rosé of Cabernet Sauvignon

- L'Aventure winery in Paso Robles offers a highly polished example of New World rosé. Wines such as this move rosé wine onto an equal footing with quality red and white wines.

- L'Aventure's estate vineyard features a geology known as "linne calodo," a sedimentary limestone soil containing chalky stones that absorb and hold moisture. These soils provide an ideal wine-growing environment.

- Varietal rosés such as this display clear, understated varietal character.

and premium blends. The wines graduated from off-dry to bone dry. They ranged from light pink to light red. The most successful of the early offerings were from producers specializing in Rhône varieties. These wines were mostly blends of Rhône grapes, dominated by Grenache, Syrah, and Cinsault. One of the most successful was Bonny Doon's Vin Gris de Cigare, not a true vin gris but rather a rosé made from Rhône varieties.

Today's best New World rosé wines are often varietal rosés made from a single distinguished grape variety. They can be serious wines when great fruit is used and care is taken in vinification. Excellent rosés are also made from a blend of Rhône varieties.

New World rosés are typically very dry and exhibit aromas and flavors of strawberry, red currant, and rose petals. They should be served well chilled. New World rosés provide excellent accompaniments to light foods, sandwiches, and picnic foods. They also make splendid apéritif wines.

A Range of Rosé Wines

- Rosé wines are made in styles ranging from very light pink to light red. The lightest is sometimes called "Oeil de Perdrix" or "eye of the partridge." These wines were popular in the 1980s and have receded in popularity. The original wines were made in the Middle Ages in Champagne, France, using the saignée method.

- The Italian rosatos and Spanish rosados are deeply colored and more intensely flavored. They can be splendid wines for light food courses such as roast chicken, sautéed pork chops, and vegetarian dishes.

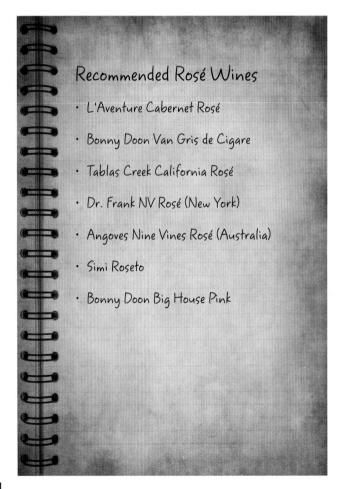

Recommended Rosé Wines

- L'Aventure Cabernet Rosé
- Bonny Doon Van Gris de Cigare
- Tablas Creek California Rosé
- Dr. Frank NV Rosé (New York)
- Angoves Nine Vines Rosé (Australia)
- Simi Roseto
- Bonny Doon Big House Pink

VIN GRIS
This pink wine is from Pinot Noir

Vin gris originated in France's Loire Valley, where light pink wines were made from the free-run juice of Cinsault and Grenache grapes. These were local wines but carried the label gris de gris (gray from gray). The wines were not gray, of course, but very light pink. They were not made by the saignée process, using the free-run juice from unpressed fruit, but rather from pressed grapes that were not allowed to macerate in their juice. The resulting juice was very lightly colored, giving rise to the designation Oeil de Perdrix (eye of the partridge).

In the New World, and especially in California, the term vin gris became associated specifically with light rosé wines made from Pinot Noir. When you see a California rosé labeled vin gris, it is very likely Pinot Noir. A very notable exception

Crusher Showing Free-run Juice

- Free-run juice, or saignée, is the juice that is released from the grapes by virtue of the weight of the fruit.

- The juice of all major grape varieties is clear. Color is imparted by extended contact with the skins. Minimal skin contact results in white or pink wines. Many Cham-

pagne wines are made from dark-skinned Pinot Noir but show no color if disallowed skin contact after pressing.

- Free-run juice carries very little, if any, tannin and must be enjoyed soon after release.

Two Pinot Noirs

- These wines were made from the same grape variety. They differ in color, dryness, and flavor intensity.

- Both are fermented to dryness, but the vin gris on the right is very dry and delicate because it didn't have time to absorb the flavor-imparting phenolics that

long maceration imparts.

- The Pinot Noir on the left has been made to express the full potential of the grape's aroma and flavor. Its aspect is slightly sweeter because of the rich fruit component.

- Lighter-styled Pinot Noirs can be as aromatic as richer ones.

is Bonny Doon's Vin Gris de Cigare, an exquisite pink Rhône blend.

Vin gris is always very dry and always very light pink, and the best examples carry a clear suggestion of the Pinot Noir flavor profile. It is often considered to be the most elegant of New World rosé wines by wine lovers because of its complex flavor profile and striking aromatics.

Oddly, vin gris is not always associated with the major Pinot Noir regions of California and Oregon. The finest fruit is necessarily reserved for red Pinot Noir. No winemaker would direct premium Pinot Noir fruit into a vin gris program because the bottle price of a fine California Pinot Noir is about three or four times higher than that of a vin gris. But there are some notable exceptions. When a producer is confronted with more fruit than he thinks he can market as varietal Pinot Noir, he may direct the surplus to a vin gris program. Or lower-quality lots of an estate vineyard may be reserved for vin gris.

Bonny Doon Vin Gris de Cigare

- Bonny Doon's Vin Gris de Cigare is one of the earliest introductions of vin gris to America. It is made from Rhône varieties, not Pinot Noir.

- The "Cigare" reference is to flying saucers and, specifically, their supposed shape. Vin Gris de Cigare introduced many Americans to dry rosé wines after decades of sweet pink wines had flooded the market. Bonny Doon was not the first to introduce dry rosé wines to the U.S. market, but it sparked a renewed interest in European-styled rosés.

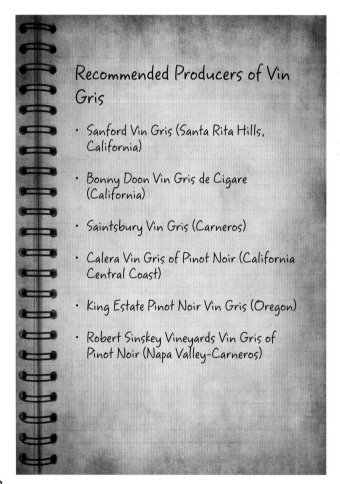

Recommended Producers of Vin Gris

- Sanford Vin Gris (Santa Rita Hills, California)

- Bonny Doon Vin Gris de Cigare (California)

- Saintsbury Vin Gris (Carneros)

- Calera Vin Gris of Pinot Noir (California Central Coast)

- King Estate Pinot Noir Vin Gris (Oregon)

- Robert Sinskey Vineyards Vin Gris of Pinot Noir (Napa Valley-Carneros)

CHAMPAGNE: THE REAL THING

An accidental discovery led to one of the world's most-honored wines

Champagne is the name given to a region that is 125 miles northeast of Paris and a part of the larger Paris Basin. Its major cities, Rheims and Épernay, preside over four cuestas, or low chalky hills that provide a unique terroir for grapes intended for sparkling wines.

Sparkling wine was originally an accident of nature. Fermentation often stopped short of dryness in the region's cold autumn climate. Nevertheless, the wines were bottled for shipment to England. When the wines warmed up, fermentation resumed, and the carbon dioxide gas went into solution. When the wine was uncorked, it was naturally carbonated, and the English loved it. Because of the high incidence of exploding bottles, the English developed the special thick bottles still used for sparkling wines.

A Typical Vineyard in Champagne

Champagne—The Real Thing

- The cold, northern climate in Champagne leads to underripe fruit unsuitable for still wine but perfect for sparkling wines.

- Germans such as Krug, Bollinger, and Roederer founded many of the well-known Champagne houses in the nineteenth century.

- Champagne was the birthplace of the world's first wine industry dominated by large-scale branded producers.

- Mme. Clicquot, who outlived her husband and became known as "veuve," or widow, founded the oldest major house.

- Because there are so many steps in the production of Champagne, the wine is necessarily expensive.

- Most Champagne is blended from different vineyard sources and from different vintages in order to maintain a consistent house style.

- Two or three times in a decade a vintage year is declared. These wines will be kept separate from the house blend and will be extremely expensive. Vintage Champagne is aged on the lees (or spent yeast cells) for five to seven years before finishing and release.

During the first four decades of the seventeenth century the technique of controlled secondary fermentation was developed by the founders of some of the great Champagne houses such as Madame (Veuve) Clicquot. The new method, known as "méthode champenoise," requires a precise ripeness level at harvest that will lead to a wine with around 8 percent alcohol when fermented to dryness. The still wine, called "clairette," is bottled, and a precise amount of yeast and sugar is added. The wine is corked, and a second fermentation takes place. When this stage is completed, the bottles are held in a downward position so the dead yeast cells can collect in the neck of the bottle, which is then frozen. The plug of dead yeast cells is removed, and a dosage is added before recorking. The dosage consists of Champagne wine, dissolved sugar, and sometimes brandy. Every house guards its dosage formula carefully. Different amounts of the dosage lead to the various styles of Champagne—Naturel, Brut, Extra Dry, and Doux.

Grape varieties used for Champagne include Pinot Noir, Chardonnay, and Pinot Meuniere.

A Coupe of Champagne

- The short, wide glass known as a "coupe" was fashionable for serving Champagne up to the 1980s, when crystal manufacturers began offering more suitably shaped glassware.

- The coupe was said to have been molded from the breast of Marie Antoinette.

- But modern research has shown that it was designed specifically for Champagne by an English glassmaker in 1663.

- The coupe was never a satisfactory design for any kind of wine because its straight or outward-sloping sides lead to spillage.

A Flute of Champagne

- The tall, narrow Champagne flute has largely replaced the coupe as the glassware of choice for all sparkling wines.

- The main attractions of the flute are its ability to promote the visual appearance of Champagne and its small surface area, which aids bubble retention.

- The flute is preferred over the coupe by caterers and servers as more glasses can be placed on a tray.

- Except for visual presentation, Champagne is best served in a standard white wine glass.

SPARKLING VOUVRAY

Here is a French alternative to Champagne at a fraction of the price

Throughout the middle Loire Valley, Chenin Blanc is king. It is one of the few grape varieties that produces the full range of wine styles, from bone dry to extremely sweet. And next to Champagne, the best-known French sparkling wines come from the heart of this region.

The western Loire Valley is best known for very dry white wines; the eastern regions produce firm reds from Cabernet Franc and benchmark whites from Sauvignon Blanc.

Sparkling Vouvray, like all the Chenin Blanc wines of the Loire, is completely dependent upon the weather. The Loire Valley is considered the dividing line between the Mediterranean climate to the south and the Atlantic climate of northern France. Harvests here are typically the latest in all of France, often running into November.

Still Vouvray

- The region around Tours, called the "Touraine," is one of France's oldest wine regions, dating back to the Middle Ages.

- Vouvray received AC (appellation controlée) status in 1939 when its wines were found to be distinct from the other wines of the Touraine. Before then, most Vouvray wines were blended into other wines of the region.

- Most of the wines of Vouvray lie on northern slopes above the Loire River and are aged in caves dug into the hillsides.

Sparkling Vouvray

- Sparkling Vouvray resembles the other sparkling wines of France, such as Blanquette de Limoux or Crémant d'Alsace, more than Champagne.

- Sparkling Vouvray is inexpensive when compared with Champagne or the better sparkling wines of the New World.

- Sparkling Vouvray uses the same style nomenclature as Champagne: Brut for very dry, Demi-sec for lightly sweet.

- Sparkling Vouvray, in any but the sweet styles, makes a perfect appetizer wine.

Vouvray producers use no new oak and no small cooperage. They prefer large old oak barrels or stainless steel because their wines are made with minimal intervention. Vintage variation is greater here than in almost any other French region. When the weather cooperates, Vouvray sings out with sweet, minerally notes. When full ripeness is not obtainable, the wines display bracing acidity and are usually used for sparkling Vouvray.

Sparkling Vouvray production follows the Champagne model. Because sparkling wines benefit from underripe grapes, most sparkling Vouvray is made from the least-satisfactory vintage years. As a result, there are large amounts of low-quality sparkling Vouvray on the market. It is essential to look for wines from the best and most dependable producers.

In good years Vouvray Mousseux, a fully sparkling wine, is produced. These can be dry, off-dry, or slightly sweet. They can express the true honeyed nature of Chenin Blanc.

Because of the decline of interest in Chenin Blanc throughout the New World over the past several decades, most Vouvray production is now sparkling.

Champagne versus Sparkling Vouvray

- The visual appearance of Champagne is strikingly different from that of sparkling Vouvray. Vouvray's larger bubbles resemble those found in most New World sparkling wines.

- The mouthfeel of Champagne is unique because of the small bubble size. The sensation in the mouth is almost electrifying. Vouvray's texture is coarser.

- Sparkling Vouvray displays some honeyed notes, baked pear, and a minerality peculiar to the Loire region. Champagne is more likely to suggest yeast or toasted bread.

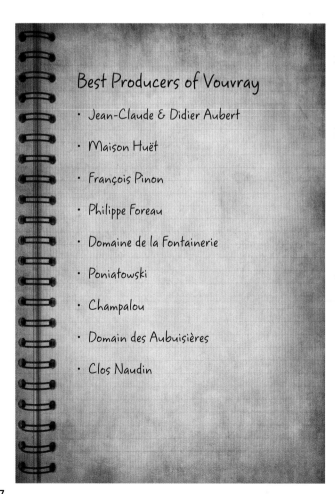

Best Producers of Vouvray

- Jean-Claude & Didier Aubert
- Maison Huët
- François Pinon
- Philippe Foreau
- Domaine de la Fontainerie
- Poniatowski
- Champalou
- Domain des Aubuisières
- Clos Naudin

CAVA: SPAIN'S INEXPENSIVE BUBBLY

It's a sparkling white wine for everyday enjoyment

Cava is a Spanish sparkling wine made in great quantity in the northeastern region of Penedés, whose major city is Barcelona. The firm of Freixenet makes an estimated 60 percent of all Spanish sparkling wine. Its major rival, Cordoniú, produces most of the remaining 40 percent. Both houses were established in the late nineteenth century, and little has changed in their wine styles over the years.

The term cava means "cellar" in Catalonia. These wines are regulated by DO (denominación de origen) rules and must be made using the traditional method, as in Champagne.

Spanish Cava is readily available in American and British marketplaces, and it is inexpensive enough to enjoy on a regular basis.

This dry, sparkling white wine makes an excellent accom-

Freixenet Carta Nevada

- Freixenet is the world's largest producer of Cava. The firm was founded in 1889. Annual production of Freixenet, including its subsidiary labels, is over 100 million bottles.

- Carta Nevada is Freixenet's medium-dry Cava. Their Brut Cava, drier and more

complex, is called "Carta Negro" and comes in a distinctive black bottle.

- Freixenet has holdings worldwide. It produces sparkling wines under several labels, including "Gloria Ferrer," made in Sonoma County, and "Sala Vivé," made in Mexico.

Segura Viudas Cava

- Segura Viudas is an artisanal, high-quality Cava made to exacting production standards by Freixenet.

- Segura Viudas is priced about two or three times as much as Freixenet's most popular brands and comes in five styles.

- Reserva Heredad, Segura Viudas's flagship wine is aged for four years on the yeast (lees). It comes in a distinctive hand-blown bottle and is available throughout America and the United Kingdom. Other Segura Viudas wines include three wines under the "Aria" label and a sparkling Pinot Noir.

paniment to appetizers, light food courses, and even desserts. American wine lovers are finding that Spanish Cava not only fills the bill for apéritifs but also makes a perfect base for sparkling wine cocktails and "Champagne" punches. It's also a good choice for wedding receptions and other festive events where guests are unlikely to pay close attention to the subtleties of a more-complex wine.

The quality of Cava varies very little from year to year because these wines are blended to conform to the house style. There are no vintage Cavas.

Spanish Cava

- Although Cava lacks the elegance and finesse of fine Champagne, it provides a very affordable alternative.

- The texture and mouth-feel of Cava are similar to those of New World sparkling wines, Cava is a DO regulated wine and, like all quality sparkling wines,

must undergo a secondary fermentation in the bottle.

- The labor-intensive process of freezing the bottle necks to remove spent yeast cells has been replaced by a gyropalette, which performs this operation mechanically on hundreds of bottles at a time.

YELLOW ● LIGHT

The most reliable Cavas are those made by the larger producers. Differences in house style are almost negligible. All Cava is made from Viura (Macabeo), Xarel-lo, and Parellada grapes grown almost exclusively in Catalonia.

Cava-based Cocktails

- Cava provides a wonderful and inexpensive base for a range of apéritif cocktails.

- Royal Kir: Add a teaspoon or more of Crème de Cassis to a flute of Cava.

- Goodnight Kiss: In a flute, place 1 sugar cube, add 1 drop Angostura bitters and a splash of Campari, and fill with Cava.

- Mimosa: Use one-third orange juice, two-thirds Cava.

- Invent your own: A very popular apéritif in Europe is made by dropping 1 spoonful of liqueur into a flute of sparkling white wine. Fruit-flavored liqueurs such as Chambord work very well. If the drink is not mixed, the denser liqueur will sink to the bottom of the glass, providing visual interest.

PROSECCO: ITALY'S FESTIVE SPARKLER

This versatile wine comes from Italy's Veneto region

Unlike Champagne (named for a region) and Cava (named after a procedure), Prosecco is an Italian sparkling wine made from the eponymous grape variety. Prosecco grapes are grown only in the Veneto region of northeastern Italy and are used to make still, frizzante, and sparkling wines. At this time the only Prosecco wines imported to the New World are of the sparkling variety.

Also, unlike Champagne and Cava, Prosecco is not made using the traditional method of secondary fermentation in the bottle but rather by the Charmat process. This wine is made in large, pressurized, stainless steel tanks, then filtered and bottled under pressure. Apart from adding carbonation to finished wine, the Charmat process is the least-expensive method of getting fizz into wine.

Zardetto Prosecco

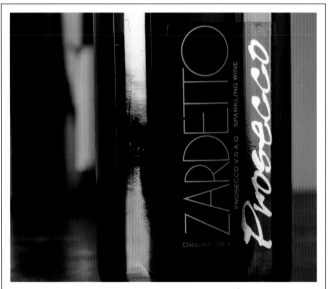

- Zardetto Prosecco is one of the most widely distributed Proseccos in the U.S. The factory is located in the heart of the finest Prosecco region—Conegliano-Valdobbiadene, 40 miles northwest of Venice.

- The term Prosecco is derived from the north Italian village of the same name.

- Approximately 150 million bottles of Prosecco are produced annually, around 60 percent from the Conegliano area.

- Zardetto markets four Prosecco wines.

Traditional Prosecco Cocktails

- The Bellini cocktail: Into a Champagne flute pour one-third part peach puree; fill with two-thirds parts Prosecco. Garnish with raspberries or cut strawberries.

- The Bellini is a classic Prosecco cocktail, invented in Venice around 1940. It was a favorite cocktail of Ernest Hemingway, Sinclair Lewis, and Orson Welles.

- The Poinsettia cocktail: This elegant Prosecco cocktail consists of $1/2$ ounce Cointreau or other orange liqueur, 3 ounces cranberry juice, and Prosecco to fill a standard Champagne flute. Garnish with orange zest.

Prosecco is one of Italy's oldest grape varieties, grown in Roman times and described by Pliny the Elder.

Prosecco was originally made in a lightly sweet style similar to Asti Spumante, but since the 1960s it has been offered almost exclusively in a very dry but not austere style. Prosecco grapes are also grown in Argentina, Brazil, Romania, and Australia.

In contrast to nonvintage Champagne, which is usually blended from a selection of base wines, Prosecco is a single-variety wine.

ZOOM

The Charmat process is used for most of the world's cheaper sparkling wines. The entire process takes place in large pressurized tanks, eliminating most of the labor-intensive steps of the traditional method. Wines made by the Charmat process will be simple and lack the complexity of traditional sparkling wines.

Prosecco Wines

- Italy is the world's largest producer of the greatest range of sparkling wines. The spectrum includes spumante (foaming) and frizzante (lightly fizzy). Many spumante wines are sweet and have large bubbles. Prosecco is dry and has finer bubbles.

- Prosecco is produced both as a lightly sparkling wine and a fully sparkling wine. Imported examples are almost always fully sparkling.

- The best Prosecco wines are labeled as "Prosecco di Conegliano."

Prosecco Profile

- Sparkling wines are normally made from barely ripened fruit, just as the herbaceousness begins to give way to varietal fruit flavors.

- Most sparkling wines are made from blends of different grape varieties. This ensures a consistent style and complex flavor palette.

- Single-variety Proseccos are characterized by that variety's flavor profile, sometimes described as lemongrass, orange blossom, peach, and tropical fruits.

- Prosecco from the Cartizze vineyard is widely thought to be the best example of Prosecco and is bottled as a vineyard-designated wine.

U.S. SPARKLING WINES

World-class wines come from California, New York State, and New Mexico

Sparkling wine in the United States enjoys a century-old tradition, beginning in Napa Valley, California. Early wines were simply carbonated still wines, but real *méthode champenoise* wines began to appear at midcentury under the labels of "Kornell" and "Schramsberg."

Because the best sparkling wine is made from barely ripe

fruit, New York State occupied center stage for much of the twentieth century, offering inexpensive mass-produced bottlings. Its history of sparkling wine goes back to the 1860s. A sparkling Catawba from the Finger Lakes region won international acclaim in 1863. Today's sparkling wines from New York State are made from a range of grape varieties.

Chandon Brut

- The Napa Valley firm of Chandon is a subsidiary of the French house of Moët et Chandon, which makes the luxury brand Dom Pérignon. Its wines are known for their richness and creamy texture.

- The California lineup from Chandon includes five

wines, including a rosé, an off-dry wine, and a sparkling red wine from Pinot Noir and Zinfandel.

- Chandon's Reserve lineup consists of seven wines, including Pinot Noir rosé, Crémant, and Twenty Year Cuvée. The winery offers vintage-dated wines as well.

Gruet Méthode Champenoise Rosé

- Rosé sparkling wines are made by adding a small amount of red Pinot Noir juice to the lightly colored free-run juice of the other grapes. Rosé sparkling wines can be complex and elegant.

- Gruet is one of the most distinguished wineries in

the southwestern United States. It specializes in sparkling wines. Gruet's NV Brut, NV Blanc de Noirs (from Pinot Noir), Demi-sec (lightly sweet), and Rosé are all value priced.

- A second tier of Blanc de Blancs, Grand Rosé and Reserve, is also offered.

A sea change in sparkling wine quality occurred when several traditional French houses set up shop in California: Moët & Chandon, Mumm, Piper-Hiedsick, Deutz, and Roederer. Their products rose to the front ranks of New World sparkling wine, along with the already established Schramsberg wines. J Vineyards & Winery joined the effort in 1986 and offers a range of excellent sparkling wines.

Washington State's Chateau Ste.-Michelle entered sparkling wine production and swept up the low-end market almost overnight with three excellent value sparklers that are inexpensive enough for everyday enjoyment. Perhaps the biggest surprise in American sparkling wine comes from a very unlikely place. In 1983 a French winemaker from Champagne passed through the Rio Grande Valley town of Truth or Consequences, New Mexico. He then proceeded to buy land and plant a vineyard devoted to sparkling wine made in the Champagne tradition. Thus was born the New Mexico house of Gruet, whose sparkling wines now rival some of the best from California.

Chateau Frank Blanc de Blancs

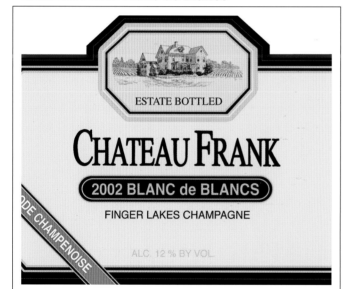

- Chateau Frank Blanc de Blancs is an example of the higher-quality *méthode champenoise* wines from New York. This winery earned the accolade "Greatest Wine Producer in the Atlantic Northeast" five years in a row in Stevenson's annual Wine Report.

- Chateau Frank offers five sparkling wines, all made in the classic style using traditional French techniques.

- Chateau Frank installed the gyropalette used in Spanish Cava production, leading to lower costs and lower retail prices.

U.S. Sparkling Wines versus Champagne

- The term Champagne is properly used only for wines originating in the Champagne region of France.

- Champagne has a fine texture that is not duplicated anywhere else in the world.

- U.S. sparkling wines occupy the low- to mid-range sector of the market. In recent years some California houses with French ties have introduced super-premium bottlings intended to rival true Champagne.

- Champagne mousse (foam) is more delicate and long-lived than most U.S. sparkling wines.

SPARKLING WINE STYLES
The world's most versatile wine comes in a range of styles

Sparkling wine provides a good, sometimes even great, accompaniment to almost all food courses, from appetizers to desserts, from savory to sweet. It is the world's most versatile wine type. But there are many styles within the sparkling wine spectrum. They may be simple fizzy dry white wines such as those encountered at "Champagne" brunches or elegant, serious, complex masterpieces such as quality vintage Champagnes. Delicious sparkling wines are available at every price point.

The least-expensive sparkling wines are simply finished still wines into which carbonation has been introduced. They are known as "soda pop" wines. Bulk processes in which a secondary fermentation takes place in large stainless steel tanks are used to make many value-priced wines.

Brut Champagne

- The term brut ("coarse" in French) was originally used to describe Champagne that was given a lower level of added sweetening, or dosage, leading to a drier wine.

- Wines labeled brut will always seem to be bone dry, even when a very light dosage has been added.

- Wines containing no dosage at all may be labeled "natural," "naturel," or "brut nature." These are the driest sparkling wines of all.

- Natural sparkling wines are most commonly produced in California. The largest producer of these wines is Korbel.

Blanc de Noirs Crémant de Bourgogne

- Wines labeled "extra dry" are sweeter than brut or natural wines but appear to be dry. A slightly more generous dosage adds roundness and removes some of the bright acidity that characterizes most brut wines.

- Wines labeled crémant are French sparkling wines made outside the Champagne region. They lack the finesse of Champagne but are relatively inexpensive. The main regions for crémant are Alsace, Burgundy, and the Limoux region of southern France.

All fine sparkling wines are refermented in the bottle. These wines will say "méthode champenoise" or "methode traditionelle" or "fermented in the bottle."

Here are the major styles: *Brut:* These are very dry and usually made from a blend of Chardonnay, Pinot Noir, and Pinot Meuniere. *Extra Dry:* Brut wines are sweetened slightly with a "dosage" of sugar after fermentation. Blanc de Blancs: These are white wines from white grapes. They are 100 percent Chardonnay and made bone dry. *Blanc de Noirs:* These white wines are made from red grapes, usually Pinot Noir and Pinot Meuniere. *Rosé:* This pink wine is usually made from a white base wine blended with a small amount of Pinot Noir. *Demi-sec:* This is an off-dry, slightly sweet wine, sweeter than Extra Dry. *Doux:* This wine is sweet. Sparkling reds are becoming fashionable, particularly in Italy. *Crémant:* This is the term used for all *méthode champenoise* sparkling wines made in France but outside the Champagne region. The most widely exported examples are from Burgundy, Alsace, and Limoux.

A Sparkling Wine Closure

- All sparkling wines come in extra thick bottles with special closures. The closure consists of a mushroom-head cork, cage, and foil covering.

- A metal ring is always included in the cage design. It twists out to provide a handle for loosening the cage. The ring can usually be seen through the foil.

- Sparkling wine bottles and closures are more expensive than traditional bottles and corks. In the case of very inexpensive wines, the cost of the bottle and closure far exceeds that of its contents.

Popping the Cork

- Don't do it! Popping Champagne corks is dangerous and causes the wine to foam out of the bottle.

- To open a sparkling wine, look for a tab or opening in the foil covering. Pull the foil away, exposing the cage. If you can't find a way to remove the foil, cut an opening and pull back the foil.

- Bend out the ring and twist to loosen the cage. It will require six turns. Lift off the cage to access the cork.

- Hold the bottle firmly with one hand, the cork with the other. Twist the bottle while gripping the cork. Keep holding the cork until it is removed. The wine will pop but probably remain inside the bottle. Always have a glass nearby in case the wine foams out of the bottle.

WHAT WINE LABELS TELL YOU

Learn how to read foreign and domestic wine labels and what to look for

There are still places in rural Europe where bulk wine is dispensed into decanters for purchase. But most people look to a wine label to provide the necessary information to evaluate the contents of a bottle. Every wine sold commercially must carry a main label. Back labels offer further information, and neck labels are sometimes used for vintage dates.

Wine labels began to appear in the late nineteenth century after the introduction of glues that would bind paper to glass. Labels used for sparkling wines use special water-resistant glue because these wines are likely to spend some time submerged in an ice bucket.

Labels can be straightforward, providing only the basic

What Every Wine Label Must Show

- Name of the wine: European wines are often named after the winery; New World wines are usually named after the grape variety.

- Geographical reference: name of country or region of origin. If the wine is from a regulated area, it will carry an AC, DO, or AVA reference.

- Volume of wine: usually given in metric designation, such as 750 milliliters.

- Alcoholic strength: Table wines will contain from 8.5 percent to around 15 percent alcohol.

- Name of producer

- Vintage or nonvintage

- Bottling designation: estate bottled or otherwise

A Basic American Wine Label

Name of wine or variety

Geographic reference

2007
FERRARI·CARANO
Fumé Blanc
SAUVIGNON BLANC
SONOMA COUNTY

(AVA)

- This is a typical, uncomplicated wine label, showing only the basic information required.

- A back label is needed to show the volume, address or location of the winery, bottling information, and the requisite government warning mandated for all wines sold in the United States.

- Unlike European labels, American wine labels highlight the producer, rather than the appellation.

information necessary to identify the wine, or they may be "artist labels" that are designed by artists specifically for a particular vintage. Château Mouton-Rothschild in Bordeaux was the first winery to commission label art from the world's best-known contemporary artists and continues to do that up to the present. Featured artists include Braque, Picasso, Motherwell, Miró, Chagall, Dalí, and Warhol. Many wineries offer their finest wines using custom artist labels. Apart from a label's design, the information given is tightly regulated to protect the consumer from fraud.

Back labels are especially common in New World wines. They can be informative when they supply objective specifics, such as the composition of a blended wine or information about the winery. But often they offer inflated "tasting notes" designed to lure customers to purchase the product.

A Typical Back Label

- Required information is sometimes moved to a back label to promote clean front label design. These items include volume of the wine, its alcoholic strength, bottling information, and government warnings.

- The phrase *Produced and Bottled by . . .* is equivalent to the phrases *Estate Bottled* and *mis en bouteilles au château.*

- French bottlings rarely use back labels. New World bottlings almost always do. Back labels provide space for a description of the wine or to inform the purchaser of its unique provenance.

About Government Warnings and Sulfites

- U.S. wine labels must warn women not to drink alcoholic beverages during pregnancy, warn of the risk of driving or operating machinery after consuming alcohol, and warn of possible deleterious health effects.

- If sulfites such as SO_2 have been added, the warning "Contains Sulfites" must appear. Sulfites are almost always used to prevent oxidation and to kill unwanted bacteria.

- Government warnings must appear in capital letters in a designated type size.

- All wines commercially sold in the United States must carry these warnings even if they are imported from other countries.

FRENCH & AMERICAN WINE LABELS
U.S. Tax and Trade Bureau controls everything a wine label says; France is even pickier

The French were not the first to provide government regulation over wine labeling. That distinction falls to Italy (Chianti). But the French were the first to develop a systematic delineation and control of geographical wine regions.

The French appellation contrôlée regulations have become the model worldwide. But unlike most other regions, the French system is based on terroir, not grape variety. Alsace is the only exception.

The French system incorporates four basic designations: Vin de Table (undesignated ordinary wines, rarely exported), Vin du Pays (country wines), VDQS (midgrade wines not entitled to the highest designation), and AC (appellation controlée)

A Typical American Label

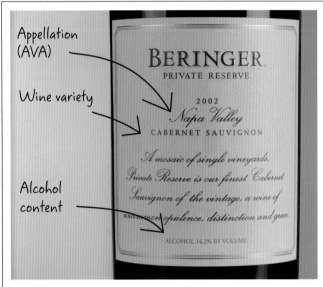

Appellation (AVA)

Wine variety

Alcohol content

A Proprietary Label

- American wine labels give a clear indication of what's inside the bottle. Purchasers need not know the specific rules that govern the wine's contents.

- The appellation or AVA is always given. ATF rules, like French AC rules, use a concentric system. For wines blended from more than one state, "America" will be the appellation.

- Narrowly defined appellations, such as "Temecula Valley," usually ensure higher-quality wine. In blended wines, ATF rules do not require labels to reveal blend specifics.

- Many American and Italian wines use proprietary names, which fall outside some government regulations and are often used to circumvent limiting restrictions.

- The required items—winery name, vintage, alcohol content, volume, appellation— must still appear on labels. If the term *meritage* is used, the wine's composition must be approved by the Meritage Association and must be a classic Bordeaux blend. American labeling may include any items the winery chooses to include as long as the required items also appear.

wines. Most exports are AC wines. It is necessary to understand the AC requirements of an appellation to know what's inside the bottle.

The AC system is administered by the INAO (Institut National des Appellations d'Origine). The INAO grants AC status to a geographic region based on its history of superior performance. The region may be a single vineyard, a region surrounding a village, or an entire region such as Bourgogne (Burgundy).

The INAO rules govern every aspect of winemaking within an appellation, including which grapes may be planted and minimum alcohol potential at harvest. American wine labeling is governed by the ATF (Bureau of Alcohol, Tobacco, and Firearms). ATF rules allow a wide range of labeling practices within specific guidelines. ATF grants appellation status based on regional distinctions. These are called "AVAs" (American Viticultural Areas). Unlike French ACs, AVAs do not extend to single vineyards, but if a wine is vineyard-designated, all fruit must come from that source. If an appellation appears on the label, all wine must come from the region. And if a varietal name is used, 75 percent of the wine must be of the named variety.

Beaujolais Label

- Grape varieties are not allowed to appear on French AC wines except for Alsatian wines. The name of the wine is the same as the name of a single vineyard that enjoys AC status. In the Beaujolais region there are thirteen vineyards that receive this coveted designation.

- The composition of the wine is known only to those who understand the AC rules that govern this particular appellation. This wine is 100 percent Gamay Noir because the rules require it.

Bordeaux Label

- Bordeaux appellations are named for villages. The Bordeaux label gives no information about the wine itself. We know this wine is a blend of Cabernet Sauvignon, Cabernet Franc, Merlot, and Petite Verdot because those are the grape varieties mandated by AC rules. If the winemaker chose to add a touch of some other variety to the blend, the label could not contain the words *appellation contrôlée*.

- French AC rules do not mandate the composition of the blend, only the grape varieties that may be used.

GERMAN & ITALIAN WINE LABELS

They're easy to decipher if you know a few terms

Of all the wines sold in America, Canada, and the United Kingdom, the hardest labels to decipher are those from Germany and Italy. Much of the most important information is in the native language

Germany does not use the appellation system to ensure specific geographics. Instead, it recognizes thirteen wine regions whose names appear on every quality German wine.

Also unique to the German labeling system is an A.P. number that identifies the specific wine and gives details surrounding its official approval.

Tafelwein (table wine) is the lowest classification of German wines; landwein (country wine) is a cut above. These wines are generally not exported. Qualitätswein bestimmter Anbaugebiete (QbA) is the lowest classification of wines

German Wine Terms

- Weingut: winery

- Abfüllung: bottled

- Erzeugerabfüllung: estate bottled

- Trocken: dry

- Halbtrocken: semi-dry

- Qualitätswein: quality wine

- Qualitätswein mit Prädikat: quality wine with special designation

- Kabinett: off-dry

- Spätlese: later harvest, sweeter

- Auslese: late harvest, sweet

- Beerenauslese: very late harvest, very sweet, grapes handpicked individually

- Trockenbeerenauslese: extremely sweet, raisined, botrytised grapes individually picked

A German Wine Label

Producer
Vintage
Name of wine
Alcohol content
A.P. number

- The name of a quality German wine consists of the village followed by the vineyard, as in Piesporter Goldtropfchen, where Piesport is the village; Goldtropfchen is the vineyard.

- German wine-growing regions are divided into 150 grosslagen, or vineyard cooperatives. Wines that do not rise to the highest standards may use the village name followed by the name of the grosslage, as in Piesporter Michelsberg.

- Common grosslage wine imports include Zeller Schwarze Katz and Bernkasteler Kurfürtslay.

70

worthy of export. Rising above these classifications is Qualitätswein mit Prädikat (QmP). This is the highest classification, and the "Prädikat" describes sweetness levels.

Quality German wines are usually named after the village and vineyard: Zeltinger Schlossberg is a wine from the Schlossberg vineyard in the village of Zeltingen.

Italian wine labels will carry one of three classifications: DOC (Denominazione di Origine Controllata), DOCG (Denominazione di Origine Controllata e Garantita), and IGT (Indicazione Geografica Tipica). DOC is the Italian version of controlled appellation and is similar to the French rules, adding a taste test and chemical evaluation. DOCG is reserved for the highest-quality areas within a DOC region and incorporates stricter guidelines. IGT suggests that the wine is typical of its region. Wines not meeting the strict DOC or DOCG guidelines are classified as *vino da tavola*. These may be either simple, uncomplicated wines or Italy's best wines. They are wines that either don't qualify for DOC status or that disregard the stringent official rules. The very expensive so-called Super-Tuscan wines of the Chianti region exemplify the latter.

A Typical Italian Wine Label

- Italian wine labels are particularly difficult to understand because of the common use of proprietary names.

- The terms *tenuta, podere, agricola, azienda, cantina, fattoria,* and *badia* mean winery, farm, or abbey.

- The largest type is usually used for the name of the wine. The producer's name may not be prominent.

- Grape varieties may be indicated if the wine is a single variety wine; otherwise a DOC name may be used, such as Chianti Classico or Salice Salentino.

Basic Italian Wine Terms

- Amara: bitter
- Bianco: white
- Classico: the historic center of a DOC region
- Dolce: sweet
- Frizzante: fizzy
- Secco: dry
- Spumante: sparkling
- Vino: wine

MENDOCINO COUNTY

California's most northerly major wine region boasts ripe reds, crisp whites, and excellent Pinot Noir

The counties of Napa, Sonoma, Marin, and Mendocino comprise California's North Coast AVA. Any wines made from fruit in these counties are entitled to use the AVA on their labels.

Mendocino is one of California's larger counties, known for its spectacular rocky coastline and ancient redwood forests. There are two main wine-growing areas: Anderson Valley, which runs from near U.S. 101 northwest to the coast, and three inland valleys east of U.S. 101.

Wineries operated in Mendocino as early as 1900, but all disappeared during Prohibition. The first to open after Prohibition was Parducci in 1932. John Parducci, along with his father, founded the modern wine industry in Mendocino County,

Mendocino County's Three Wine-growing Zones

- Anderson Valley: one of California's coolest growing regions. Beautiful, crisp, and complex whites and stunning sparkling wines.

- Mendocino Ridge: high-elevation vineyards (1,200-plus feet), some with ocean views. Superb Pinot Noir and great Zinfandel.

- Inland Valleys: legendary Petite Sirah, Syrah, and Zinfandel

Anderson Valley Vineyard

- Anderson Valley is California's coolest major wine-growing region. White varieties do especially well here.

- Anderson Valley white wines are light, complex, and crisp. Valley reds are lean, but hilltop reds are amazing, especially Pinot Noir and Zinfandel.

- Anderson Valley enjoys a strong coastal influence, making it a prime region for sparkling wine, which requires barely ripe grapes.

- Anderson Valley wines are hard to find, but they offer excellent value because the region is less known.

making artisanal Cabernet Sauvignon and Zinfandel. He was the first to source grapes from Anderson Valley and use that label designation even before it became an official AVA.

Mendocino County established itself as a premium wine-growing area with the development of Anderson Valley in the 1980s when the French Champagne house Roederer doubled the valley's area under vine. Soon after, wonderful Zinfandel and Pinot Noir growing in the hilltop vineyards led to a new Mendocino Ridge AVA. These vineyards lie above the coastal fog that shrouds the valley floor. Anderson Valley is one of California's coolest wine-growing regions.

Excellent Riesling, Gewürztraminer, and Chardonnay are made from valley fruit by wineries such as Navarro, Edmeades, Brutocao, Greenwood Ridge, and Husch. For this reason, Anderson Valley is often compared with Alsace, even though its wines are not as meaty.

Rich red wines are produced in the eastern vineyards of Potter Valley, Redwood Valley, and McDowell Valley. These wines are great value because vineyard property here is about one-third as expensive as comparable property in Napa Valley.

Mendocino Ridge Vineyard

- The ridges above Anderson Valley lie above the fog and enjoy a cool, sunny climate.

- Mendocino Ridge enjoys a separate AVA from Anderson Valley. It runs northwest to the Pacific Ocean. The appellation is the second in the United States to be based on elevation.

- Some of California's finest Pinot Noir vineyards are found here and in the coastal ridges in neighboring Sonoma County.

- Greenwood Ridge is the best-known winery that offers estate-bottled wines. Its wines are well made and attractively priced.

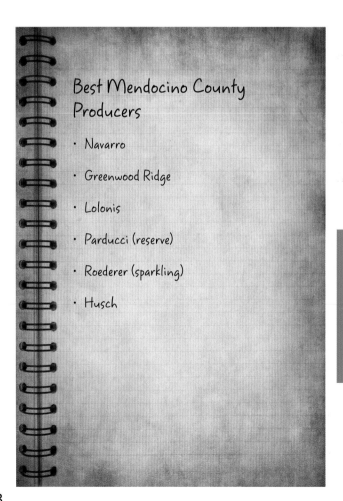

Best Mendocino County Producers

- Navarro
- Greenwood Ridge
- Lolonis
- Parducci (reserve)
- Roederer (sparkling)
- Husch

SONOMA COUNTY

California's oldest wine region is home of the world's best Zinfandel

Sonoma County is the cradle of the California wine industry. In 1834 General Mariano Vallejo planted the first vineyard in California devoted to the production of table wine. In 1857 Agoston Haraszthy established the first commercial winery, Buena Vista, in the Carneros district of Sonoma County. In the decade following, a bevy of vineyards and wineries appeared all over the state.

In contrast to Napa Valley, Sonoma County has largely been able to maintain its original, casual, rural character. It's possible to walk into most tasting rooms without making a reservation, waiting in line, taking a guided tour, or paying an expensive tasting fee.

Situated less than an hour's drive north from San Francisco, Sonoma Country enjoys a wider spectrum of AVAs than any

Sonoma County

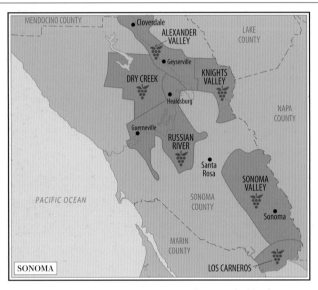

A Russian River Vineyard

- The Sonoma Coast AVA lies on hilltops above the Pacific Ocean. Many of Sonoma's best Pinot Noir's are grown here.

- Carneros is the oldest wine region in Sonoma County. This AVA spills over into Napa County. Carneros vineyards are near sea level

and are cooled by foggy mornings. Alexander Valley is home to more than forty wineries. It is bisected by U.S. 101 and runs up to the Mendocino County border.

- Knights Valley is the highest and warmest of Sonoma County's wine-growing regions.

- The Russian River AVA extends from near the coast up to Healdsburg on U.S. 101. This region produces great Pinot Noir, Chardonnay, and Zinfandel.

- The best Russian River vineyard locations are in the western part of the watershed near Guerneville

and Forestville. The Russian River Wine Road runs from Healdsburg to Guerneville.

- This appellation is known for sparkling wine production. Iron Horse, Korbel, and J are based here. Most of the wineries along the Russian River Wine Road offer complimentary tastings.

other county in California. The chilly Sonoma Coast and Russian River AVAs produce some of California's finest Pinot Noir. The most-celebrated Zinfandels in the world hail from Dry Creek and Sonoma Valley. More than 450 wines now carry "Sonoma County" appellations. These wines occupy the full spectrum of grape varietals but focus most extensively on Chardonnay, Cabernet Sauvignon, Merlot, Pinot Noir, and Zinfandel. Sonoma County wines often offer better value than those from neighboring Napa Valley because the price of vineyard land is considerably less expensive.

ZOOM

Exceptional Wines of Sonoma County
Siduri Pinot Noir
Twomey Merlot
Matanzas Creek Sauvignon Blanc
Silver Oak Cabernet Sauvignon
Jordan Cabernet Sauvignon
Rosenblum Zinfandel
Ravenscroft Zinfandel

Ferrari-Carano Winery, Dry Creek

- Ferrari-Carano is a Sonoma County luxury wine estate. With more Americans embracing fine wine as a part of their lifestyle, these opulent visitor centers are appearing in Sonoma County.

- Ferrari-Carano sources its fruit from nineteen estate vineyards in four appellations. Although this winery offers twenty-five wines, its Fumé Blanc is legendary, both for its high quality and its value. Larger wineries offer excellent products at very competitive prices. The house style here typifies that of Sonoma County: full flavored, round, and rich.

Buena Vista Winery

- Buena Vista is California's oldest continuously operating winery. It typifies the traditional Sonoma winery: casual, small to medium in size, and surrounded by an estate vineyard.

- The original Buena Vista vineyard was planted from rootstock hand-carried from Europe by its founder, Agonton Haraszthy. These vines became the source for most varieties planted in California in the mid-nineteenth century.

- The Buena Vista Carneros winery is a popular tourist attraction, located just miles from Sonoma.

CALIFORNIA

NAPA VALLEY

America's most-celebrated wine region is home to some of the world's greatest wines

Napa Valley is America's Bordeaux. It's like a giant amusement park for wine lovers and unlike every other American wine region. The cost of vineyard land in the Napa River drainage is the highest anywhere in the United States. Consequently, only highly capitalized wineries can set up shop here.

The typical Napa Valley winery is a lavish château-like estate with a visitor's center, guided tours, and substantial tasting fees. The great wines that gave Napa Valley its reputation will not be poured anywhere without a significant charge.

There are over three hundred wineries in Napa Valley, nearly one-quarter of the total number of bonded wineries in the entire state. Around 5 million people visit each year.

Napa Valley

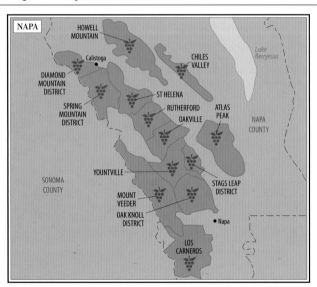

Napa Valley Tasting Room

- Napa Valley shares the Carneros AVA with Sonoma County. Wines made in the Napa County portion may use either a "Napa Valley" or a "Carneros" appellation.

- The Mayacamus Mountains line the west side of the valley and separate Napa Valley from Sonoma County. They are home to the Mount Veeder, Spring Mountain, and Diamond Mountain AVAs.

- The eastern mountains are dominated by Atlas Peak (south) and Howell Mountain (north). Great cabernet comes from Oakville and Rutherford.

- Wine tasting here is more structured and more expensive than that in other regions. Typical tasting fees range from $5 to $40, with most wineries charging $10.

- Premium wines from better producers are not included in a general tasting. The Sterling Winery offers a short aerial tram ride up to its tasting room in Calistoga. The basic fee is $20 including the tram ride. "Cult" wineries are generally not open to the public. But Opus One offers one taste of its current release Cabernet Sauvignon for $30.

The uniqueness of Napa Valley is its heterogeneity of geography and climate. The temperature change from the cool south to the hot north can easily be as much as 20° or even more. Mountain ranges on each side of the valley provide entirely different growing conditions. This wide range of wine-growing conditions has made it possible to obtain optimum sites for specific varieties. Chardonnay thrives in cool Carneros, whereas Cabernet Sauvignon is king of the midvalley. Mountain sites are ideal for Syrah and Zinfandel.

Wine Cave

- Nearly sixty Napa Valley wineries age their wines in wine caves. Many offer special tours and tastings.

- A typical wine cave tour lasts an hour and a half and includes a barrel tasting as well as a tasting of finished wine. A picnic lunch is often included.

- Wine cave tours are priced around $50 per person and require reservations.

- Well-known wineries that offer exceptional wine cave tours include Flora Springs and Pine Ridge.

A Napa Valley Picnic

- Many Napa Valley wineries offer free use of their picnic facilities. It is customary for users to purchase a bottle of wine.

- There are around fifty Napa Valley wineries that include picnic facilities. Some wineries have onsite delicatessens to supply cheese, meats, and French bread, but most visitors stock up in Oakville, where there is a Dean and DeLuca store.

- Oakville Grocery, on the corner of Oakville Crossing and SR 29, is a "must stop" location for picnic supplies. It has operated continuously since 1881.

CALIFORNIA

MONTEREY COUNTY

You'll find a beautiful coast, upscale resorts, and high-altitude wineries

When we think of Monterey County, images of the Big Sur coast come to mind, along with the charming town of Carmel, luxurious ocean-view hotels, and several of the world's most beautiful golf courses.

Surprisingly, Monterey County produces about one-fifth more wine grapes than Napa Valley and has about one-fifth as many wineries. Almost all the vineyards are in the Salinas Valley, which runs from the crescent of Monterey Bay southeast 85 miles to the San Luis Obispo County line.

The Salinas Valley, south of King City, is home to the world's largest contiguous vineyard—San Bernabe Ranch. Here 7,000 acres form a carpet of vines as far as the eye can see, 11 miles

Monterey County

- This county is sparsely populated and largely agricultural. There are five important AVAs, all but one in or above the Salinas Valley.

- U.S. 101 runs the length of the Salinas Valley. The vineyards of the Santa Lucia Mountains AVA are conspicuously visible in the west.

- A long, winding road leads through the mountains from Greenfield to Carmel, passing through the Arroyo Seco AVA, Carmel Highlands AVA, and Carmel Valley. Most Carmel Valley tasting rooms are located in Carmel Valley Village, not at the wineries.

A Santa Lucia Highlands Vineyard

- This is Monterey County's premier wine-growing region and the first U.S. AVA to be based on elevation.

- The Salinas Valley experiences cold winds and fog throughout the growing season, but the vineyards in the "SLH" appellation lie above the marine layer.

- The Santa Lucia Highlands enjoys the latest harvest dates of any American region because of its cool climate and lack of autumn rain. The Santa Lucia Mountains form the spectacular Big Sur coast on the west as they drop precipitously to the rocky coastline.

long and 5 miles wide. This region is Monterey County's work-horse, providing a huge amount of fruit destined for "fighting varietal" wines under the umbrella "California" appellation.

The regions of greatest interest lie in the mountains that rise precipitously on each side of the valley. High in the eastern Gavilan Mountains, near Pinnacles National Monument, is the Chalone Vineyard, now an AVA. It was planted in the 1920s and now produces some of Monterey County's finest Chardonnay and Pinot Noir. The Santa Lucia Mountains to the west rise steeply from the valley floor and contain enormous alluvial fans, some 1,000 feet high. This is the Santa Lucia Highlands AVA. Pinot Noir and Chardonnay here rival California's finest and most expensive.

Monterey County's fourth important AVA is Carmel Valley. This is a mountain top region above the valley with ten high-quality wineries. Monterey County's high-elevation vineyards supply fruit for Chardonnay and Pinot Noir. Lower-elevation vineyards supply the value-oriented market. An exception is the Arroyo Seco AVA west of Greenfield. The special soils and terrain aspect support fifteen different varieties.

Cannery Row Tasting Room

- Visitors to Monterey need not make the long trip out to the wineries to experience Monterey County wines. Monterey's famed Cannery Row offers five opportunities to taste regional wines.

- The Cannery Row Bay View Tasting Room offers a standard and premium tasting with a view for $10–15.

- Baywood, Bargetto, and Schied Wineries have tasting rooms on Cannery Row. Cannery Row offers tasting rooms, restaurants, hotels, and the Monterey Bay Aquarium, all within walking distance.

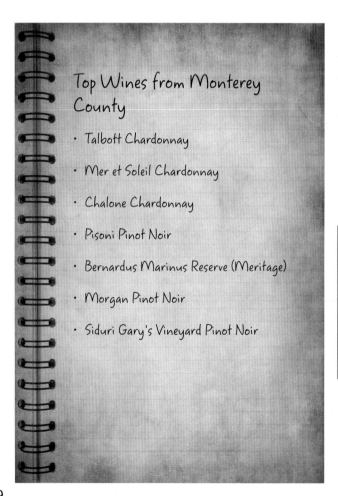

Top Wines from Monterey County

- Talbott Chardonnay

- Mer et Soleil Chardonnay

- Chalone Chardonnay

- Pisoni Pinot Noir

- Bernardus Marinus Reserve (Meritage)

- Morgan Pinot Noir

- Siduri Gary's Vineyard Pinot Noir

CALIFORNIA

SAN LUIS OBISPO COUNTY
It's California's fastest-growing wine region

If you drove north on U.S. 101 through San Luis Obispo County twenty years ago, you would probably not have noticed any vineyards. Today vineyards carpet the region. It is the fastest-growing wine-growing area in California.

Whereas Santa Barbara County and Monterey County are mostly cool regions, San Luis Obispo vineyard areas are largely planted in warmer areas more suited to red grapes.

Paso Robles was the county's first wine-growing area, but the vineyards were largely in the western hills and away from public view. Zinfandel was the main grape, and up into the 1980s local patrons would bring their own jugs to the wineries to be filled with wine for little more than a handshake. Even in the 1990s one could buy a half gallon of old-vine, dry-farmed Zinfandel at the winery for $5. Those very grapes

San Luis Obispo County

- San Luis Obispo wine-growing regions consist of four AVAs: Paso Robles, York Mountain, Edna Valley, and Arroyo Grande Valley.

- Paso Robles is the main AVA. U.S. 101 separates it into rolling benchlands on the east and rugged limestone hills on the west.

- Edna Valley lies southeast of the city of San Luis Obispo. It enjoys some maritime influence and is known for Chardonnay and Pinot Noir.

- York Mountain is populated by a single winery. It is associated with famed pianist and Polish prime minister Ignacy Paderewski.

Westside Paso Robles Vineyard

- The term Westside refers to all the wine-growing areas west of U.S. 101. The terrain here is very mountainous and enjoys a limestone soil similar to the southern Rhône Valley.

- Many of Paso Robles' finest wines come from Westside vineyards. Zinfandel is a specialty of this region.

- No Westside vineyard can be machine harvested. Grapes are kept to low yields, often around 2 tons per acre. A group of Westside wineries known as the "Far Out Wineries" has applied for a Paso Robles Westside AVA.

now produce wine made to more exacting standards and offered in fancier bottles for more than $50 a piece.

The rising star in San Luis Obispo is Syrah. Gary Eberle, whose original Paso Robles winery has morphed into giant Meridian, made the earliest California Syrah here. Cuttings from his vineyard gave rise to many of the fine Syrah vineyards on the Central Coast.

Edna Valley Vineyard

- Edna Valley runs from San Luis Obispo city limits southeast to Arroyo Grande Valley. The northern end is 15 miles from the sea and enjoys a moderate marine influence.

- Edna Valley's geology is dominated by volcanic soils, the result of ancient eruptions of a string of volcanoes whose remnants still dominate the skyline. San Luis Obispo County's largest contiguous vineyard, the Paragon-Pacific Vineyard, is located here. It is planted mostly to Chardonnay. Edna Valley produces the county's finest Syrah from Alban Vineyard.

Talley Rincon Vineyard

- Arroyo Grande Valley climate ranges from very cool in the west to very hot in the east. The best vineyards are located on hillsides.

- Arroyo Grande Valley AVA is home to the oldest vineyard in California's Central Coast region, Saucelito Canyon, planted to Zinfandel in the early 1880s. Saucelito Canyon and Toucan Wines, both Zinfandel producers, occupy the east end.

- Laetitia Winery and Talley Vineyards and Winery dominate the west. Talley's Pinot Noir from Rosemary's Vineyard consistently receives high ratings in wine.

CALIFORNIA

SANTA BARBARA COUNTY
You'll find upscale ranches and world-class Pinot Noir

The story of Santa Barbara County wine begins in an unlikely, remote Foxen Canyon property in 1972. A group of investors purchased land and planted it to the usual varieties. The Zaca Mesa Winery was established in 1978 as one of the county's first, and Ken Byron Brown was engaged as winemaker. This winery is less known for its wines than for the pantheon of Central Coast winemakers who interned there. The list includes seven of the top winemakers in the region. Brown went on to establish Byron Winery in Santa Maria. It's now one of the county's most-prestigious labels.

A parallel story took place about the same time in the Santa Ynez Valley east of Buellton when Richard Sanford and his partner planted the famous Sanford & Benedict Vineyard in what is now the Santa Rita Hills. This vineyard remains one of

Santa Ynez Valley

Cambria Winery

- Santa Barbara County has three distinct wine-growing regions: Santa Ynez Valley, Santa Maria Valley, and Los Alamos. There are also large vineyards north of Lompoc devoted to Chardonnay.

- SR 154 runs from Santa Barbara northwest to reconnect with U.S. 101 north of Buellton. It passes near several noteworthy wineries such as Brander, Gainey, and Rideau.

- Several wineries maintain tasting rooms in the quaint Danish village of Solvang. Other wineries operate tasting rooms in Los Olivos.

- Cambria Winery is located on the historic Santa Maria Mesa, which overlooks Santa Maria Valley. The finest wine grapes are grown on the mesa.

- Principal vineyards and wineries on the mesa are Bien Nacido Vineyard, Cambria Winery, Byron Winery, and Kenneth Volk Vineyards and Winery.

- The grape varieties grown here are Pinot Noir and Chardonnay. To reach the mesa, drive east on Betteravia Road to Santa Maria Mesa Road. Cambria, Byron, and Volk welcome visitors to their tasting rooms.

the prime Pinot Noir vineyards in California.

The two areas pioneered by these people—Santa Maria Mesa and Santa Rita Hills—are now the crown jewels of Santa Barbara wine-growing regions.

In the early 1970s extensive land on the Santa Maria Mesa was planted by the Miller family, who renamed the property "Bien Nacido" (wellborn). It is now one of the county's largest and most-celebrated vineyards.

Santa Rita Hills

- Santa Rita Hills is one of California's smallest and most-recent AVAs. It was granted AVA status in 2001 as a result of its unique terroir and impressive wines.

- Santa Rita Hills occupies the center portion of the Santa Ynez River corridor running from the ocean eastward.

- Its geology is unique, containing a rare soil type called "botella," consisting of a mixture of clay and loam with a high calcareous content.

- Pinot Noir and Chardonnay grown here possess a high degree of complexity with mineral overtones.

The Brander Vineyard

- The Brander Vineyard in Los Olivos was inspired by the châteaux of Bordeaux and originally planted to Bordeaux varieties.

- Brander's Sauvignons are among the finest in California. The winery offers a range of styles, including wines made from free-run

- juice of grapes that have macerated with twenty-four-hour skin contact—a highly unusual procedure for white wines.

- Brander was an early devotee of close-spaced vine planting, resulting in lower yields and more concentrated flavors.

CALIFORNIA

83

SOUTHERN CALIFORNIA
California's forgotten wine region is staging an epic comeback

Although it is true that the modern California wine industry traces its roots back to the vineyard of Mariano Vallejo in 1834, many people are surprised to learn that the earliest commercial wineries were established in Los Angeles County just four years after Vallejo planted his first vine and nineteen years before Agoston Haraszthy began to plant grape cuttings imported from Europe at Buena Vista Vineyard in

Sonoma County. The first commercial orange grove had not yet been planted.

The region chosen as best suited to viticulture was hard against the San Gabriel Mountains, about 45 miles east of Los Angeles, which had been granted "city" status just three years earlier.

This region, known as "Rancho Cucamonga," quickly

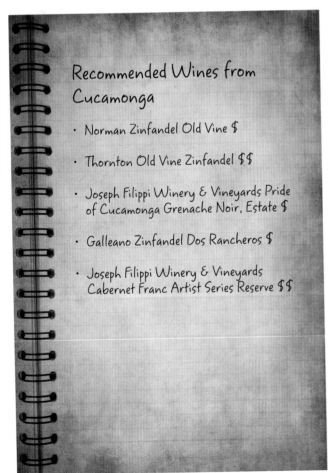

Recommended Wines from Cucamonga

- Norman Zinfandel Old Vine $

- Thornton Old Vine Zinfandel $$

- Joseph Filippi Winery & Vineyards Pride of Cucamonga Grenache Noir, Estate $

- Galleano Zinfandel Dos Rancheros $

- Joseph Filippi Winery & Vineyards Cabernet Franc Artist Series Reserve $$

Rancho Cucamonga

- Gnarled vines over a century old were planted when Los Angeles County was undeveloped.

- Old vines produce low yields, resulting in intense wines of great complexity. Under the right soil conditions their root systems reach 20 or even 30 feet

into the ground, searching for water and nutrients.

- Most old-vine vineyards are head pruned, not trellised, and are farmed without irrigation when possible.

- Cucamonga now has only two operating wineries: Galleano and Filippi.

became the largest viticultural area in the United States. In 1920 Cucamonga had two times more acreage under vine than Napa and Sonoma Counties combined. Some of these old vines still produce, and Zinfandel from the Cucamonga AVA is sourced by top wineries throughout the state.

About 40 miles south of Cucamonga lies the city of Temecula. A wind gap in the coast range brings marine influence to this region, mitigating what would otherwise be a very hot region and making it ideal for viticulture. Temecula Valley now boasts more than forty wineries, ranging from rustic mom-and-pop operations to lavish palaces. There are stylish hotels, spas, and four-star restaurants there as well. The wineries are located along a strip paralleling Rancho California Road, which runs east from Interstate 15.

In the 1990s Pierce's disease destroyed nearly half of the entire vineyard area. After years of recovery, Temecula winemakers are still resigned to losing around 20 percent of their vines each year. Nevertheless, Temecula wines remain attractively priced for the high quality they deliver.

Thornton Winery, Temecula

- Thornton is one of Temecula's largest and most attractive wineries for visitors.

- Thornton, like many other Temecula wineries, enjoys a hilltop location that provides sweeping views of neighboring vineyards and wineries. The specialty of this winery is sparkling wines. Thornton offers seven excellent sparkling wines, including a true Brut Natural, a rosé, and an almond-flavored sparkler.

- Several larger Temecula wineries have restaurants on their premises. Thornton's restaurant is Café Champagne.

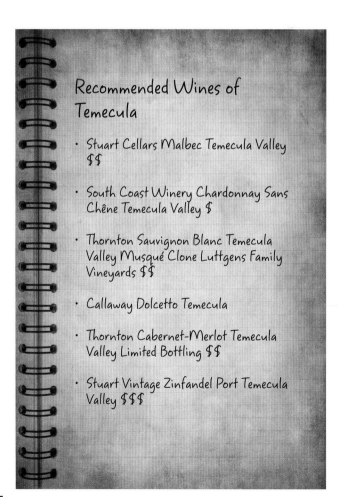

Recommended Wines of Temecula

- Stuart Cellars Malbec Temecula Valley $$

- South Coast Winery Chardonnay Sans Chêne Temecula Valley $

- Thornton Sauvignon Blanc Temecula Valley Musqué Clone Luttgens Family Vineyards $$

- Callaway Dolcetto Temecula

- Thornton Cabernet-Merlot Temecula Valley Limited Bottling $$

- Stuart Vintage Zinfandel Port Temecula Valley $$$

SACRAMENTO VALLEY

This region is mitigated by San Francisco Bay and the Sacramento/ San Joaquin River Delta

The Sacramento Valley comprises the northern half of California's Central Valley. It is bisected by the Sacramento River, California's largest. This region has two unique distinctions: ample water and some maritime influence flowing eastward from San Francisco Bay. The valley runs 140 miles from Red Bluff in the north to Lodi in the delta.

There are eighty-six wineries in the valley, largely producing Chardonnay, Zinfandel, Petite Sirah, and Chenin Blanc.

The main wine-growing regions are Lodi in the delta area and Clarksburg, between Lodi and Sacramento. Although a few Sacramento Valley wineries source fruit from outside the region, the overwhelming amount of Sacramento Valley fruit

Sacramento Valley AVAs

- Lodi AVA (sixty wineries)
- Clarksburg AVA (ten wineries)
- North Yuba AVA (three wineries)
- Sloughhouse AVA (no wineries)
- Cosumnes River AVA (no wineries)

Woodbridge Vineyard

- The Lodi-Woodbridge region is located in the Sacramento/San Joaquin River Delta, directly east of San Francisco Bay.

- Woodbridge is a small village on the outskirts of Lodi with a rich history of winemaking. The Mondavi family started its first

winemaking operation here in 1923. The Lodi region is cooler in temperature, offering an excellent terroir for wine grapes.

- Lodi is the first California AVA to adopt regionwide sustainable farming practices, known as the "Lodi Rules."

is sourced by wineries outside the area.

The area with the greatest concentration of wineries is Lodi. There are sixty wineries operating here. This is the coolest growing region in the Sacramento Valley. It is also the area's oldest, going back to the 1850s.

The Mondavi family began its historic rise to fame in Woodbridge, a suburb of Lodi, and wines made under the "Mondavi" umbrella are still labeled "Woodbridge." The best of these is their Port. Everything else under this label is good, value-oriented varietal wine.

Lodi possesses splendid old-vine Zinfandel vineyards and offers Zinfandel wines that are round, fruity, and mouthfilling. Clarksburg AVA, north of Lodi, enjoys cooling fogs and mists, keeping the region about 9 degrees cooler than the city of Sacramento. The stars here are Chenin Blanc and Petite Sirah. Around 90 percent of Clarksburg fruit is sourced by wineries outside the appellation. Clarksburg currently produces some of the best Chenin Blanc fruit in California. Ten wineries are located here. The best known are Bogle, which specializes in Petite Sirah, and Ehrhardt, which specializes in Chenin Blanc.

Bogle Petite Sirah

- Bogle is the most widely distributed producer in the Clarksburg region, north of Lodi. The Bogle family has farmed this soil since the mid-1800s and is in its sixth generation.

- This producer is best known for its Petite Sirah. It carries a "California" appellation because it sources fruit from Lodi as well as from its own Clarksburg vineyard.

- Bogle also offers Zinfandel from eighty-year-old vines typical of this region.

Petite Sirah Food Pairings

- Roast leg of lamb
- Richly sauced beef stew
- Cheddar cheese
- Tex-Mex chili
- Barbecued steaks

SAN JOAQUIN VALLEY

Discover California's largest and hottest wine-growing region

The San Joaquin Valley is the southern half of California's Central Valley and is among America's largest agricultural regions. It extends 220 miles from Stockton near the delta to Bakersfield in the south and is 40–50 miles wide. Most of California's wine, table, and raisin grapes are grown here.

San Joaquin Valley soils are very deep and fertile because the valley is a repository of alluvial runoff from both the Sierra Nevada on its east and the coast range on its west. Overcropping is common here, with yields approaching four or five times that of premium coastal and mountain vineyards. This leads to an excellent table grape crop, but fruit quality is low for winemaking. As a consequence, almost all San Joaquin wine grapes are used as base wine for the least-expensive blends. Wines that are labeled "California Chablis," "California

San Joaquin Valley Vineyard

- California's Central Valley is home to the largest winery operations in the world. Wineries here often resemble oil refinery tank farms. These massive operations utilize large-scale agricultural practices such as aerial spraying, mechanical pruning, and mechanical harvesting.

- Many wineries located elsewhere in the state offer value wines with "California" appellations. Many of these wines are made in huge Central Valley wineries.

- White Zinfandel under the "Sutter Home" label is made in Manteca by Delicato, the sixth-largest U.S. winery.

Thompson Seedless

- Thompson Seedless is the primary grape of Central Valley. It is a heavy bearing variety used for table grapes and raisins.

- Thompson Seedless is ill suited for winemaking because its flavors are too monodimensional, and its acids too low.

- Until 1973 Thompson Seedless was the main grape used for blending Central Valley white wines. It gave way to French Colombard, another heavy bearing variety with better potential for winemaking.

Burgundy," or "Rhine Wine" probably originated here. High-producing varietals are preferred: French Colombard, Chardonnay, and Thompson Seedless for whites, Zinfandel for reds.

The San Joaquin Valley provides 80 percent of the entire wine grape crush for the state of California. Napa Valley, in contrast, provides 3 percent.

The San Joaquin Valley is home to E & J Gallo, until recently the world's largest wine company.

In recent years there has been an advance in grape and wine quality in some valley vineyards because of viticultural refinements, new varieties, rootstocks, and trellis systems. These advances are attempting to transform the San Joaquin Valley from a generic into a varietal wine producer. Fresno State University is championing the effort. The wines produced from the university's vineyard are remarkably good.

The University of California at Davis developed a hybrid of Cabernet Sauvignon and Carignane called "Ruby Cabernet." It was intended to withstand the heat of the Central Valley. It found a happier home in Texas.

Ruby Cabernet

- The San Joaquin Valley proved too hot to successfully grow Cabernet Sauvignon, the red variety most in demand. Ruby Cabernet was hybridized to solve this problem.

- Carignane, a heavy bearing heat-tolerant grape from southern France, was crossed with Cabernet Sauvignon at the University of California at Davis and enjoyed limited success in high-elevation vineyards southeast of Bakersfield.

- Ruby cabernet is rarely offered as a pure varietal wine.

Fresno State University

- Fresno State University occupies the cutting edge of research into vineyard management and trains large number of California's finest winemakers.

- The commercial side of wine production is the focus of California State University at Fresno. The University of California at Berkeley pioneered wine research in the early twentieth century. After the repeal of Prohibition, that task fell to the University of California at Davis, whose faculty impacted every aspect of wine growing and winemaking worldwide.

COLUMBIA VALLEY

It's America's second-largest wine-growing region and home of many value wines

The Columbia River, with its tributaries, drains all of eastern Washington and passes through one of the most scenic river gorges in the United States en route to the Pacific Ocean. The Columbia Valley was created when ice dams on ancient Lake Missoula gave way, sending a torrent of water from Montana through Idaho and Washington State. Geologists estimate that the flow of this remarkable event more than equaled the modern flow of all the world's rivers combined. Topsoils were completely washed away. This catastrophe, in combination with continuous volcanic events, resulted in the unique, if thin, soils of the Columbia River Basin.

The Columbia Valley AVA encompasses 11 million acres

KNACK WINE BASICS

The Columbia River

A Yakima Valley Vineyard

- The Columbia River forms the boundary between most of Washington and Oregon. There are wineries on both sides of the river.

- The Walla Walla AVA, near the 90-degree bend in the Columbia River, is shared by Washington and Oregon. Most wineries in this appel-

lation are in Washington.

- The Puget Sound AVA encompasses a large area, but few wineries offer wine from this appellation.

- The Columbia Gorge AVA lies equally in Washington and Oregon. It is centered in the Hood River area.

- Nearly 40 percent of Washington's annual wine production comes from grapes grown in the Yakima Valley. The valley is unlike the rest of the Columbia River Basin in soil type and climate. It is usually 5–10 degrees cooler here than in other regions, leading to better acidity in wine grapes.

- The soils here are sandy, with little water retention. Irrigation is necessary.

- The valley is surrounded by several of the state's most prestigious sub-appellations: Rattlesnake Hills AVA, Horse Heaven AVA, and Red Mountain AVA.

of land and includes all other Washington State appellations except for Puget Sound AVA and Columbia Gorge AVA. Much of the wine labeled with the "Columbia Valley" appellation is made in the greater Seattle area from fruit grown in eastern Washington. Although around 250 wineries release wine under this appellation, few wineries receive visitors and offer wine sales. Columbia Valley wines tend to be polarized between ultrapremium bottlings and value-oriented wines. Giant Château Ste.-Michelle, located in a Seattle suburb, owns a majority of Columbia Valley vineyard land.

Wahluke Slope

- The new Wahluke Slope AVA is Washington State's warmest wine-growing region. It lies east of Yakima on the Columbia River.

- This is the only Pacific Northwest appellation consisting of a single landform. The Wahluke Slope is a giant alluvial fan.

- Merlot, Syrah, and Cabernet Sauvignon do especially well here, but white varieties are also grown.

- There are twenty vineyards in this AVA but only two small wineries. About 20 percent of Washington wine originates in this region but is made elsewhere.

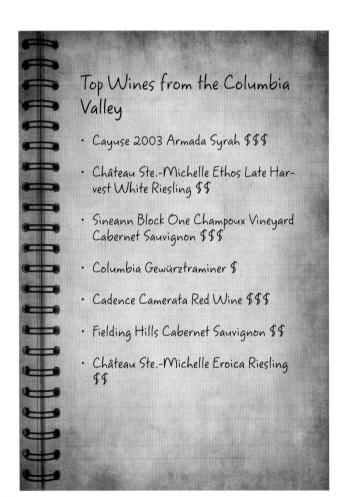

Top Wines from the Columbia Valley

- Cayuse 2003 Armada Syrah $$$

- Château Ste.-Michelle Ethos Late Harvest White Riesling $$

- Sineann Block One Champoux Vineyard Cabernet Sauvignon $$$

- Columbia Gewürztraminer $

- Cadence Camerata Red Wine $$$

- Fielding Hills Cabernet Sauvignon $$

- Château Ste.-Michelle Eroica Riesling $$

PACIFIC NORTHWEST

PUGET SOUND

This wet, foggy region offers wine from cold-weather grapes and world-class reds from other regions

Although the Puget Sound AVA was recognized in 1995, the history of wine growing there goes back to 1872, when Lambert Evans, a retired soldier from the Civil War, planted a vineyard on Stretch Island. Wine growing became firmly established there, based on a French-American hybrid called "Island Belle." This red grape was developed with very cool, wet climates in mind and quickly became the most widely planted grape variety in Washington. Wine growing virtually ceased with Prohibition but resumed in the 1980s.

Small vineyards dot many of Puget Sound's islands, but the main growing areas are on Bainbridge Island and Whidbey Island, where they enjoy some protection by the Olympic

Puget Sound Vineyard

- Puget Sound is cold and wet between November and April. Grapevines are dormant during this time.

- Rainfall is abundant here, averaging 60 inches a year. Many vineyards can be dry farmed.

- The wines of Puget Sound are unlike those of the rest of Washington State. They are naturally high in acids, a quality that many Columbia Valley wine growers have difficulty achieving.

- Twenty-five wineries operate in the Puget Sound AVA. Most use imported grapes for their red wines.

Muscadet Cluster

- High-acid white varietals are well suited to Puget Sound. Muscadet shows great promise. Like Washington State Viognier, Washington State Muscadet could outperform its French counterpart.

- Sieggerebe is the most common white varietal in Puget Sound vineyards. Hybridized in Germany in 1929, Gewürztraminer is a parent, and Sieggerebe possesses characteristics reminiscent of Gewürztraminer.

- Madeleine Angevine is a variety that reaches its fullest potential in Puget Sound.

Mountains. All the best vineyard sites on both sides of the sound are planted in microclimates that offer the protection of mountains.

French varieties have not done very well in this marginal climate, but the German varieties ripen well, producing light, crisp wines. Preferred varieties include Müller-Thurgau and Sieggerebe. Pinot Gris, which performs exquisitely in the cool Willamette Valley of Oregon, is appearing in the sound, as well as Muscadet. Red grapes include Pinot Noir and Island Belle. Hoodsport Winery offers island Belle as a varietal wine.

Quilceda Creek Winery

- Puget Sound's Quilceda Creek Winery, founded in 1979, was named by wine authority Robert Parker Jr. as Washington State's premier Cabernet Sauvignon producer.

- Quilceda Creek produces Cabernet Sauvignon, Merlot, and a Columbia Valley red. Its wines have achieved "cult" status and are sold only to the winery's subscriber list.

- Quilceda Creek wines are known for their ageability in spite of their abundant ripeness. They consistently rate at the top of "top wines of Washington State" lists.

Notable Puget Sound Wineries

- Bainbridge Island Winery: Only 100 percent Puget Sound wines are produced. Visitors are received.

- Andrew Will: This winery makes some of the finest Merlots in Washington State from Columbia Valley fruit.

- Hoodsport Winery: Hoodsport offers a wide spectrum of traditional and nontraditional varieties, including Lemberger and Island Belle/Merlot.

WALLA WALLA

Here is the source of many of Washington State's finest red wines

The Walla Walla AVA is one of Washington State's most celebrated, with more than ninety wineries producing many of the state's top-rated wines.

The soils here are a complex mix of sand, silt, and volcanic ash. The climate is arid, requiring irrigation. The landscape consists mostly of barren, grassy, rolling hills. Rainfall is around 10 inches a year (compare with Puget Sound's 60 inches). And summers are hot. Oddly, this other-worldly region proves to be an ideal location for controlled viticulture. Walla Walla lies on a latitude midway between Burgundy and Bordeaux. From June to October, the region enjoys extended daylight; and rainfall at harvest time is rare, allowing longer hang time than in many other regions.

The Walla Walla AVA supports a wide range of traditional

Where the Wineries Are

- Lowden: On SR 12 2 miles before the city of Walla Walla. L'Ecole No. 41 and Woodward Canyon are on the north side of the highway.

- Walla Walla and outskirts: Here you will find dozens of wineries and tasting rooms, including Pepper Bridge and Seven Hills.

- Oregon: On SR 11 a few miles south of Walla Walla you will cross the Oregon border. There are four wineries here. There are two tasting rooms on SR 11.

L'Ecole No. 41 Winery

- L'Ecole No. 41 is a "must stop" for Walla Walla visitors. Housed in a schoolhouse built in 1915, it offers a full spectrum of high-quality Walla Walla wines.

- L'Ecole No. 41 is the first winery on U.S. 12 on the approach to Walla Walla from the west. Its label was designed by an eight-year-old child.

- Most of L'Ecole No. 41's fruit is sourced from the region's finest vineyards.

- L'Ecole's wines are exceptional and attractively priced. Woodward Canyon is located next door.

varieties, from Sémillon to Cabernet Sauvignon. And the wines are almost uniformly superior. The best are among Washington State's finest.

The pioneer wineries of this appellation still exist and are among the finest producers: Leonetti, Woodward Canyon, and L'Ecole No. 41.

Walla Walla boasts at least two "cult" wineries. Leonetti was the region's first winery, established in 1977. It sells only to a subscriber list, but its wines can be found on the Internet. Established in 1996, Cayuse Vineyards has consistently produced the top Syrah in all of Washington State. The small winery (2,500 cases per year) owns five vineyards south of the city of Walla Walla. All are biodynamically farmed. The wines are sold only to a subscriber list.

The Walla Walla AVA is largely in Washington but dips down into Oregon to include several outstanding vineyards of the region. There are no large estate wineries here and no luxury wine châteaux. Winery-owned vineyards certainly exist, but most Walla Walla wineries source fruit from the celebrated privately owned vineyards in the region.

Walla Walla Vineyard

- The best vineyards of this region are planted largely on gently rolling hills with excellent drainage. All Walla Walla vineyards are irrigated.

- Walla Walla vines grow in infertile, thin soils that coax them to produce small, richly flavored berries.

- The unique Walla Walla soils allow the grapes to express the special characteristic minerality of this region.

- The Walla Walla AVA produces uniformly excellent fruit for Washington State's quality wines. Little or none is destined for the value wine market.

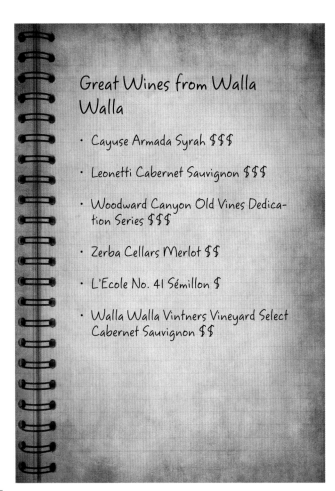

Great Wines from Walla Walla

- Cayuse Armada Syrah $$$
- Leonetti Cabernet Sauvignon $$$
- Woodward Canyon Old Vines Dedication Series $$$
- Zerba Cellars Merlot $$
- L'Ecole No. 41 Sémillon $
- Walla Walla Vintners Vineyard Select Cabernet Sauvignon $$

LAKE CHELAN

Washington State's newest wine-growing region has sixteen wineries

Lake Chelan is one of Washington State's oldest grape-growing areas—and newest, in spite of a wine-growing history going back to 1881. The area was first settled by Italian immigrants, one of whom owned a vineyard in California. Louis Conti probably obtained cuttings from Agoston Haraszthy's Buena Vista Vineyard in Sonoma. The first Lake Chelan vineyard was planted with cuttings from Conti's California vineyard. Today

there are sixteen lakeside wineries, and the region received official AVA status in 2009.

Lake Chelan is a 50-mile-long narrow fjord-like lake in north-central Washington, rimmed by high mountains. The majestic Cascade Mountains rise at its northwest end; a fertile valley occupies the southeast end. At an elevation of 1,486 feet and a depth of nearly 400 feet, Lake Chelan is

North Shore Wineries with Tasting Rooms

- Benson Vineyards

- Four Lakes Winery

- Tildio Winery

- Wapato Point Cellars

Lake Chelan Winery

- With a backdrop of the Cascade Mountains, Lake Chelan is one of Washington State's most scenic wine-growing regions.

- Wineries are located on the north and south sides of the lake near the town of Chelan.

- Benson Vineyards, on Lake Chelan's north side, is the only 100 percent estate winery in the region. It offers fourteen wines, covering the full spectrum—including Ice Wine. Comfortable accommodations and a variety of restaurants are located in Chelan and Manson.

the third-deepest lake in the United States. The region is very rural, sparsely populated, and pristine.

Lake Chelan enjoys a climate similar to the Columbia Valley, but the lake provides a moderating influence on the vines. Consequently, all the Lake Chelan wineries are located on hillsides overlooking the water.

The modern era of winemaking in Lake Chelan dates back to the 1990s. The first bonded winery opened in 2000. Growers have planted to Pinot Noir, Chardonnay, Syrah, Merlot, Malbec, Riesling, Pinot Gris, and Gewürztraminer.

The Lake Chelan wineries have engaged some of Washington's finest winemakers, and Lake Chelan wines are beginning to receive accolades from wine reviewers and medals in major wine competitions. With only around 200 acres under vine, most local wineries expand their offerings with wines made from Columbia Valley fruit. Wine touring in this area is very different from in the better-known and more-established wine destinations in the state. Wineries are small and eager to receive visitors. Many roads are unpaved, and sometimes the only transportation is by ferry or seaplane.

Wine Touring at Lake Chelan

- Lake Chelan offers a full range of tourist services. Off-road vehicles take visitors to scenic locations at attractive prices.

- W.A.V.E. (Winery Assault Vehicle Excursion) tours take groups to eight wineries. Pinzgauer vehicles hold up to nine people. Tours are booked for four or six hours at reasonable rates.

- Private limousine service is available in the town of Chelan. The Lady of the Lake and Lady Express ferries take visitors to Stehekin, at the far end of Lake Chelan. The round trip occupies a full day.

South Shore Wineries with Tasting Rooms

- Karma Vineyards & Cave

- Lake Chelan Winery

- Nefarious Cellars

- Rio Vista Winery and Vineyards

- Tsillan Cellars

- Vin du Lac/Chelan Wine Co.

- Please note that days and hours of operation vary.

COLUMBIA GORGE

This scenic region produces crisp white wines from Hood River and complex reds from the Dalles

The Columbia River Gorge is one of the Pacific Northwest's most scenic and geologically interesting regions. The Columbia River is walled in by mountains on both sides. More than seventy waterfalls grace the Oregon side. The region was declared the nation's first National Scenic Area in 1986.

The sea-level Columbia River cuts through the Cascade Mountains to eastern Washington and passes through two distinct climatic regions. The forested gorge area is cool, wet, and windy, but beyond the Cascades a desert climate dominates. This clear regional distinction led to the establishment of a separate AVA for the Columbia Gorge in 2004.

The Columbia River Gorge AVA includes vineyard areas in

A Columbia Gorge Vineyard

- Cool air flows from the Cascade Mountains and picks up moisture from the Pacific Ocean, making this region one of the Northwest's coolest wine-growing areas. The soils are volcanic.

- Although this region enjoys abundant rainfall, the growing season is typified by cool, sunny days, providing an excellent environment for grape varieties.

- Grapes must be hand pruned and hand harvested. The best wines carrying a "Columbia Gorge" appellation are lean and complex, with mineral notes.

Cathedral Ridge Winery

- Cathedral Ridge, one of the gorge's first wineries, is a ten minute drive from Hood River and is one of the few area wineries open to visitors year round.

- Originally specializing in white wines, especially German varieties, this winery has switched its winemaking emphasis largely to reds, especially Pinot Noir.

- Cathedral Ridge is one of the few Pacific Northwest wineries offering a Zinfandel. Cathedral Ridge's winemaker for the past decade is Michael Sebastiani, of the eponymous California wine family.

Oregon and Washington. Wineries are found on both sides of the river from the city of Hood River in the west to the Dalles. More than fifty wineries are located in the western 40 miles near Hood River. The cool, western end of the Gorge produces delicate Pinot Noir, Chardonnay, and white German varieties; moving eastward, warmer-weather red grapes such as Syrah, Zinfandel, Cabernet, and Barbera dominate. Most of the gorge wineries make white wines from gorge fruit and import red varieties from warmer eastern regions.

Wineries range from rustic family operations to modern tourist-oriented facilities with spectacular views of the Columbia River. There are no large-scale wineries here. The finest wines are made both in tiny wineries and midsized commercial wineries. Maryhill Winery on the Washington side is a consistent medalist in wine competitions. It is best known for its red wines. Some of the Pacific Northwest's finest Viognier and Syrah are made by Syncline, a two-person operation on the Washington side. Syncline wines have scored in the *Seattle Times*'s top twenty-five Washington State wines and number four in that newspaper's listing of "Best Value Producers."

Cascade Cliffs Winery

- Volcanic escarpments appear on both sides of the gorge. They erode into basaltic soils highly favored for wine growing. In contrast, flood deposits dominate the soils of the eastern Columbia Valley.

- Cascade Cliffs Winery is farther east and on the Washington side. It enjoys a moderate climate and specializes in Italian varieties such as Barbera.

- Its Columbia Valley–designated Barbera was awarded a double-platinum medal and named "Best of the Best" by the Pacific Northwest Wine Press.

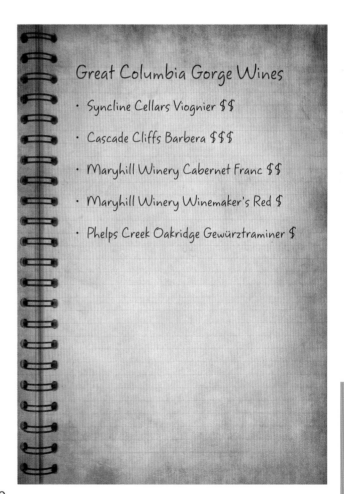

Great Columbia Gorge Wines

- Syncline Cellars Viognier $$
- Cascade Cliffs Barbera $$$
- Maryhill Winery Cabernet Franc $$
- Maryhill Winery Winemaker's Red $
- Phelps Creek Oakridge Gewürztraminer $

WILLAMETTE VALLEY

You'll find a world-class Pinot Noir and superb Pinot Gris

Oregon's Willamette (pronounced Will-a-met) Valley is one of America's most important appellations for Pinot Noir and Pinot Gris. The valley runs from Portland south to Eugene, a distance of 100 miles, and includes most of Oregon's largest cities. It is bounded on the west by the Coast Ranges and on the east by the Cascade Mountains. The 3.3-million-acre AVA contains a half-dozen smaller AVAs with regional distinctions.

These include the famous red Dundee Hills, where many of Oregon's finest Pinot Noirs are produced.

Lying to the west of the Cascades, the Willamette Valley is a marginal wine-growing region suitable for only a narrow range of cool-weather varieties. In contrast, most of Washington State's viticultural areas are found east of the Cascades and are drier and warmer.

The Oregon Wine Tasting Room

- The Oregon Wine Tasting Room, which stocks 350 Oregon wines, is located 9 miles south of McMinnville on SR 18. It contains the largest collection of Oregon wines anywhere.

- McMinnville hosts the International Pinot Noir Celebration, the largest event of its kind in the world each July.

- The Willamette Valley AVA was subdivided in 2005 and 2006 into areas that showed specific characteristics: McMinnville Foothills, Dundee Hills, Ribbon Ridge, the Yamhill-Carlton District, Eola-Amity Hills District, and Chehalem Mountains.

Hilltop Vineyards

- The best vineyard sites in this region are on gentle to fairly steep hillsides. Visitors to these wineries are treated to panoramic views of the surrounding countryside.

- The wineries of the Willamette Valley are all small to medium in size. Many do not have public tasting rooms, so call ahead.

- Most of Oregon's finest vineyards are meticulously farmed. A high percentage of these vineyards is organically farmed, and an increasing number of biodynamic vineyards are beginning to appear.

The Willamette Valley was never considered a suitable region for viticulture until David Lett, a graduate of the University of California at Davis, arrived with three thousand grapevine cuttings and made the first effort to make wine here. In 1979 Lett's Oregon Pinot Noir bested the finest red Burgundies in a blind tasting in Paris. This single event generated a wine industry that now boasts over three hundred wineries. Lett also planted the first Pinot Gris in America. Oregon Pinot Gris has earned an international reputation for quality and style.

ZOOM

Pinot Noir is extremely sensitive to soil type. In Burgundy it grows best on gentle slopes underlain by chalky limestone that originated in the Jurassic period. In California's Santa Rita Hills, the best Pinot Noir grows on a specific type of limestone soil called "botella." Oregon's Pinot Noir prefers iron-rich basaltic soils such as those found in the famous Red Hills of Dundee.

Argyle—an Oregon Farmhouse Winery

- Oregon boasts few modern wineries with luxurious reception areas. Most are small wineries based in farmhouses or barns.

- Most of the winery production is limited to small estate vineyards. Much of it never leaves the state. Only larger wineries enjoy wide distribution, and even those wines can be difficult to find outside of major metropolitan wine stores.

- Because the Oregon wine industry dates back only to the mid-1980s, all the vineyards were planted to Burgundian clones of Pinot Noir and Chardonnay.

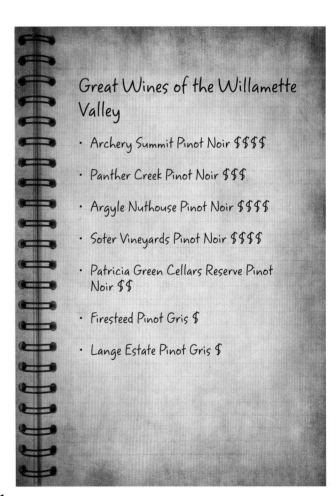

Great Wines of the Willamette Valley

- Archery Summit Pinot Noir $$$$
- Panther Creek Pinot Noir $$$
- Argyle Nuthouse Pinot Noir $$$$
- Soter Vineyards Pinot Noir $$$$
- Patricia Green Cellars Reserve Pinot Noir $$
- Firesteed Pinot Gris $
- Lange Estate Pinot Gris $

101

SOUTHERN OREGON

Explore Oregon's little-known Cabernet country

The earliest attempt at commercial winemaking in Oregon occurred after the California Gold Rush when Peter Britt, a pioneer settler in the Rogue Valley, planted around two hundred varieties and pressed his first grapes in 1858. Wine at that time sold for 50 cents a gallon, but customers brought their own jugs because bottling lines had not yet been invented. The most successful variety was Riesling. Britt had little, if any, competition, and all commercial winemaking in southern Oregon ceased with the advent of Prohibition. It lay fallow until Richard Sommers, a University of California at Davis graduate, opened the region's first post-Prohibition winery in 1961.

The wine-growing regions of southern Oregon are lumped together into one large AVA that runs from just south of

Southern Oregon Wine Country

- The sub-appellations of southern Oregon lie in four valleys, each enjoying AVA status: Red Hill–Douglas County, Rogue Valley, Applegate Valley, and Umpqua Valley.

- The Rogue Valley encompasses two tributary valleys: The cool Illinois Valley supports Burgundian varieties. Bear Creek Valley, which runs parallel to the Interstate 5 corridor, enjoys a Bordeaux-like climate.

- Applegate Valley, south of Grants Pass, is one of Oregon's newest appellations and is planted to Cabernet Sauvignon, Merlot, Chardonnay, Syrah, and Zinfandel.

- The Umpqua Valley is the oldest appellation in the region, created in 1984. It enjoys the greatest diversity of terroirs and climates.

Valley View Winery and Vineyard

- Valley View Winery is a restoration of the original 1850-era Peter Britt winery of the same name that ceased operating after Britt's death in 1906.

- Valley View was the first bonded winery in the Rogue Valley AVA since the repeal of Prohibition.

- This estate vineyard is sustainably farmed. Varieties offered are Merlot, Cabernet Sauvignon, Cabernet Franc, Tempranillo, Viognier, Sauvignon Blanc, Roussanne, Chardonnay, and Syrah. Its wines are not distributed outside Oregon but can be obtained through the winery's web site.

Eugene 125 miles to the California border. In 1984–2006 four sub-appellations were recognized to reflect the diversity of soils and climate. The vineyard areas occupy high mountain valleys. High elevation and a marine influence, spilling over the coastal mountains to the west, are major elements of this region's distinct terroir. Westerly valleys are cool enough for German varieties. Easterly valleys are warm enough to ripen Cabernet Sauvignon and Syrah.

A large number of high-quality wines emanate from this region. There are twenty wineries and 120 vineyards that supply not only local producers but also Willamette Valley wineries whose estate vineyards are unable to ripen many red wines. Southern Oregon soils are varied, but most vineyards are planted on marine sedimentary formations derived from 200-million-year-old bedrock eroded from the Klamath Mountains. Both the soils and climate stand in stark contrast to those of the Willamette Valley. The grape varieties grown here include Merlot, Cabernet Sauvignon, Syrah, Chardonnay, Cabernet Franc, Riesling, Tempranillo, Gewürztraminer, and Viognier. There is also some Pinot Noir and Pinot Gris.

Weisinger's of Ashland

- Weisinger's Vineyard-Winery typifies the small modern winery that has taken root in southern Oregon since the growth of viticulture there in the 1980s.

- Located off U.S. 99 just south of Ashland, Weisinger's is a favorite tourist stop that caters to those wishing to discover wines of the Rogue Valley. Its tasting room is open year round.

- Weisinger's produces Cabernet Sauvignon, Merlot, and Syrah, along with red and white blends, all from Rogue Valley fruit. The winery does not have distribution outside Oregon.

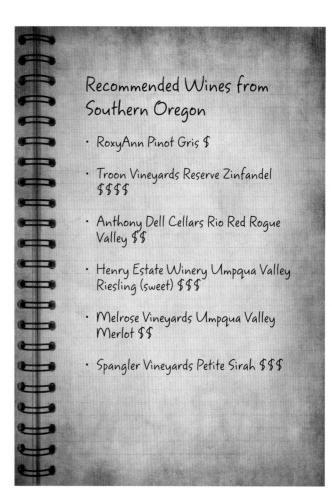

Recommended Wines from Southern Oregon

- RoxyAnn Pinot Gris $

- Troon Vineyards Reserve Zinfandel $$$$

- Anthony Dell Cellars Rio Red Rogue Valley $$

- Henry Estate Winery Umpqua Valley Riesling (sweet) $$$

- Melrose Vineyards Umpqua Valley Merlot $$

- Spangler Vineyards Petite Sirah $$$

FINGER LAKES
Here lies New York State's premier wine-growing region

In central New York State lies a group of long, narrow, deep glacial lakes that suggests on a map the outstretched fingers of a hand. These are the Finger Lakes. The lakes enjoy a micro-climate suitable for viticulture in a region otherwise too cold. The lakes, along with the mountains that surround them, moderate both summer and winter climates.

In 1882 the Geneva Agriculture Experiment Station was established here to assist in the development of a growing wine industry. The station grew to become the largest and most important agricultural research center in the United States and still operates as an arm of Cornell University.

Until 1959 the Finger Lakes region was dominated by five large wineries: Taylor, Gold Seal, Widmer's, Canandaigua, and Pleasant Valley, which sold wine under the "Great Western"

Common French-American Hybrid Grapes

- Seyval Blanc: crisp white, medium body

- Vidal Blanc: high-acid white, excellent for Ice Wine

- Chancellor: well-balanced red blending grape

- Chamboursin: medium body red grape

- Marechal Foch: very dark red, velvety

- Baco Noir: smoky, deep red

A Finger Lakes Vineyard

- Wineries line the shores of the four main lakes: Keuka, Seneca, Cayuga, and Canandaigua. Most Finger Lakes wineries are open to visitors year round.

- The majority of Finger Lakes wineries lie on one of four "wine trails." The longest of these is the Seneca Lake Wine Trail, which includes over sixty wineries.

- The Finger Lakes region is a very popular tourist desti-nation. Its beautiful scenery appeals to regular tourists and wine lovers alike. Tasting rooms are crowded on weekends, much less so on weekdays.

label. These wineries supplied most of the sparkling wine sold in the United States. Still wines were made from native American and French-American hybrid grapes known for their winter hardiness. Canandaigua, through a series of acquisitions, has become the world's largest wine entity, operating under the name "Constellation Brands."

The first commercial Finger Lakes wine made from European varieties *(v. vinifera)* was released under the "Gold Seal" label in 1959, but the most important advocate and pioneer of European varieties in the Finger Lakes was a Russian immigrant, Dr. Konstantin Frank, who established his Vinifera Cellars in 1962. This proved to be a turning point, not only for the Finger Lakes but also for all eastern U.S. wineries. Frank's research into grafting the European varieties onto American native rootstock proved to be a key factor in growing these varieties in cold climates and protecting the more delicate European vines against pests and diseases that had hindered all previous efforts. With over one hundred wineries here and four "wine trails," the Finger Lakes AVA has become the largest wine-producing region in America outside of California.

Belhurst Castle and Winery

- Begun in 1889, Belhurst Castle and Winery on the west shore of Seneca Lake was one of the first wine estates in the Finger Lakes.

- The castle overlooks Seneca Lake and offers a wide array of unique modern accommodations along with the opportunity to experience the region's historic wines, made largely from French-American hybrid grapes.

- The Belhurst Castle estate includes three hotels, two restaurants, and a winery.

Wine Trails of the Finger Lakes AVA with Recommended Wineries

- Canandaigua Wine Trail: Widmer Wine Cellars

- Keuka Wine Trail: Dr. Konstantin Frank's Vinifera Cellars

- Seneca Wine Trail: Belhurst Castle and Winery

- Cayuga Wine Trail: Goose Watch Winery, Hosmer Winery

LONG ISLAND

This premier wine-touring destination is less than three hours from New York City

Unlike all other New York State wine regions that enjoy wine-growing traditions going back as far as the eighteenth century, the first commercial Long Island vineyard was planted in 1973. This new, dynamic wine region escaped the decades of experimentation associated with the Finger Lakes and Hudson River districts and was in a position to plant the most

suitable varieties from its inception. Wine growing here has been based on the Bordeaux model, with Long Island vintners engaged in frequent consultation with French vignerons. Consequently, Long Island wines have more in common with European wines than with western U.S. wines.

Long Island enjoys a unique climate among northeast

Distinctions of Long Island

- It's the newest major wine region in the north-eastern United States.

- It's the Northeast's warmest wine-growing district.

- Unlike those of other New York regions, Long Island vineyards are dominated by European varieties.

- Long Island produces a full spectrum of wines, from Cabernet Sauvignon to Ice Wine.

A Lyre Trellis

- The Lyre Trellising system is commonly used in Long Island vineyards. It is a variation on the widely used Geneva Double Cordon system developed at the Geneva (New York) Agriculture Experiment Station.

- Vines are split into two

cordons, which are trained vertically on four wires, while the grape clusters hang down and receive continual sunlight.

- This method discourages vine diseases by opening up the center area, much like the standard approach to pruning hybrid tea roses.

regions. The 120-mile-long island splits into North and South Forks at its eastern end, separated by Peconic Bay. The North Fork AVA is home to around thirty wineries whose vineyards enjoy a mild climate during the growing season as a result of the influences of the Gulf Stream, Long Island Sound, and Peconic Bay. This AVA includes the entire North Fork. Wines from this appellation are rounder and more fruit-forward than those of any other New York State wine region, including the South Fork.

The Hamptons AVA occupies a smaller region in the western portion of the South Fork. The climate here is substantially colder, foggier, and more heavily influenced by winds off the Atlantic Ocean. Wines from the Hamptons are leaner than those from the North Fork, and white wines are more dominant. There are presently only four wineries that occupy this appellation.

The main varieties grown on Long Island are the classic Bordeaux grapes, led by Merlot and Cabernet Franc. Chardonnay is the most widely planted white variety in both North and South Fork regions.

A Long Island Winery

- All the wineries on Long Island are small- to medium-sized operations. Most make their wine from their estate vineyards, but some import fruit from neighboring vineyards.

- In 2001 a general Long Island AVA was created so fruit from vineyards outside the North or South Fork AVAs could be used in wines carrying a "Long Island" appellation.

- Twenty-nine North Fork wineries feature public tasting rooms, and tourism is encouraged. More than a million people visit Long Island wineries annually.

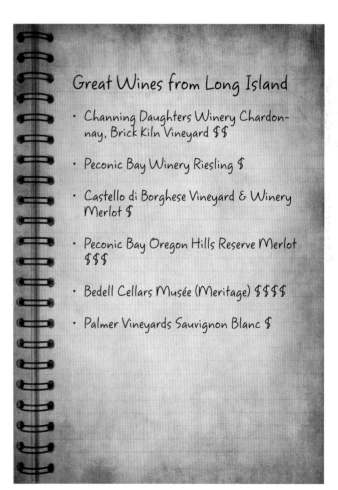

Great Wines from Long Island

- Channing Daughters Winery Chardonnay, Brick Kiln Vineyard $$

- Peconic Bay Winery Riesling $

- Castello di Borghese Vineyard & Winery Merlot $

- Peconic Bay Oregon Hills Reserve Merlot $$$

- Bedell Cellars Musée (Meritage) $$$$

- Palmer Vineyards Sauvignon Blanc $

HUDSON RIVER VALLEY
America's oldest wine region comes of age

This historic region has both the oldest continuously active winery in America, the Brotherhood Winery (1839), and the oldest operating commercial vineyard in America (1827), now occupied by the Benmarl Winery. The original vineyard of the Brotherhood Winery no longer exists, but the winery survived Prohibition by making sacramental wine, as did Beaulieu Vineyards in California, and continues operating today.

Climatic conditions here are reminiscent of those of Germany's Rhineland, which experiences milder winters and cooler summers, mitigated by the proximity of the river. Water plays a dominant role in all of New York State's wine-growing regions—Finger Lakes, Hudson River Valley, Lake Erie, and Long Island.

Early settlers from Germany's Rheinpfalz, noting the region's

Main Grape Varieties of the Hudson River in Order of Prominence

- Seyval Blanc
- Cabernet Franc
- De Chaunac
- Chardonnay
- Cayuga
- Frontenac
- Pinot Noir

The Hudson River Wine Region

- The scenic Hudson River features a complex geology and topography. The climate becomes harsher as one travels north.

- Soils are dominated by schist, slate, and limestone, which, along with the hilly terrain, create many microclimates.

- Total vineyard acreage here reached an all-time low in 1996, with only 650 acres under vine. As suburban sprawl spreads north from New York City, vineyard land has become increasingly expensive, forcing some wineries to abandon riparian sites in favor of inland sites.

resemblance to the Rhine River, attempted to establish vineyards based on native American varieties in the eighteenth century. As with all the early efforts at viticulture in the eastern United States, their success was limited until the introduction of cold-tolerant, pest- and disease-resistant French-American hybrids in the late nineteenth century. The Hudson River region was slow to regain its footing in the years following Prohibition until the success of French-American hybrids in the Finger Lakes was established, around 1945. The star variety was Seyval Blanc, characterized by a pleasant citrus aroma and minerality. Seyval Blanc is the most widely planted variety in the Hudson River AVA, but cold-tolerant European varieties *(v. vinifera)* began to appear in the early 1970s. Today the region produces good Pinot Noir and Chardonnay.

Thirty-three bonded wineries occupy the valley, most on the west side of the river and situated to take advantage of the morning sunshine. Almost all are found within a mile of the river's edge. The Shawangunk Wine Trail runs up the western bank; the Dutchess Wine Trail is on the eastern side.

Benmarl Barrel Room

- Although Benmarl vineyard is the oldest continuously producing vineyard in America, the winery was thoroughly modernized by its new owners after 1957.

- The Miller family's vision is to promote and develop American wines not based on European models.

- Until recently, Benmarl specialized in wines made from French-American hybrids. These varieties still form the core of production. Benmarl has won prestigious awards and has been favorably reviewed by the New York Times's wine reviewer Frank Prial.

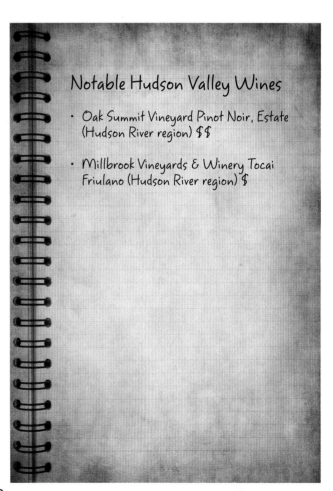

Notable Hudson Valley Wines

- Oak Summit Vineyard Pinot Noir, Estate (Hudson River region) $$

- Millbrook Vineyards & Winery Tocai Friulano (Hudson River region) $

VIRGINIA
The effort of four centuries begins to flower

If New York State can claim to be the cradle of commercial winemaking in the United States, Virginia can claim to have made the first effort at wine grape growing in North America, if unsuccessful.

The settlers of Jamestown in 1607 found a rich supply of Native American grapevines growing wild throughout the region. English King James I of "King James" Bible fame became so intrigued at the notion of importing wine from America that he decreed that every householder in the Virginia colony would be required to plant ten vines on his property. Eight French vignerons were sent to Virginia in 1619 with a supply of cuttings "of the best sort."

All these early efforts were doomed to failure. The native grapes produced wine admitted to be "sour." And the French

Virginia's Most Widely Planted Varieties

- Cabernet Franc
- Chardonnay
- Cabernet Sauvignon
- Merlot
- Viognier
- Seyval Blanc
- Rkatsiteli

Jefferson Vineyards

- Jefferson Vineyards is a modern vineyard planted on the original site of Thomas Jefferson's 1774 site, 1 mile from Monticello. Early investors included George Washington and George Mason.

- The modern vineyard planted dates back to 1981.

- Thomas Jefferson made the earliest effort to produce wine commercially in America after the failed attempt at Jamestown 155 years earlier.

- The Jefferson Vineyard lies within the Monticello AVA, one of Virginia's six appellations.

varieties were ill equipped to deal with Virginia's harsh winters and humid summers. The average life of an imported vine in Virginia at that time was three seasons—just the time needed to produce its first crop. After heroic efforts, winemaking in Virginia languished for more than three centuries.

Observing the success of wine growing in several regions outside of California in the 1970s, Virginians took up the cause again, searching out their most suitable locations and grape varieties. In 1993 shock waves spread through the American wine industry when top awards for Viognier, a little-known variety at the time, were won by Virginia's Horton Vineyards. Nearby, Barboursville Vineyards expanded its vineyard to 126 acres after its acquisition by the Zonin family of Italy's Veneto.

In the years following, Virginia has found its stride in the community of mid-Atlantic wine regions and now boasts more than 150 vineyards and more than fifty farm-style wineries.

Although there is still some devotion to French-American hybrids such as Seyval Blanc, most Virginia wineries have replaced these varieties with European vines and offer the usual array of wines.

Barboursville Vineyard & Winery

- Barboursville, with a case production of around fifteen thousand, is one of Virginia's largest wineries. It is Italian owned; the winemaker hails from Italy's Piedmont region.

- Barboursville was one of the first examples in a wave of European investment in Virginia in the 1970s–1980s.

During this time the number of bonded wineries in Virginia rose from six to thirty-six.

- Barboursville is one of the only eastern wineries focusing on Italian varieties. Its Nebbiolo—one of the most difficult of varieties—is a gold medal winner.

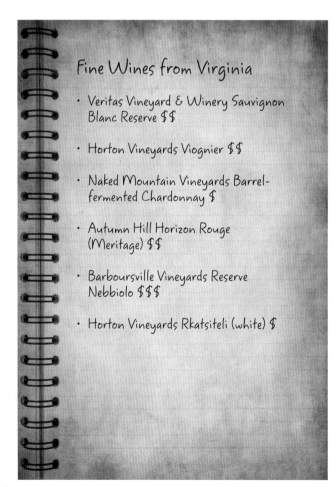

Fine Wines from Virginia

- Veritas Vineyard & Winery Sauvignon Blanc Reserve $$

- Horton Vineyards Viognier $$

- Naked Mountain Vineyards Barrel-fermented Chardonnay $

- Autumn Hill Horizon Rouge (Meritage) $$

- Barboursville Vineyards Reserve Nebbiolo $$$

- Horton Vineyards Rkatsiteli (white) $

NEW MEXICO & COLORADO

Here is America's oldest vinifera wine-growing region

KNACK WINE BASICS

Although wineries are found in every state, nowhere is grape growing more difficult than in the Rocky Mountain West. Here, in addition to the usual ravages of pest and diseases, grapevines must contend with high altitude, difficult soils, severe weather, and a short growing season.

A narrow corridor suitable for viticulture runs from central New Mexico through western Colorado. This corridor varies in width from around 150 miles down to 2 miles. Grape growing is largely confined to the Rio Grande Valley, but there are extensive plantings in the high desert near Deming and east of Albuquerque. Commercial viticulture begins near the city of Truth or Consequences, with European varieties (*v. vinifera*) dominating. As elevation increases north of Albuquerque, French hybrids become more prominent.

High-altitude Grape Growing

- Vines must be cold-tolerant.

- Dry climate discourages diseases.

- Vineyards must be irrigated in regions where water is scarce.

- Vines experience a wide daily temperature shift, with intense sun and cold nights.

- Winds up to 100 miles per hour and baseball-sized hail are common.

A New Mexico Vineyard

- New Mexico is home to a burgeoning wine industry. Grapes are grown in five appellations. Three border Texas and Mexico; one occupies the central portion of the Rio Grande Valley; and the fifth is located near Santa Fe, the state capital.

- New Mexico soils consist of silty, clay-loam from ancient river deposits and areideal for grape growing. The most widely planted varieties are Cabernet Sauvignon, Chardonnay, Syrah, Baco Noir, and Vidal Blanc. Zinfandel is appearing in increasing numbers, as is Chenin Blanc.

New Mexico lays claim to the first vinifera vineyard in the United States. There are records of European vines growing in the Mesilla Valley as early as 1580. Grape growing began in earnest in 1629 when the local padres required ever-increasing quantities of sacramental wine. The vines they brought from Mexico came to be known as the "Mission" grape and were used to make brandy as well as sacramental wine.

There are around thirty wineries in New Mexico today. All are small, most with case production around two thousand or less. Gruet, specializing in sparkling wines, is the only sizeable winery. Its case production is in excess of fifty thousand.

Viticulture in Colorado is found in two appellations: Grand Valley and West Elks. West Elks is home to Terror Creek Winery and the highest vineyard in the Northern Hemisphere (6,400 feet). Riesling, Gewürztraminer, and Pinot Noir are especially suited to this terroir, but the most widely grown varieties are Merlot, Chardonnay, and Cabernet Sauvignon. The number of wineries in Colorado doubled over the past decade, now exceeding eighty.

Gruet Winery

- Established in 1984, Gruet was one of the first wineries associated with the modern renaissance of New Mexico's wine industry.

- Gilbert Gruet was a partner in the Champagne house of Gruet et Fils and saw New Mexico as an ideal location for sparkling wine produc-

tion. Gruet's vineyards grow at an elevation of 4,300 feet.

- Gruet Winery produces some of America's finest sparkling wines. It has taken dozens of gold medals in national and international competitions. The lineup includes seven attractively priced sparkling wines.

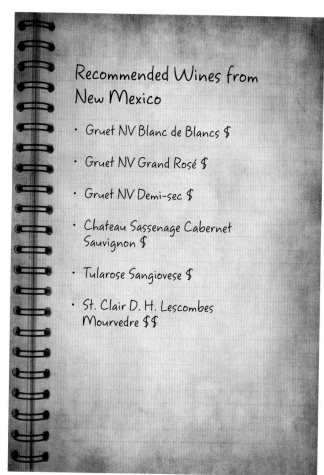

Recommended Wines from New Mexico

- Gruet NV Blanc de Blancs $
- Gruet NV Grand Rosé $
- Gruet NV Demi-sec $
- Chateau Sassenage Cabernet Sauvignon $
- Tularose Sangiovese $
- St. Clair D. H. Lescombes Mourvedre $$

TEXAS

The Lone Star State is America's fifth-largest wine producer

The Texas wine industry traces its history back to 1659, when the first of four missions was established in what is now Ciudad Juarez, just across the Mexican border from El Paso, in west Texas. The padres brought cuttings of the Criolla Chica grapevine, said to have originated in Spain, Sardinia, or Chile. This became known as the "Mission grape" and was planted at every mission where grape growing was sustainable.

Visitors to the El Paso region called this valley "the Eden of the Grape," and the first commercially successful winery in the American Southwest was located here. Pass Wine, as it was called, sold in 1847 for $2 a gallon. The padres compared it favorably with the best of Germany and France. Around 200,000 gallons were made each year, and Pass Wine was exported within a radius of 200 miles.

Recommended Wines from Texas

· Fall Creek Chenin Blanc $

· Fall Creek Chardonnay $

· Messina Hof Wine Cellars Gewürztraminer $

· Inwood Estates Vineyards Palomino-Chardonnay $$$

· Woodrose Winery Cabernet Sauvignon, Estate $

Fall Creek Vineyards

- Fall Creek Vineyards has grown from disastrous beginnings in 1975 to one of Texas's premier winery operations with a case production topping thirty thousand.

- Fall Creek evokes the charm of an old Hill Country ranch house but with state-of-the-art facilities.

- Fall Creek utilizes the Lyre Trellis system more common to Long Island, New York, than to the American Southwest. It produces many high-quality wines. It is known for its Sauvignon Blanc, Chenin Blanc, and Chardonnay; its Meritus red blend is a double gold medal winner.

Just before Prohibition 2,900 acres of Texas land was under vine, and twenty commercial wineries were operating. Wine-making ceased with the advent of Prohibition and was not seriously resumed until the 1970s.

The number of Texas wineries nearly quadrupled in the years following 2000 and now stands at more than 160. Approximately 86 percent of Texas wine is consumed within the state. The Texas Hill Country, west of Austin, is the nation's second-most-visited wine region after Napa Valley, California. It is also the largest AVA in the United States.

The Balcones fault system, running from south-central Texas northeast to Oklahoma, bisects Texas into two regions. The eastern region is humid and highly susceptible to vine diseases. Consequently, almost all the vineyard areas are in central and west Texas. Wineries, however, are found in every region of the state.

Primary grape varieties grown in Texas are (in order of dominance) Cabernet Sauvignon, Merlot, Chardonnay, and Chenin Blanc. Texas Chenin Blanc is a rising star and generally priced very attractively.

Wine Touring in the Hill Country

- Of the six Texas appellations, the Hill Country in central Texas receives the most visitors and is the most popular region for bus and limo tours.

- Twenty-four Hill Country wineries receive 5 million visitors each year. Many Hill Country wineries offer wine tasting without charge.

- The Texas Wine Trail runs from Fredericksburg north to Austin. This is the most popular area for wine touring. Elegantly appointed touring vans service the Texas Wine Trail, operating out of Fredericksburg.

Becker Vineyards Barrel Room

- Texas Hill Country wineries are small- to medium-sized operations, but they typically feature modern winemaking facilities.

- In spite of the cost of French and American oak barrels (as high as $1,000 each), these wines are very attractively priced. There are few exceptions.

- Some wineries offer guests the opportunity to taste wines in various stages of development in their barrel rooms. Some of the larger barrel rooms are designed for dinner parties and wedding receptions in addition to wine storage.

MISSOURI

Splendid reds and delicious whites flow from American hybrid grapes

Missouri is the superstar among American Midwestern wine-growing states. First, it saved the Bordeaux vineyards from total and permanent devastation from the phylloxera pest in the late nineteenth century by supplying a vast quantity of American rootstock that was phylloxera resistant. Second, it became a primary viticultural region for American hybrid varieties.

The Missouri wine regions are located along benchlands above the western reach of the Missouri River and in the Ozark Mountains. The most important wine region is the Hermann and Augusta AVAs. This land was settled in the early nineteenth century by German immigrants who planted American and French hybrids that had an increasingly successful track record. It may have been pure luck that guided

Norton and Vignoles Characteristics

- Norton: declared in 1873 the "Best Red Wine of All Nations" at a worldwide wine competition in Vienna. Deep purple-red wine reminiscent of Australian Shiraz. Flavor profile: wild blackberries, black currants, chocolate, and spice.

- Vignoles: a white Pinot Noir hybrid, created in France in the nineteenth century. Most examples are semisweet with tropical fruits dominating. It's especially susceptible to the noble rot. It then renders a luscious dessert wine with complex honey, peach, and floral aromas and flavors that linger toward infinity on the palate.

Stone Hill Winery

- Established in 1847, Stone Hill Winery is the oldest, most-awarded, and largest winery in Missouri. In 1900 it was the nation's second-largest winery. It won gold medals in various competitions.

- Stone Hill's 160-plus-year-old vaulted cellars are the nation's largest. During

Prohibition they were used for mushroom cultivation.

- Stone Hill focuses on French-American hybrids: Chardonel, Vidal Blanc, Vignoles, Norton, Chamboursin, and Concord. The Norton and Late Harvest Vignoles are the highest-rated wines of their type.

the early wine growers to plant two hybrid varieties that have since become signature varieties of the state of Missouri: Norton and Vignoles.

These varieties are almost unknown west of the Rockies and internationally, but when grown in Missouri's best vineyards they render exquisite and unusual wines. The deep red Norton grape originated in a Richmond, Virginia, vineyard as a natural cross between a native American grape and a European variety planted nearby. It exhibited the best characteristics of both parents. It became commercially available in 1830, around the time of the German immigration to western Missouri. Simply put, Missouri is the world's best source for wine made from the Norton grape. The grape Cynthiana is believed to be a mutation of Norton and has a similar flavor profile. Vignoles (VEEN-yole) is a manufactured French hybrid grown widely in the Midwest. The finest examples are from Missouri. It's a flowery, semisweet or semidry wine, sometimes made into a late-harvest dessert wine. That's where it shines, competing with classy German and Canadian Ice Wines at a fraction of the price.

Cluster of Norton Grapes

- The Norton grape, a product of an accidental natural crossing of *v. aestivalis* and a *v. vinifera* in a Virginia vineyard, is America's most distinguished native red grape variety.

- Norton grapes are grown largely in Virginia and Missouri, but the best examples so far come from Missouri. Virginia wineries are working hard to surpass the current standard.

- Wines from Norton grapes are deeply colored, moderate in tannin, and richly flavored. Enjoy them with foods appropriate to California Petite Sirah.

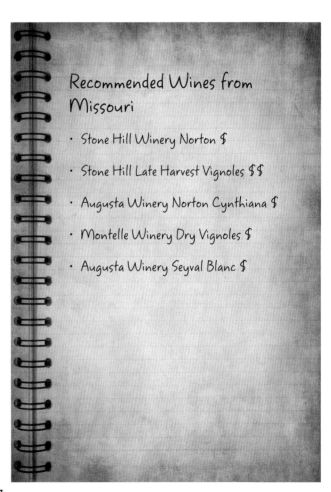

Recommended Wines from Missouri

- Stone Hill Winery Norton $
- Stone Hill Late Harvest Vignoles $$
- Augusta Winery Norton Cynthiana $
- Montelle Winery Dry Vignoles $
- Augusta Winery Seyval Blanc $

CANADA

North America's most unlikely wine-growing region produces one of the world's finest dessert wines

The center of Canada's wine industry is in Ontario and British Columbia. The story of winemaking in Canada is a rocky one. After much experimentation, largely in Ontario, sixty-seven wineries flourished in Canada in 1925. All but six were decimated by inclement weather and Prohibition. After Canadian repeal, wineries were slow to recover. Even as late as 1980 most Canadian vineyards were planted to labrusca varieties and American hybrids. Elvira was the most widely planted grape.

Typical Canadian wines before the 1980s were fortified, sweet wines that used Port, Sherry, and Madeira as a model. Liquor laws in Canada have been among the most restrictive

The Making of Ice Wine

- Grapes are left on the vine into the winter months to freeze, thaw, and refreeze.

- The juice becomes concentrated and intensely flavored.

- The grapes are hand harvested and pressed in a frozen state.

- Approximately one drop of concentrated juice remains in each grape. Ice Wines are necessarily very expensive.

British Columbia's Okanagan Valley

- The Okanagan Valley, an extension of Washington State's Columbia River Valley, produces most of Canada's quality red and white wines.

- The valley contains a 90-mile-long lake that provides a microclimate suitable for viticulture.

More than 150 wineries are located in this valley. This region is desert, with abundant sunshine. Geographers call it the "northern terminus" of the Sonoran Desert that originates in Mexico. Okanagan wines resemble European wines more than the rich, fruit-forward wines of the American West.

in the modern world, varying from province to province. Wide variance still exists, as in the United States.

Canada hit paydirt when Walter Hainle attempted to re-create German Eiswein from Ontario grapes in 1973. In 1978 Hainle Vineyards first offered Canadian Ice Wine to the world. Over the next several decades Canadians have perfected this style of wine, and it has now taken its place alongside the world's best examples. Canada's most scenic vineyards lie in the western province of British Columbia. Nearly two hundred of Canada's five hundred wineries have taken root here. The main wine-growing region is the Okanagan Valley, a northern extension of Washington State's Columbia Valley. This is red wine country, with 52 percent red wine varieties. Most widely planted here are Merlot, Pinot Noir, Cabernet Sauvignon, Syrah, and Cabernet Franc. Among white varieties, Chardonnay, Pinot Gris, and Gewürztraminer lead the pack.

Although wine was made in Nova Scotia as early as 1611, the province established its first commercial winery, Grand Pré, in 1978. Since then more than a dozen wineries have sprouted, catering to the tourist trade.

An Ontario Vineyard in Winter

- Frozen grapes are the source of Canada's most celebrated and expensive wine.

- Ice Wine (the rest of the world calls it "icewine" or "eiswein") was an accidental discovery in Germany in 1794.

- The great European sweet wines are the result of the noble rot—botrytis. Ice Wine is not a botrytised wine and has a different flavor profile.

- Canadian Ice Wine is usually made from Vidal Blanc or Cabernet Franc in contrast to German eisweins that are usually made from Riesling.

Inniskillin Ice Wine

- In 1975 Inniskillin Wines received the first winery license in Ontario since Prohibition.

- The first Canadian Ice Wine was made here in 1984 from Vidal Blanc grapes. In 1991 an Inniskillin Ice Wine captured the Grand Prix d'Honneur at Vinexpo in Bordeaux, bringing Canadian wines into the international spotlight.

- Inniskillin has acquired property in the Okanagan Valley, British Columbia, and Napa Valley, California.

ALSACE

Germany meets France to produce the world's best Pinot Gris and Gewürztraminer

Lying in the far northeast corner of France and bordering Germany's Rhineland, Alsace is unique among all of France's wine regions. Alsace is bilingual and shares its food and wine culture with Germany. Its wines are different from all other French wines. Alsatian wines are made mostly from Germanic varieties in a climate that has much more in common with Germany than France; yet the wines are distinct from both French and German models.

The Rhine River forms the eastern border of Alsace, and the Alsatian vineyards lie on the western side of the river in the foothills of the Vosges Mountains, which form a boundary between northern France's cold and wet Atlantic climate and

Alsatian Wine Terms

- Edelzwicker: a proprietary blended white wine. The name means "noble mixture."

- Crémant d'Alsace: sparkling wine usually based on Pinot Blanc

- Vendange Tardive: late harvested. These can range from bone dry to moderately sweet.

- Sélection des Grains Nobles (SGN): very sweet late-harvest wine from the finest grapes

Rangen Vineyard

- Rangen is the most southerly Grand Cru vineyard in Alsace and one of the steepest.

- Vineyards on steep slopes are terraced. Most Alsatian vineyards are planted on rolling hillocks farther down the slopes.

- The Rangen Vineyard is maintained by the house of Zind-Humbrecht, which uses horses to work the vineyard because it is too steep for tractors.

- Mechanical harvesting is used only in vineyards planted on the alluvial plains closer to the Rhine River.

the more moderate climate of Germany's Rhine River Valley. Although Alsace lies on the same latitude as the vineyards of Champagne, the geology and climate could hardly be more different.

The Alsatian vineyards lie in a 90-mile-long, narrow strip running north and south along the foothills of the Vosges west of the city of Colmar. The region is intersected by faults that created a kaleidoscope of unique microclimates and soils that allows a single grape variety to express distinctly different characteristics.

Alsatian wines are named after the grape variety, and only three types of cultivars are allowed to use the "Alsace" appellation: Traditional varieties (Riesling, Chasselas), Burgundian varieties (Pinot Noir, Pinot Blanc, Pinot Gris), and Swiss/Austrian varieties (Traminer, Gewürztraminer, Sylvaner, Muscat Ottonel). Pinot Noir is Alsace's only red variety.

The white varieties here are vinted at a higher alcohol level than the German whites and display a regional quality that is often described as complex, with notes of gunflint, minerals, crisp acidity, and very pure fruit flavors.

Alsatian Barrel Room

- Alsatian producers have traditionally used large oval neutral wood barrels for wine storage.

- After many years of repeated use, these barrels develop a glassy lining from tartrates in the wine. This increases the inert quality of the barrel.

- Because 90 percent of all Alsatian wines are white, small barrels (barriques) and new oak are avoided because they impart their own flavors to the wine.

- When new barrels are necessary, they are thoroughly cleansed and used for edelzwicker for several years.

Alsatian Pinot Gris

- Alsace is the world's premier region for Pinot Gris. Alsatian Pinot Gris expresses the unique soils of the region and is distinct from New World versions.

- Alsatian Pinot Gris is made in styles ranging from bone dry to intensely sweet. The most successful ones are Vendange Tardive wines.

- Vendange Tardive Pinot Gris may not be labeled as "VT." It is often impossible to know whether it's a dry or sweet version from the label information. Until recently, Alsatian Pinot Gris was labeled Tokay Pinot Gris.

LOIRE VALLEY
It's the land of castles and world-class Chenin Blanc

The Loire is France's longest river. It flows from the Central Massif near the northern Rhône Valley west to the sea at Nantes. It is considered the northern limit of traditional grape growing in France. Champagne and Alsace are exceptions, the former not needing to fully ripen its fruit, and the latter enjoying a Germanic climate.

The Loire is a region of great contrasts. Here we find France's driest and most acidic wines—and its sweetest. The varietal list of Loire wines is too long to list here, but there are two standouts: Sauvignon Blanc and Chenin Blanc.

Sancerre and Pouilly Fumé, on opposite sides of the river, are standard-bearers for Sauvignon Blanc and inspired Robert Mondavi to adopt the name Fumé Blanc for his Sauvignon Blanc that performed sluggishly in the California market of 1968.

Food Pairings for Loire Wines

- Muscadet: raw oysters, poached white fish

- Dry Vouvray: scallops, grilled fish, pasta with olive oil-based sauces

- Off-dry Vouvray: ham, Indian and Pakistani dishes, grilled chicken

- Sancerre/Pouilly Fumé: seared tuna, roast chicken, sautéed pork chops

- Quarts de Chaume: blue-veined cheeses, fresh fruit, custards

The Hill of Sancerre

- Sancerre is a dramatically situated hilltop village on the Loire's eastern reaches.

- Grapes have been grown here since Roman times. Until the middle of the twentieth century, red wines dominated, along with whites from the Chasselas grape.

- By 1980 Sauvignon Blanc from Sancerre replaced all whites as the most commonly ordered wine in restaurants worldwide for reasons of distinction and economy. Sancerre is the quintessential expression of the Sauvignon grape, with its alluring flavors of gooseberry and flint.

The midvalley region around Tours is where Chenin Blanc reaches its greatest expression. It renders a crisp, bone-dry version in the biodynamically farmed vineyards of Savennières and a luscious off-dry wine with flavors of peach, lemon, minerals, apples, and pears in Vouvray. These wines are made only in suitable years. The fruit from off-years goes into sparkling Vouvray production.

The superstars of the Loire are the unctuous botrytised dessert wines of Bonnezeau and Quarts de Chaume.

Quarts de Chaume

- Quarts de Chaume takes its place alongside the great Sauternes of Bordeaux and the Sélection des Grains Noble of Alsace as one of France's great dessert wines.

- The "Quarts de Chaume" appellation is around 100 acres, and yields are kept to a maximum of 1.2 tons per acre—half that of most of the world's finest vineyards.

- The Chenin Blanc grape reaches its finest expression in this wine and in neighboring Bonnezeau. Wines from surrounding vineyards carry the appellation "Côteaux de Layon." These are lighter sweet wines.

Great Wines of the Loire

- Savennières (bone-dry)

- Muscadet de Sèvres et Maine (very dry)

- Sancerre (dry)

- Pouilly-Fumé (dry)

- Vouvray (off-dry)

- Montlouis (slightly sweet)

- Quarts de Chaumes (very sweet)

BURGUNDY
Original home of Pinot Noir and Chardonnay

Burgundy is an ancient wine-growing region in eastern France. Records of viticulture go back to the second century when the Romans conquered the Celtic inhabitants, who were already making wine.

The indigenous grapes of Burgundy are Pinot Noir, Gamay, Chardonnay, Pinot Blanc, and Aligoté. These are the only grapes allowed in Burgundy's Côte d'Or (Golden Slope), a narrow strip of vineyard land running from Dijon south to Santenay, a distance of about 30 miles.

The Côte d'Or is divided into a northern half (Côte de Nuits) and a southern half (Côte de Beaune). The city of Beaune is the center of winemaking and distribution; it lies between the two regions.

The Côte de Nuits is known for great red wines made from

Burgundy

- Burgundy, a tiny wine region, 30 miles long and 11 miles wide, contains more classified sub-appellations than any other region in the world of comparable size.

- The northern part, the "Côte de Nuits," produces red wines from Pinot Noir almost exclusively. Great

vineyards here are Chambertin, Bonnes Mares, Musigny, Clos Vougeot, and Eschezeaux Pere.

- The Côte de Beaune produces the great white Burgundies of Meursault, Corton-Charlemagne, and Montrachet.

Clos Vougeot

- Clos Vougeot is one of Burgundy's most famous vineyards and the largest. The "Clos" refers to the stone wall that was erected by Cistercian monks in 1336 to enclose their vineyard.

- Clos Vougeot is a Grand Cru property owned by eighty négociants. Each is respon-

sible for farming his portion of the property.

- This historic vineyard is situated on a gently sloping hillside. Not every part of the vineyard renders the highest-quality fruit, so prices for wines under this label vary considerably.

Pinot Noir. The Côte de Beaune is home to the world's most-esteemed, full-bodied dry white wines made from Chardonnay. The Côte d'Or has been the gold standard for the finest wines in the world, both red and white.

There are no large estate wineries in Burgundy, only négociants—houses with partial ownership in an array of vineyard properties. A given vineyard may be owned and farmed by dozens of négociants, some owning only a row or two of vines. So you will see Clos Vougeot, for example, offered under many different labels.

The Burgundian classification system is fourfold. Wine made from grapes grown inside the "Burgundy" appellation may be labeled "Bourgogne," the lowest level of classification. Above that are the village wines that take their name from a village appellation and are made from fruit sourced from multiple vineyards within the village appellation. They may contain fruit from superior vineyards but only in poor years. Premiere Cru wines are single-vineyard wines from good sites. The label includes the words "Premiere Cru." The best wines are from thirty vineyards classified as "Grand Cru."

The Great Romanée-Conti

- For a century or more Romanée-Conti has been considered the world's finest expression of the Pinot Noir grape.

- Romanée-Conti and five other contiguous Vosne-Romanée properties are under single ownership, called a "monopole."

- At one time half the production of Romanée-Conti was on standing order by film director Alfred Hitchcock.

- One bottle of Romanée-Conti is currently priced well over $10,000. Older vintages are substantially more costly.

Burgundy's Star Négociants

- Louis Jadot
- Drouhin
- Faively
- Bouchard Per et Fils
- Chartron et Trebuchet
- Olivier Leflaive
- Compte de Vogué
- Domaine Leroy
- Henri Jayer
- Domaine Armand Rousseau
- Louis Latour

BEAUJOLAIS

Excellent and affordable red wines come from the Gamay grape

Beaujolais is the region north of Lyons and south of Burgundy. It's home to France's most approachable, vivacious, and fruity red wines. When French law expelled the Gamay Noir grape from Burgundy, the grape found a very happy home here. In fact, all of the world's best Gamay wines originate here. The "Beaujolais" appellation is one of France's largest, about twice the size of the state of Rhode Island.

Unlike every other French wine region, a single grape dominates, and almost all wine produced here is from the unblended Gamay grape. There is a small amount of white wine also (1 percent) because the varietal restrictions are not quite as limiting as in the Burgundian region. White Beaujolais is made from Chardonnay, Pinot Blanc, Pinot Gris, and Aligoté. It's a simple wine and inexpensive when it can be found.

Beaujolais Vineyards

- The best vineyards in Beaujolais are in the northern hills. The soils here are granitic in contrast to the Jurassic limestone soils of the Côte d'Or to the north.

- These vineyards produced what is frequently called "the only white wine that happens to be red" because

of its light body, low tannins, and fruity appeal.

- Beaujolais is meant to be drunk upon release, not cellared. The Cru Beaujolais can be held for a year or two; Beaujolais Nouveau must be consumed within months of its release.

Georges Duboeuf Winery

- Georges Duboeuf is the major player in Beaujolais. The products of this winery encompass the entire scope of Beaujolais wine from Beaujolais AOC to all the Cru Beaujolais wines.

- Founded in 1964, the firm of Georges Duboeuf produces 30 million bottles of

Beaujolais wine each year.

- Georges Duboeuf Beaujolais Nouveau is the most widely distributed wine of its kind in the world. It becomes available every November, just in time for American Thanksgiving dinner, where it is particularly appropriate.

Gamay is a thin-skinned grape with limited tannins. It resulted from a natural crossing of Pinot Noir and an indigenous white variety called "Gouais." Consequently, Gamay displays the bright fruitiness of Pinot Noir and the light body of Gouais. It's the ideal red wine for people who dislike the heaviness and tannins of popular red varieties. The wines of Beaujolais are made to be enjoyed soon after release.

There are four quality tiers of Beaujolais wine. Wines labeled *Beaujolais* can originate anywhere in the appellation but as a rule are products of the least-desirable vineyards lying on lower elevations. There are sixty villages entitled to make wine under this appellation. *Beaujolais Villages* is a cut above it; originated in thirty-nine of the better villages in the northern portion of the appellation. The term *Cru Beaujolais* is reserved for ten specific wines that represent the best the region has to offer. In Beaujolais, the term cru may or may not refer to a particular vineyard.

Beaujolais Nouveau

- This unique wine is made to be enjoyed within weeks of the harvest. It is released the third Thursday of November following harvest.

- Beaujolais Nouveau is bright, very fruity, light, very aromatic, and refreshing. Its estery aroma suggests banana and pear.

- This style was created to celebrate the harvest. The French law governing it was established in 1951.

- Beaujolais Nouveau is best served as an apéritif wine or as an accompaniment to picnic sandwiches. It is best served slightly chilled.

The Ten Cru Beaujolais Wines

- Brouilly (light)

- Régnié (light)

- Chiroubles (light)

- Côte de Brouilly (light)

- Fleurie (light)

- Saint-Amour (light)

- Chénas (medium-light)

- Juliénas (medium-light)

- Morgon (medium)

- Moulin-à-Vent (medium)

RHÔNE VALLEY

Luscious, mouth-filling wines from Syrah and Grenache grapes

The Rhône Valley is France's oldest wine-growing region. The Romans cultivated wine grapes here as early as the first century AD. Some sources suggest that Phoenicians may have planted the earliest vineyards many centuries earlier.

The Rhône Valley runs from Switzerland south to the Mediterranean Sea, but the main areas of interest are two stretches south of Lyons, separated by a 30-mile reach with little or no vineyard areas. The best vineyard sites are on hillsides.

The northern Rhône contains some of the world's steepest vineyard properties. Syrah is the only red variety allowed. Viognier is the superstar white, but Marsanne and Roussanne are also grown. The great appellations for red wine here are "Côte-Rotie" and "Hermitage." These wines represent the finest expression of the Syrah grape anywhere in the world and are

The Rhône Valley

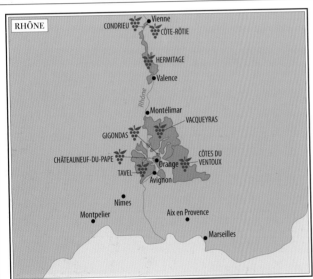

A Northern Rhône Vineyard

- The principal wine-growing region of the Rhône Valley is around 100 miles long.

- Steep hillside vineyards that require manual tending characterize the northern portion. Wines from this region are expensive. Syrah and Viognier are the only dominant grape varieties.

- The southern portion is less hilly and enjoys a more moderate climate. The southern appellations allow as many as twenty different red and white grape varieties, but Grenache is the main red grape and is required to be used as the base wine in appellation-labeled blends.

- The "Côte-Rotie" (roasted slope) appellation produces the finest and most expensive Syrah wines in the world.

- The main producer here is E. Guigal, whose top Côte-Rotie Syrahs cost hundreds of dollars.

- As throughout France, individual vineyards determine the price of wine. The greatest vineyards are La Landonne, La Mouline, and La Turque.

- Côte Brune et Blonde is a blend of wines not destined for vineyard designation and is less expensive.

priced accordingly. Condrieu and Château Grillet are planted to Viognier. The finest producers here are Chave, Guigal, Jaboulet, and Chapoutier. Croze-Hermitage is a large appellation surrounding the Hill of Hermitage. These wines never rise to the stature of Hermitage but are much less costly.

Much less expensive are the Syrahs from neighboring regions, such as Cornas, St.-Joseph, and St.-Peray.

The southern Rhône offers a completely different array of wines. Whereas the wines of the northern Rhône are fundamentally single-variety wines, the wines of the south are often elaborate blends. The main red grape of the southern Rhône is Grenache. The most important wine here is Châteauneuf-du-Pape, a blend of up to thirteen red and white varieties.

Gigondas and Vacqueras offer Grenache blends similar to Châteauneuf-du-Pape at much lower prices. Tavel and Lirac, across the river from Châteauneuf-du-Pape, are the only appellations in France for rosé wine. The lower-elevation vineyards throughout this region are entitled to the "Côtes-du-Rhône" appellation and are made in vast quantity. Around 80 percent of all southern Rhône wines bear this appellation.

The Hill of Hermitage

- This famous site is named for a medieval monk who built a chapel for solitary meditation.

- The most noteworthy wine is named after this chapel, Hermitage La Chapelle. The flat land surrounding the Hill of Hermitage is entitled to use the "Croze-Hermitage" appellation. It's a large appellation, and the wines vary in quality from average to very good.

- An Australian vintner, using the Syrah grape for premium quality wine, named the wine to associate it with this French wine. It was called "Grange-Hermitage."

A Vineyard in Châteauneuf-du-Pape

- The vineyards of Châteauneuf-du-Pape are characterized by a profusion of white, quartzite pebbles, often several inches across. This pebbly surface absorbs the sun's heat and warms soil, promoting vine growth.

- This vineyard was established by the Avignon Pope Clément V in 1309, and bottles of Châteauneuf-du-Pape bear an embossed papal symbol.

- The wines of Châteauneuf-du-Pape vary in quality, but a 2004 reserve bottling from Ch. de Beaucastel brought a price of $485.

129

BORDEAUX

It's the original home of Cabernet Sauvignon and Merlot

The Bordeaux region in southwest France produces more high-quality wine than any other, with a quarter-million acres under vine and more than thirteen thousand producers. It is a region of large wine estates that has historically supplied most of the world's luxury wines.

The most famous examples of Bordeaux wine represent around 5 percent of the region's production.

Viticulture in Bordeaux can be traced back to Roman times, but there is compelling evidence that grapevines were in place long before. The Latin poet Ausonius, a Bordeaux resident, established a private vineyard here in the fourth century. St. Emilion's Château Ausone is named for him.

Great wine did not flow from this region until the Dutch drained the marshland that characterized the Médoc in the

Bordeaux

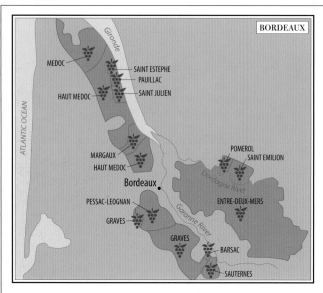

- The wine-growing areas of this region occupy the Gironde Estuary, a confluence of two rivers: Dordogne and Garonne.

- The great winelands of the south (left) bank lie in the "Médoc" region. Its main villages are St. Estéphe, Paulliac, St. Julien, and Margaux.

- The great north (right) bank vineyards lie in the "St. Emilion" and "Pomerol" appellations in the Dordogne River drainage.

- The "Entre-Deux-Mers" appellation lies between these two regions. This appellation produces wines of lesser quality.

Gravelly Soils of Pessac-Leognan

- Just beyond the city limits of Bordeaux lie the special soils that produce the world's most precious and costly dessert wines.

- This region is dominated by gravelly soils that gave rise to the term Graves. A sub-appellation—"Pessac-Leognan"—was created

- within the larger Graves region to recognize the best growing areas.

- Sauternes and Barsac are made from grapes dehydrated by the noble rot (botrytis), yielding one drop of juice per grape seventeenth century. The great wine estates of Ch. Lafite, Ch. Margaux, and Ch. Latour were planted soon after this event. These wine estates then introduced the greatest red wines then known to the world.

Unlike most other French wine regions, the wines of Bordeaux are rarely made from a single variety. They are almost always blends. Red wines made in the left bank wineries (Médoc) are predominately Cabernet Sauvignon with small amounts of Merlot, Cabernet Franc, and Petite Verdot. The red wines of the right bank are usually Merlot based. The sweet wines of Sauternes and Barsac are blends of Sauvignon Blanc and Sémillon.

The red wines of Bordeaux are known for their ageability. Those from good vintages should never be drunk before ten years and will improve for at least twenty. Unlike New World Cabernets, red Bordeaux often declines into a funky state during the first decade, after which it emerges like a butterfly from the cocoon. Sauternes are delicious upon release but will develop character over time. They can be held under proper conditions for decades.

The Most Highly Prized Bordeaux Wine

- Ch. Pétrus is Bordeaux's most expensive wine. Annual production is less than three thousand cases.

- The Ch. Pétrus vineyard is planted to 95 percent Merlot and 5 percent Cabernet Franc.

- The Ch. Pétrus vineyard is geologically unique among its Pomerol neighbors, featuring an upwelling of Jurassic soils unknown anywhere else in the region.

- The Merlot grape reaches its finest expression in the wines of Ch. Pétrus.

A Bordeaux Château

- Large wine estates and flamboyant châteaux dominate Bordeaux, in contrast to Burgundy and all other French wine regions.

- The estate vineyards are planted to reflect the house blend of Cabernet Sauvignon, Merlot, Cabernet Franc, Petite Verdot, and occasionally Malbec.

- All the Premiere Grand Cru Bordeaux wines are made from estate fruit. There are five in the Médoc: Ch. Lafite Rothschild, Ch. Mouton-Rothschild, Ch. Latour, Ch. Margaux, and Ch. Haut-Brion.

131

SOUTHERN FRANCE
Here is the world's most productive wine-growing region

France's Mediterranean coast contains that nation's largest wine-growing region. The Languedoc-Roussillon region extends from the Spanish border to the mouth of the Rhône River. To the east of the Rhône the vinelands of Provence are found. Combined, this region has more acreage under vine than all the vineyards in the United States. It produces one-third of France's total wine output.

One reason for the region's burgeoning success is the comparative lack of government regulation. Those stringent regulations—the most restrictive in the world—are meant to maintain the quality and identity of France's great wines. But in most of the south, vineyard owners have a freer hand over grape varieties, winemaking standards, and labeling. Whereas wines from France's traditional appellations must

KNACK WINE BASICS

Wine Regions of France

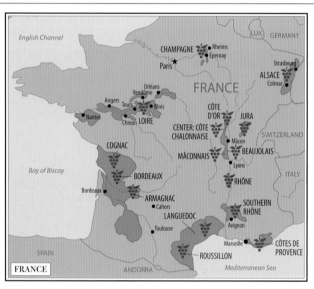

- Although each of the France regions enjoys its particular distinctions, all southern regions are blessed with abundant sunshine and the coastal influence of the Mediterranean Sea.

- The climate of southern France is heavily influenced by the dry mistral winds

- that blow throughout the year, clearing the skies and preventing the humid conditions that lead to vine disease.

- Corbières is one of the few AC regions in the area. Its best red wines have won many national honors and offer great value.

Bush-pruned Vines in Pic St.-Loup

- Vines in the region are pruned to grow as bushes rather than trained on vertical trellises. This limits the yield, concentrating flavors in the remaining grapes.

- Bush-pruned vines have grapes that hang low, close to the ground under a circular canopy.

- Bush pruning protects the fruit from both the heat of the summer sun and the destructive mistral winds.

- Pic St.-Loup has around fifty wineries, the most notable of which are Domaine L'Hortus and Ch. de Lascours.

132

use the name of the vineyard to identify the wine, most wineries of southern France are free to use varietal labeling. The only other French region to enjoy this latitude is Alsace.

Another reason for the growth of the wine industry in southern France is the relatively low cost of its products. These wines are competitively priced with the inexpensive table wines of Australia, South America, and the United States.

Less than 10 percent of Languedoc-Roussillon and Provence is under *appellation controlée* restrictions. The remaining wine is sold as Vins de Pays (VdP, Country Wines). The quality of the wines of this region has improved steadily over the past two decades. Languedoc-Roussillon, sometimes lumped together as "Languedoc," is red wine country. Carignan is the most widely planted red grape, but there is plenty of Grenache, Mourvedre, Syrah, Merlot, and Cabernet Sauvignon. White wines are made mostly from varieties not well known outside the region, but there are Viogniers that rival those of the northern Rhône at a fraction of the price. "Limoux" is the region's appellation for sparkling wine called "Blanquette." Provence is known for its crisp, dry rosé wines.

A Farmhouse Winery in Languedoc

- Although vast quantities of wine flow from Languedoc, almost all is produced by small family wineries.

- Some farmhouse wineries have remained in family ownership since the French Revolution.

- Wine regulations here are so relaxed that wineries are prone to experimentation with different varieties and blends.

- Most family wineries do not have public tasting rooms but are happy to receive visitors who call ahead.

Main Appellations in Languedoc and Provence (West to East)

- Banyuls (rich, sweet dessert wine)

- Rivesaltes (fortified wine)

- Blanquette de Limoux (sparkling wine)

- Fitou-Corbières (red wine)

- Minervois (red wine)

- St.-Chinian (red and rosé wine)

- Pic St.-Loup (red, white, and rosé wine)

SAUTERNES & BARSAC

Luscious dessert wines pair wonderfully with seafood, patés, rich organ meats, and strong cheeses

The Sauternes and Barsac districts southeast of the city of Bordeaux are unique among all France's appellations. They are classified exclusively for sweet wines. In most other French appellations late-harvest sweet wines are an exception.

Sauternes lies in the Graves district that runs upriver from the city limits of Bordeaux on the south bank. Graves is the only French appellation that takes its name from the predominant soil type, gravelly alluvium. But the unique success enjoyed by Sauternes and neighboring Barsac has more to do with its unique microclimate than with its soils.

The Ciron River flows out from the forested hills, delivering cool water that mixes with the warmer water of the Gironde,

Château d'Yquem

- The "Graves" appellation derives its name from the characteristics of its soil, which is gravelly clay.

- The bedrock soil of Graves is Calcaire d'Asteries, a limestone embedded with fossilized starfish that reaches the surface in Barsac.

- Graves topsoil is alluvial deposits from millennia of flooding of the Garonne and other rivers. These are geologically recent soils in contrast to those of Burgundy and Ch. Pétrus in Pomerol. The Sémillon grape thrives here more than in any other wine region in the world.

Botrytised Sémillon Grapes

- The noble rot works its miracles only on the skins of healthy, ripe grapes. If the skins are damaged, gray rot develops.

- The noble rot dehydrates individual grape berries, turning them brownish; they resemble moist raisins when the process is com- plete. Botrytis reduces acid levels, so the wines of Sauternes are usually blends of Sémillon and the higher-acid Sauvignon Blanc.

- Botrytised vineyards take several harvesting passes because each cluster will not be infected to the same degree at the same time.

creating an evening mist that remains through the night and into the late morning. This climatic condition, unique to the southern Graves, promotes the noble rot—botrytis. It infects Sauvignon Blanc grapes, then the Sémillon, which is particularly susceptible. The noble rot desiccates grapes and concentrates flavors of the little remaining juice. It also imparts a spectacular flavor spectrum of its own, making the wines of Sauternes and Barsac the most prized of all the world's dessert wines. Neighboring Barsac, across the Ciron River, enjoys different soils, and the wines display a slightly flinty element.

ZOOM

Botrytis, the "noble rot," is found throughout the world's major wine-growing regions but especially in Sauternes and Barsac. The spores are present in the vineyards and spring into action when the climatic conditions are favorable. Botrytis mold destroys the grape's physical structure. Late-harvest and Ice Wines are made from healthy fruit and do not exhibit the prized flavor profile of botrytised fruit.

Ch. d'Yquem–the World's Premier Dessert Wine

- Ever since the classification of 1855, the wine of Ch. d'Yquem has been regarded as the greatest wine of Sauternes.

- The vineyard is planted to 80 percent Sémillon/20 percent Sauvignon Blanc.

- The maximum yield here is $1/2$ ton per acre, compared with the usual 1.2 tons per acre in other Sauternes vineyards.

- Ch. d'Yquem is the world's costliest wine to produce and the most expensive sweet wine, costing more than $600 a bottle.

The Premiere Cru Wines of Sauternes and Barsac:

Sauternes

- Château La Tour Blanche

- Château Lafaurie-Peyraguey

- Château Clos Haut-Peyraguey

- Château de Rayne-Vigneau

- Château Suduiraut

- Château Guiraud

- Château Rieussec

- Château Rabaud-Promis

- Château Sigalas-Rabaud

Barsac

- Château Coutet

- Château Climens

135

PIEDMONT/PIEMONTE

Welcome to the land of truffles and the "King of Wines and the Wine of Kings"

The Italian province of Piedmont, known in Italy as "Piemonte," is the nation's most-distinguished wine region. It is distinguished by its history and the unique array of indigenous grape varieties that grows better on its home soil than anywhere else in the world.

Piedmont lies at the same latitude as Burgundy and shares a similar summer climate. But there is one particular distinction here: a preponderance of fog in certain vineyard areas during the growing season. Evening and morning fog is a critical factor in many of the world's premium wine regions. Sauternes depends on it to promote the botrytis mold that is essential for its wines. In the Piedmont the fog performs a

The Italian DOC/DOCG System

- DOC: Denominazione di Origine Controllata. Wine must originate from the named region and conform to strict government regulations.

- DOCG: Denominazione di Origine Controllata e Garantita. Term is reserved for Italy's finest wines whose quality is guaranteed by the government.

- IGT: Indicazione Geografica Tipica. Wine is representative of its region. Similar to the French Vin de Pays.

A Nebbiolo Vineyard in Piedmont

- Nebbiolo is the grape of Barolo and Barbaresco. Along with Sangiovese of Chianti, Nebbiolo is Italy's most noble grape variety.

- Traditionally made Nebbiolo wine is brick red and lightly pigmented but very tannic. It takes years of cellaring for the tannins to soften and the true glory of this variety to become expressive.

- Modern Nebbiolos are made in a style that minimizes the tannins and maximizes the youthful fruitiness. These wines are darker than traditionally made wines.

different function. It mitigates the hot summer temperatures and promotes an ideal climate for the Nebbiolo grape to ripen to perfection. So particular is this grape that it hasn't been grown with complete success anywhere else in the world. And to the chagrin of the international wine community, this grape produces two of the world's greatest wines—Barolo and Barbaresco, known for centuries as "the king of wines and the wine of kings." Tokaji Azsú and Chablis have also claimed the title. Barolo and Barbaresco are capable of great longevity when kept under proper temperature control.

Nebbiolo, Chianti, and Cabernet Sauvignon

- The color of wines comes from pigments in the grape skins. The thicker the skins, the more pigment is available to color the wine.

- Most of the pigment is released into the fermenting wine within two days.

- Thin-skinned grapes such as Pinot Noir and Barbera contain less pigment and less tannin. They provide wines with lighter color and medium body.

- Nebbiolo's skin is thin and lightly pigmented, but unlike other red grapes, it possesses strong tannins.

Piedmont is home to one of the world's most food-friendly red wines: Barbera. This is a thin-skinned, low-tannin red that is an ideal accompaniment to Italian dishes in particular, especially those involving tomatoes. Dolcetto is a fruity, soft red designed for early consumption. Piedmont is also home to the white truffle. Typical visitors to the region come primarily for the food and wine. White wines include Gavi, a soft, delicate dry wine; Roero Arneis, a more-complex, substantial wine similar to Tocai Friulano; and Moscato, a semisweet wine finished in a sparkling style called "Asti Spumante."

Traditional Wines of Piedmont

- Moscato d'Asti: fragrant, fruity, suggestive of orange blossoms and lychee, slightly sparkling white wine

- Roero Arneis: fragrant peach and pear aromas

- Barbera: abundant fruit, medium body, lively acidity. Great food wine.

- Dolcetto: deep red, mild tannins, reminiscent of blackberries and plums

- Nebbiolo: distinctive, great wines of Barolo and Barbaresco. Best drunk after five to ten years or more.

ITALY

TRENTINO–ALTO ADIGE

Fresh, bright white wines come from the Italian Alps and home of Pinot Grigio

Trentino and Alto Adige are two contiguous provinces in north-central Italy that, although separate in language and culture, are considered as a single entity for political reasons. These are the most northerly of all Italian provinces and two of the most scenic. They occupy an alpine region deeply cut through by the Adige River and its tributaries. Almost all the vineyard areas lie on steep slopes above the river valley.

The southern province of Trentino is home to some of Italy's largest wine cooperatives such as Mezzacorona and Cavit, whose products are exported worldwide.

The wines here largely reflect the simple tastes of former generations. Grapes are harvested earlier rather than later,

Major Varieties of Trentino-Alto Adige

- Gewürztraminer (It originated here.)
- Chardonnay
- Pinot Grigio
- Mueller-Thurgau
- Schiava
- Lagrein
- Teroldego
- Marzemino

Vineyards in Trentino–Alto Adige

- The best vineyard sites are located on steep hillsides surrounded by the Dolomites and southern Alps.

- Flat lands near the river bank are planted to fruit orchards and the large commercial vineyards that can be mechanically harvested.

- Traditional pergola vine trellising, where the vines form a canopy with the grape clusters hanging down, is gradually giving way to more modern trellising systems.

when flavors and sugars are more mature; wines are tank fermented in large stainless steel fermenters. These inexpensive wines are found on supermarket shelves throughout the United States, Canada, and the United Kingdom. They stand in contrast to the artisanal products of the smaller producers who grow the best-suited varieties in the most-favorable locations and utilize labor-intensive methods to craft the best possible wines.

Alto Adige (upper Adige River Valley) was a part of the Austro-Hungarian empire until it was transferred to Italy after World War I. It's much more German than Italian with respect to language and cuisine. The vineyards here are planted accordingly to accommodate the tourist appetite for light, dry red wine. More than 50 percent of vineyard land is devoted to Schiava, a fairly simple light red wine that pairs well with the Germanic foods that proliferate here but has no place in the export market.

Trentino's outstanding export red varieties include Teroldego, a full-bodied spicy wine with snappy acidity, and Lagrein, a rich, fruity wine with notes of leather, mushroom, and spice.

Mezzacorona Winery, Trentino

- This winery, founded in 1904, is Italy's oldest commercial winery and one of the largest in the nation.

- Its estate vineyards employ both the traditional pergola trellising system and the more modern espalier system that allows mechanical harvesting.

- It receives fruit from 1,300 local growers and vinifies only grapes of its own production.

- Mezzacorona offers a range of quality wines from affordable everyday wines to prestige reserve bottlings.

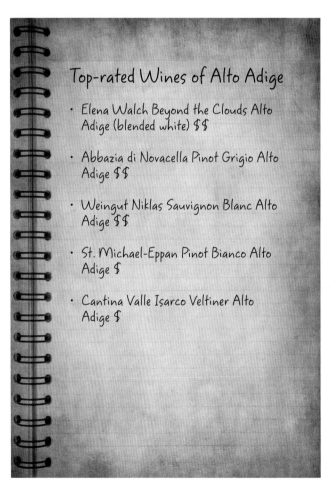

Top-rated Wines of Alto Adige

- Elena Walch Beyond the Clouds Alto Adige (blended white) $$

- Abbazia di Novacella Pinot Grigio Alto Adige $$

- Weingut Niklas Sauvignon Blanc Alto Adige $$

- St. Michael-Eppan Pinot Bianco Alto Adige $

- Cantina Valle Isarco Veltiner Alto Adige $

ITALY

FRIULI-VENEZIA GIULIA
Tocai Friulano is Italy's delicious mystery grape

KNACK WINE BASICS

Friuli-Venezia Giulia is Italy's most northeastern province, bordering Austria and Slovenia. Like Alto Adige, it was a part of the Austro-Hungarian empire until the end of World War I. Some scholars contend that the Hungarian Furmint grape of Tokaji might have either originated in Friuli or been brought to the region from Hungary.

Tocai Friulano is the dominant grape of the region today and is under fire from the Hungarian government for using the "Tocai" name. The name "Tokay" has already been excised from Alsatian wines.

The Friuli region is surrounded by low hills called "Collio" and "Colli Orientali" (eastern hills). The best vineyard sites are in these hilly regions.

Many wine writers consider Friuli to be Italy's finest region

Recommended Wines of Friuli

- Rodaro Ribolla Gialla

- Vie di Romans Dolee Isonzo del Friuli

- Bastianich Tocai Friulano

- Mario Schiopetto Collio Sauvignon

- Mario Schiopetto Collio Pinot Bianco

- Ronco Del Gelso Friuli Isonzo Tocai Friulano

A Wine Village in Friuli

- Friuli population is a mixture of Slovenians, Austrians, and Italians, but the Italian language and culture are dominant.

- Friuli enjoys a unique climate because of cool winds blowing south from the Alps mixing with the moderate breezes coming off the Adriatic Sea. The entire region is said to enjoy "natural air-conditioning." There are ten DOC regions in Friuli and one DOCG, Ramandolo, inside the Collio Orientali DOC.

- Wineries are small. The best ones are located on hillsides, Collio and Collio Orientali.

for white wine. Tocai Friulano, its signature grape, yields a medium-bodied dry white wine with aromas and flavors of wildflowers, pears, citrus, and herbs.

Before the late 1960s Italian white wines were either thin, acidic, and monodimensional wines or rustic, sweet wines requiring fortification to make them palatable. The white wine revolution in Italy began when meticulous winemakers like Schiopetti modernized winemaking in Friuli.

In 2009 the name "Tocai" was disallowed because of Hungarian objections. This lovely wine is searching for a new name. It's been grown elsewhere as "Sauvignon Vert" and "Sauvinonasse" in Chile, but the current preference in Italy is to call it "Friulano." This practice will certainly lead to confusion because there are six California wineries that offer it under the "Tocai Friulano" label.

The white wines are made in stainless steel, but Western-educated winemakers are experimenting with expensive oak barrels and malolactic fermentation, which will certainly drive up the price of these wines. The Friulanos of the future are likely to be fatter and more Chardonnay-like.

Tocai Friulano

- Tocai Friulano is a fleshy white wine with flavors of peach, pear, and almonds. It finishes with a zing of mineral notes and good acidity.

- Tocai Friulano is thought to be related to the Hungarian Furmint grape or Sauvignon Blanc, but its origins have yet to be confirmed.

- New World Tocai Friulanos are often very good but are not surviving the economics of the market. Only six U.S. wineries offer them.

Friuli's Super-whites

- Friuli's top white wines are not varietally labeled. They are blends. These are among the world's finest full-bodied white wines. Some distinguished examples:

- Jermann Vintage Tunina (Chardonnay, Sauvignon, Tocai, Picolit)

- Bastianich Vespa Bianco (Chardonnay, Sauvignon, Picolit)

- Zamò Tre Vigne (Chardonnay, Sauvignon, Tocai)

VENETO

Enjoy everyday light red wines, round and savory whites, and rich wines "for reflection"

Veneto is a northeastern province whose wine-growing regions are dominated by the lower Adige River. Its capital city is Venice, and the center of its wine industry is Verona. It is the largest producer of DOC wine in Italy.

Nowhere else in Italy can we find a richer palette of wine types and styles. No single variety dominates, and all the highest-quality wines are blends. It's difficult to differentiate the fine wines of the Veneto from the sea of ordinary wines found on the export market. The more than twenty DOC regions have been expanded to the point of meaningless-ness. The producer is the key.

The best known Veneto wines are Soave, a Garganega wine;

Great Producers of the Veneto

- Speri
- Masi
- Pieropan (Soave)
- Dal Forno
- Anselmi

Drying Grapes for Amarone

- Amarone is Valpolicella, whose grapes have been dried on straw mats or racks to concentrate the flavors.

- Amarone is a thick, mouth-filling, dry wine and the fourth-best-selling wine type in Italy. It can age gracefully for decades.

- The grapes used for Valpolicella and Amarone are the indigenous varieties Corvina, Rondinella, and Molinari. Corvina is the base wine.

- The term Amarone means "bitter," reflecting the early examples, which were more rustic than the polished examples of today.

Valpolicella, a Corvina blend; and Prosecco, a sparkling wine. The best examples of these wines come from the original classified vineyard areas called "classico." All the major DOC regions have been expanded to accommodate a growing market demand. The expanded areas are not entitled to the "classico" designation. The Veneto is home to Italy's largest wine cooperatives: Santa Margherita, Bolla, Zonin, and others. Santa Margherita introduced Pinot Grigio to the U.S. market more than thirty years ago and dominated that sector until the variety became popular on the international market.

ZOOM

Ripasso—Veneto's Unique Process: Ripasso wines are made by refermenting Valpolicella wine on the skins of grapes previously used to make Amarone. The result is a richer, much more complex wine with some Amarone character. The process used was introduced by the Masi winery in 1964. The cost of Ripasso wines is usually just a little higher than that of quality Valpolicella.

Recioto—Italy's Supreme Dessert Wine

- Recioto is Italy's most-honored and expensive sweet wine.

- Recioto is made from the ripest hand-picked grapes of the finest clusters. Only the "ears" of each cluster are used. It uses the same grape combination as Valpolicella, but the grapes are dried for a longer time, leading to an intense flavor and elevated sugars.

- These wines are very expensive and so complex that they are usually not paired with food. Italians consider their Recioto "wines for contemplation."

Principal Wine Types of the Veneto

- Prosecco: inexpensive sparkling white wine made in bulk

- Soave Classico: medium-bodied, fruity and flowery white wine with mineral overtones

- Valpolicella Classico: light, fragrant dry red, most widely produced red wine in Italy after Chianti

- Bardolino: simpler, lighter version of Valpolicella from Lake Garda

- Amarone: rich, dry red made from dried grapes

ITALY

143

TUSCANY/TOSCANO

Say "ciao" to Brunello, Vino Nobile, and Chianti—Italy's most famous wine

It's been said that Tuscany is Italy's Bordeaux and that Piedmont is its Burgundy. That is to say that Tuscany is dominated by a huge production aimed at a worldwide market, whereas small, quality-oriented producers dominate Piedmont. Tuscany's capital city is Florence (Firenze) ; Siena is the center of its wine industry.

Although Tuscany is known for its red wines, white is grown as well. The overwhelming number of Tuscan Trebbiano wines are thin, acid, and fruit-lacking. They are used mainly as blending wines. But in France the grape is called "Ugni Blanc" and is one of the principal grapes used to make Cognac.

Wine Regions of Tuscany

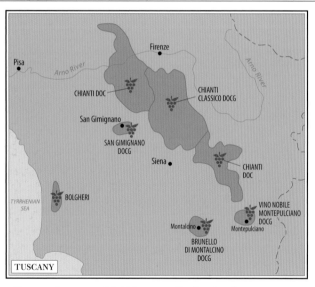

A Tuscan Vineyard

- Tuscany has more DOC(G) areas than any other Italian province—twenty-six at last count.

- Low undulating hills and stately cypress trees characterize this region. Its Mediterranean climate is moderated by breezes blowing inland from the Tyrrhenian Sea.

- Almost all of Tuscany is under vine, but the most important DOC(G) regions are Chianti (Classico), Vernaccia di San Gimignano, Brunello di Montalcino, and Vino Nobile di Montepulciano.

- Although an ocean of Chianti wine is sold to be blended by large exporters, most of the production is from small- to medium-sized wineries.

- Vine trellising systems in Chianti usually utilize the modern system of training on wires, known as the "Guyot system."

- The Italian terms podere, tenuta, azienda agricola, and fattoria are commonly used on wine labels. These terms simply mean "winery" or "farm."

The main stand-alone white Tuscan wine is Vernaccia di San Gimignano, a wine reminiscent of a light-styled Soave.

The glory of Tuscany is Chianti. Chianti is a wine-growing region near Siena. The original area, called "Chianti Classico," was the first wine region in the world to become subject to government regulation (in 1716).

Historically, Chianti was a blend of Sangiovese and various other required grapes. One hundred percent Sangiovese could not be labeled as "Chianti." These restrictions led to the thin, acidic wines of the past but also to experimental winemakers who could forgo the "Chianti" label and label their wines as simply *vini di tavola*—table wines.

The "Big Three" red wines of Tuscany are Chianti Classico Riserva, Brunello di Montalcino, and Vino Nobile di Montepulciano. Montalcino is a tiny hilltop village south of Siena with over three hundred producers, all of whom make Brunello. Brunello, a variety of Sangiovese also known as "Sangiovese Grosso," has thicker skin and yields one of Italy's most elegant red wines. Wines from lesser vintages are sold as "Rosso di Montalcino."

A Super-Tuscan Wine

- Overly restrictive regulations of the past led some Chianti producers to abandon the blending requirements in order to produce superior wine.

- These became the so-called Super-Tuscans of the late twentieth century and sported fantasy names more akin to fossils of the Burgess Shale than wine—Sassicaia, Ornellaia, and Tignanello.

- Some Super-Tuscans are 100 percent Sangiovese, but most are Cabernet/Merlot/Sangiovese blends.

Vin Santo

- Vin Santo, Tuscany's "holy wine," is a sweet dessert wine made from Trebbiano or Malvasia grapes.

- Vin Santo is made from dried grapes in a fashion similar to Amarone. It reaches alcohol levels of 16–18 percent.

- Many Italians enjoy their Vin Santo with dry desserts like biscotti or panettoni, which they dip into the wine.

- Although Vin Santo is made in other Italian provinces, it is a signature wine of Tuscany.

SARDINIA/SARDEGNA
You'll find refreshing and underrated white wines and rustic reds

The island province of Sardinia is one of Italy's most remote, rustic regions. It's just slightly smaller in area than Sicily. It was under Spanish control until the eighteenth century, and Spanish influence abounds.

The main grapes of Sardinia are of Spanish origin, and the local products include unique wines made nowhere else in the world.

Until recently the wines of Sardinia were below export quality, but the infusion of government subsidy and the creation of DOC and DOCG regions encouraged the rise of quality wineries. The best wines of Sardinia now stand alongside the fine wines of the mainland.

Sardinia is hot and dry, particularly in the unprotected south, where it receives hot sirocco winds from the African Sahara.

Major Grapes of Sardinia

• Vermentino: white, aromatic, with notes of almond and citrus

• Vernaccia: white, plump, sugar-rich, used for Sherry-style wines

• Monica: used for fresh, light, fruity reds

• Cannonau: Grenache, flavors of cherry, kirsch, wild red berries

• Carignano: deep color, rich, concentrated red

Sardinian Vineyard

• Today viticulture is the most important agricultural endeavor in Sardinia. Grapevines grow in every part of the island.

• Sardinians have sharply reduced the quantity of production in recent years, favoring lower yields that lead to optimum wines.

• Sardinia has sixteen IGTs (Indicazione Geografica Tipica) regions, the most of any Italian province.

146

Sardinia's most successful grape varieties are Cannonau, a clone of Grenache; Monica, a light red quaffable wine for local consumption; and Vermentino, a white grape that shows serious potential.

Vernaccia di Oristano (not related to Vernaccia di San Gimignano) is made in a Sherry style. It is fermented to high alcohol (19 percent), aged in chestnut barrels, filled to 90 percent capacity to encourage oxidation, and held for six years before release. It yields complex flavors of almonds, orange peel, tobacco, tea, and honey. It suggests sweetness on the palate but finishes dry. It's like no other wine in the world.

Two producers stand out from the pack and are most widely exported. Argiolas, in the far south of the island, produces a celebrated red blend from five native grapes called "Turriga." It consistently rates in the low 90s in major reviews. Argiolas was founded in 1917 and is family owned and operated.

Santadi Terre Brune is Sardinia's other celebrated red wine. It's one of the best examples of quality wine from an Italian cooperative. Terre Brune is 90 percent Carignan and one of Sardinia's finest wines.

Vermentino di Gallura

- Vermentino is Sardinia's signature white wine. Historians tell us that it arrived here in the nineteenth century BC from Corsica.

- It is one of only four Italian white wines to be awarded DOCG status.

- The best examples are from the north, particularly in the Gallura region.

- Sardinian Vermentino is crisp and citrusy with almond notes.

- Vermentino is grown in other Italian provinces as well and has become an attractive, inexpensive export.

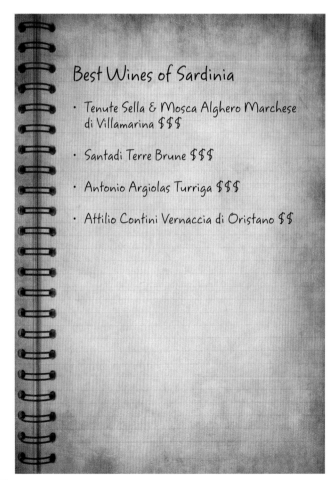

Best Wines of Sardinia

- Tenute Sella & Mosca Alghero Marchese di Villamarina $$$

- Santadi Terre Brune $$$

- Antonio Argiolas Turriga $$$

- Attilio Contini Vernaccia di Oristano $$

SOUTHERN ITALY
Robust and inexpensive red wines grow from native varieties

When you enter Italy's southern provinces you encounter a culture, terrain, and climate very different from those of other regions. Agriculture is the central industry here, and the Italian government is determined to maintain its primacy in the growing of wheat (for the pasta manufacturers in Naples), olives, lemons, and tomatoes—all products of international significance. The European Union (EU) forbids any new vineyard development, only the replanting or restructuring of existing vineyard property. This has resulted in a certain gentrification of these southern vineyards. Whereas in former days the wines of southern Italy were largely unworthy of export, today's products can be superb.

Campania, the province of which Naples is the capital, is known for its white wine made from the Greco grape and

Indigenous Grapes of Southern Italy

- Greco: refreshing white with good acidity

- Fiano: white grape reminiscent of pine nuts and herbs

- Aglianico: notes of black cherry with leather and tobacco

- Negroamara: rustic red with notes of coffee and tobacco

- Primitivo: medium acidity, soft-drinking, moderate tannins

Vineyard in Calabria

- The best vineyard sites in Calabria are on hillsides. Pugliese vineyards are mostly on level ground.

- The hot summer climate of Calabria and Puglia is moderated by cross winds emanating from the Ionian Sea and the Adriatic Sea.

- Grape-growing traditions here were heavily influenced by the Greek occupation in the eighth century BC.

- Most of southern Italy's indigenous grape varieties are of Greek origin and differ greatly from those of the north.

its red Aglianico, which grows on volcanic slopes shared by neighboring province Basilicata. Aglianico di Vulture, from the slopes of Mount Vulture, is widely exported.

Calabria is in the throes of a quality revolution, largely pioneered by two producers: Librandi and Fattoria San Francesco. These firms have introduced international varieties into their Galioppo blends, creating wines reminiscent of the Super-Tuscans of Chianti.

Of greatest interest to Western consumers are the wines of Puglia, the heel of Italy's boot. This is red wine country, and Puglia vies with the Veneto as Italy's most prodigious wine producer. This province is Italy's flattest region and enjoys an iron-rich, marly soil ideal for viticulture.

Most of Puglia's red wine is made from the richly flavored Negroamara (the name means "black and bitter") grape, usually blended with some Malvasia Nera to lighten it up. This is the formula used in Salice Salentino, Puglia's most popular export.

Puglia's Primitivo di Manduria, a Zinfandel relative, yields one of Italy's great red wines in the hands of the best producers.

Primitivo di Manduria

- Puglia's most elegant, complex, and balanced single-variety red wine is made from the Primitivo grape.

- Recent DNA fingerprinting conducted at the University of California at Davis has determined that Primitivo is genetically identical to California's Zinfandel.

- Primitivo is now considered to be a clone of Zinfandel and is planted in California vineyards alongside established California clones.

- Italian Primitivo is exported in a range of styles, quality levels. The best Italian Primitivo is the equal of the finest California Zinfandels.

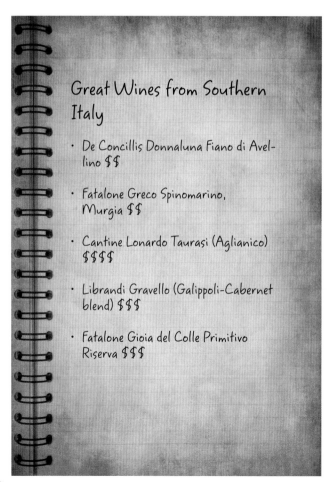

Great Wines from Southern Italy

- De Concillis Donnaluna Fiano di Avellino $$

- Fatalone Greco Spinomarino, Murgia $$

- Cantine Lonardo Taurasi (Aglianico) $$$$

- Librandi Gravello (Galippoli-Cabernet blend) $$$

- Fatalone Gioia del Colle Primitivo Riserva $$$

SICILY & PANTELLERIA
Here lies Europe's most southerly wine region

Sicily and its small southern desert island neighbor Pantelleria seem to be a different country from the rest of Italy. As a rule they experience no rainfall after February until after the harvest. Dry winds and intense summer heat eliminate vine diseases that plague other Italian regions. Sicily is often called "the California or Australia of Italy."

Prior to the 1990s Sicily was Italy's largest wine-producing region, but only 5 percent ever saw a bottle. The other 95 percent was made into grape concentrate or bulk wine to be shipped to cooperatives in northern Italy and southern France to prop up their anemic wines.

The rise in quality in Sicilian wine over the past two decades has been more than remarkable. Total wine production has dropped to 40 percent of that of previous years, and the big

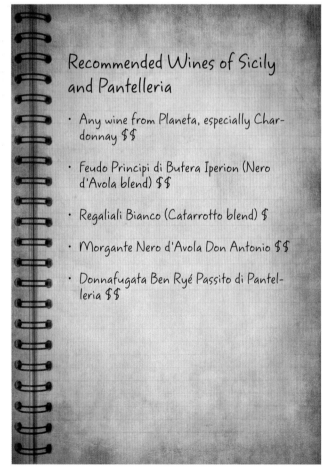

Recommended Wines of Sicily and Pantelleria

- Any wine from Planeta, especially Chardonnay $$

- Feudo Principi di Butera Iperion (Nero d'Avola blend) $$

- Regaliali Bianco (Catarrotto blend) $

- Morgante Nero d'Avola Don Antonio $$

- Donnafugata Ben Ryé Passito di Pantelleria $$

A Vineyard in Sicily

- Sicily has the largest area under vine of any region in Italy. Most vineyards lie around the island's perimeter, but some line the slopes of Mount Etna, growing at elevations up to 2,000 feet.

- Because of the strong sirocco winds that blow north from Africa's Sahara Desert, Sicilian vineyards are bush pruned except in protected areas.

- Sicily's wines are made largely from indigenous grapes, most of which grow nowhere else.

cooperatives have all but disappeared. The Sicilian wine scene is now dominated by passionate wine families devoted to raising Sicilian wine to the highest international standards.

Sixty percent of Sicilian vineyards are planted to Catarrotto, a plush, spicy, waxy white grape used in blends, Piemontese Vermouth, and Marsala. Grown only in Sicily, Catarrotto is Italy's second-most-planted grape (after Sangiovese).

Sicily's signature grape is Nero d'Avola, grown only here. This Syrah-like grape is showing exciting potential.

The island of Pantelleria, with its wind-swept, black, sandy soils, is located just 52 miles from the coast of north Africa. It produces two wines of great merit: Moscato and Passito di Pantelleria—a ripasso wine that many compare with the finest Vin Santos of Tuscany. Sipping these wines is like biting into a ripe, plump golden raisin.

Marsala is Sicily's traditional fortified wine. Dry, young Marsalas are destined for cooking. Aged versions are made in Sherry or solera style. These display a complex palette of caramel, orange peel, nuts, spice, and other exotic flavors.

Marsala—Sicily's Traditional Fortified Wine

- Like Sherry and Madeira, the English created Marsala during the War of the Spanish Succession, during which they had no access to French wine.

- Marsala is made in a range of styles, colors, and sweetness levels. Colors are gold, amber, and ruby.

Age categories are fine (for cooking), superiore, and vergine/soleras. Vergine/soleras Marsalas are aged for a minimum of five years in wood; riservas must be held for ten. Fine and superior Marsalas may be dry or sweet; vergine/soleras Madeiras are sweet on the tongue but finish dry.

The Southern Island of Pantelleria

- The term Pantelleria means "daughter of the wind," referring to the strong, hot sirocco that blows across the island.

- It is the most southerly wine-growing region in Europe.

- Moscato is the most culti-

vated grape on the island. The Arabs introduced it, and Pantellerian viticultural practices are based on Arab models, with stone-walled terraced vineyards and vines planted in sunken holes to protect from the wind.

- All the export wines of Pantelleria are sweet.

151

THE MOSEL-SAAR-RUWER

Enjoy winding rivers, steep vineyards, charming villages, and great low-alcohol Rieslings

Mosel-Saar-Ruwer is the best known of Germany's wine regions. This name identifies the principal river valley of the Mosel and its two tributaries that lie near the French border. The wines from this region bear strong similarities to each other, so they are grouped together. In 2007 German labeling law dropped "Saar" and "Ruwer" from the official name.

The Mosel-Saar-Ruwer defines the northern extent of Europe's wine-growing regions. North of Koblenz the harsh continental climate is inhospitable to viticulture. The only factor that makes wine growing possible in the Mosel Valley is its remarkable and scenic topography. The river has cut a deep valley, and the vineyards are on steeply inclined

The Mosel River Valley

- The valley of the Mosel River (French: Moselle) traces a tortuous path from Koblenz up to Trier, where it joins with its tributaries, the Saar and Ruwer.

- About a dozen tiny villages dot the riverbank between Koblenz and Trier.

- About sixty high-quality vineyards grace the steeply inclined hillsides.

Town of Zell

- The road from Koblenz to Trier passes though a series of picturesque wine villages for a distance of 125 miles.

- Wine bars and wine-tasting cellars are found in most of these villages.

- Although guest services in the villages are available, the Mosel also supports smaller cruise ships and bus tours.

- A plethora of bed and breakfasts are eager to receive guests traveling on a budget. Look for signs announcing "Zimmer Frei" (room available).

slopes that offer protection from the elements and expose the grapes to the sun. The river mitigates the climate and provides a source of water. Production costs are higher here because of the steeply inclined vineyards.

Soils of the Mosel are mostly slate and shale, giving the wines a flavor profile distinct from those of wines of other German regions. During the mid-twentieth century around 90 percent of the Mosel vineyards were planted to Riesling. After a half-century of experimentation with other varieties, the trend is back to Riesling, and Mosel producers identify that grape on their labels. Mosel wines carry the name of the village and vineyard, as in Ürziger Würzgarten, where "Ürzig" is the village, and "Würzgarten" is the vineyard. The producer is also mentioned on the label. Although vineyards and producers are small, there are around 150 German *grosslagen*—large wineries that buy huge quantities of inferior fruit. Several of these are located in the Mosel Valley. These producers are entitled to use their village name along with the name of the grosslage. It's necessary to know these grosslage names to avoid confusing them with the quality wines of the region.

A Riesling from the Mosel

- Mosel wines are among the world's lowest-alcohol dry wines. They are often as low as 6–9 percent, making them delightfully light and appealing.

- Mosel wines are traditionally bottled in what Germans call "hock"-style bottles. In Alsace these tall bottles are known as "flutes." The producers of the Mosel use green bottles to distinguish their wines from those of the Rhineland, which use brown bottles.

- The best Mosel Rieslings can be cellared for decades.

Common Grosslage Wines of the Mosel

- Zeller Schwartze Katz

- Kröver Nachtarsch

- Bernkasteler Badstube

- Bernkasteler Kurfürstlay

- Piesporter Michelsberg

- Wiltinger Scharzberg

THE GERMAN RHINELAND
Quintessential Riesling from the Rheingau, Rheinhessen, and Rheinpfalz

Although some wine authorities believe that the delicate Rieslings of the middle Mosel represent the supreme expression of that grape variety, the wines of the central Rhineland continue to enjoy their defenders as the world's greatest examples.

The German Rhineland is the Rhine River drainage from Koblenz south to the French border at Alsace. It includes three major tributaries: the Main, flowing west from Frankfurt, the Neckar, flowing west from Heidelberg and points east, and the Nahe, flowing from the southwest.

Wines here are fuller bodied and higher in alcohol than the Mosel Rieslings. They are also more likely to exhibit Riesling's

The Central German Rhineland

• Germany does not use an appellation of origin system like France and most of the world.

• The central Rhineland occupies five delimited regions from north to south: Mittel-Rhein, Rheingau, Nahe, Rheinhessen, and Rheinpfalz.

• The Rheingau, along with the Mosel, is the most-esteemed wine-growing region in Germany.

Vineyards above Rüdesheim

• The steeply inclined vineyards of the Rheingau are all south-facing and receive more sun than those of the Mosel.

• An aerial tram takes visitors from the town of Rüdesheim over the vineyards to a hilltop restaurant featuring regional dishes.

• The town of Geisenheim is home to Schloss Johannisberg and, since 1872, the Geisenheim Grape Breeding Institute. This was the most important academic institution dealing specifically with viticulture until the advent of the School of Enology and Viticulture at the University of California at Davis.

most characteristic quality—a faint aroma reminiscent of petrol or burnt rubber.

Grapes were cultivated here as early as 800 AD. The ruins of medieval castles, called "schloss," abound on the hills overlooking the river. A harvest at the time of Charlemagne yielded 6,000 liters of wine at Schloss Johannisberg, a winery that continues to operate. Schloss Johannisberg, in the Rhinegau region, is the oldest known Riesling vineyard in the world. So honored is this property that many New World Rieslings were named "Johannisberg Riesling" in order to separate the variety from incorrectly named grapes such as Grey Riesling, Emerald Riesling, and Franken Riesling—none of which is a true Riesling.

The most celebrated vineyards in the Rhineland are located in the Rheingau region: Schloss Johannisberg, Schloss Vollrads, Marcobrunn, Jesuitgarten, Klosterberg, and many others. If the wines of the Mosel might be considered feminine, these are the masculine German Rieslings.

The Rheingau vineyards are planted on fairly steep south-facing hillsides on the north side of the river.

Rheingau Rieslings

- Rheingau Rieslings represent the richest expression of the Riesling grape. They are the gold standard and tower high above all the Rieslings of the New World.

- Rieslings from the central Rhineland, like Austria, use brown-tinted hock-style bottles.

- Major producers in the Rheingau include Schloss Vollrads, Georg Breuer, Schloss Schonborn, Staatsweinguter, Kloster Eberbach, Josef Leitz, and Robert Weil, currently the rising star among Rheingau producers.

Different Regions, Different Rieslings

- Alsace: dry, graceful, balanced, moderate alcohol. It ages up to ten years.

- Mosel: full range of styles from dry to very sweet. Classic Riesling. Very low alcohol. It ages for decades.

- Rheingau: bold, rich, stylish. Full range of styles from dry to very sweet. Moderate alcohol.

- Rheinhessen: Some excellent Rieslings, but many of the grosslage wines originate here.

- Rheinpfalz: Lighter-styled Rieslings dominate.

AUSTRIA

The Wachau region provides some of the finest white wines in the world

Although Austrian wines were largely unknown in New World wine markets until the 1980s, archeological evidence shows that wine was produced there as early as 700 BC. Austrian wine was used to supply Roman troops, and viticulture prospered throughout the Middle Ages. But the wines of former times must not be confused with the sublime products we now associate with this region. The vintage of 1456 was so bad that the wine was used in mortar for building the tower of St. Stephen's Cathedral in Vienna.

Following World War I, Austria became the third-largest wine-producing country in the world after France and Italy. The modern Austrian wine industry got off to a rocky start when it was

Austria's Traditional Grape Varieties

- Grüner Veltliner: 37 percent (white)

- Welschriesling: 9 percent (white)

- Blauer Zweigelt: 9 percent (red)

- Weißer Burgunder and Chardonnay: 6 percent (white)

- Blaufränkisch: 5 percent (red)

- Blauer Portugieser: 5 percent (red)

- Riesling: 3 percent (white)

A Wachau Vineyard

- The Wachau region straddles the Danube River northwest of Vienna. Its major city is Krems.

- Grapes are grown on the sandy banks near the Danube and on steep rocky slopes.

- The finest wines of the Wachau are labeled "Smaragd." These are higher in alcohol, richer flavored, and more expensive.

- Smaragd means "having the color of emeralds," but the wine carrying this distinction is not green.

discovered in 1985 that unscrupulous winemakers had "sweetened" their low-quality wines with poisonous diethylene-glycol (antifreeze) to try to pass them for higher-quality wine. This scandal ruined international sales, and Austrian wines didn't enjoy wide export until the 1990s.

From 2000 to 2005 Austria refashioned its wine industry to conform to EU wine regulations and adopted the appellation of origin system, known in Austria as "DAC" (Districtus Austriae Controllatus).

Most Austrian vineyards lie in the southern and eastern parts of the country. Twenty red grape varieties and ten whites are widely grown, but the star is Grüner Veltliner—Austria's national grape. In the Wachau region, this grape produces dry white wine on a par with the world's best. About 75 percent of Austrian vineyards are planted to white varieties, but reds are on the rise.

A new generation of winemakers is reshaping the industry. Only since the 1990s have Austrian winemakers traveled abroad to study at the world's great schools of enology and viticulture. As a result, modern approaches, techniques, and equipment are now being utilized.

Grüner Veltliner

- Grüner Veltliner is indigenous to Austria and has been cultivated there since Roman times.

- It is Austria's most distinguished wine, It's stunningly powerful and intense; when subjected to low yields it offers flavors and aromas of citrus, tropical fruits, and white pepper.

- Grüner Veltliner is one of the world's most versatile wines, pairing effectively with a wide range of foods from Asian cuisine to "difficult" foods such as asparagus and artichokes.

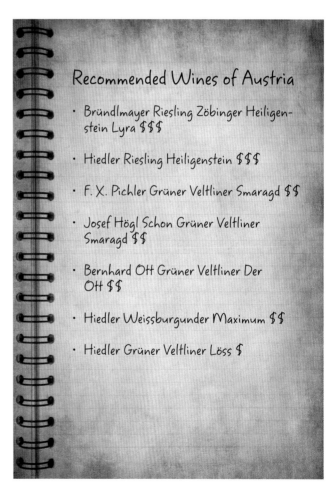

Recommended Wines of Austria

- Bründlmayer Riesling Zöbinger Heiligenstein Lyra $$$

- Hiedler Riesling Heiligenstein $$$

- F. X. Pichler Grüner Veltliner Smaragd $$

- Josef Högl Schon Grüner Veltliner Smaragd $$

- Bernhard Ott Grüner Veltliner Der Ott $$

- Hiedler Weissburgunder Maximum $$

- Hiedler Grüner Veltliner Löss $

NORTHWEST SPAIN: GALICIA
Soft, aromatic whites come from Rías Baixas

Galicia is Spain's most northwestern province and completely different from the rest of the country. With the Atlantic Ocean to its west and the Bay of Biscay to its north, Galicia is the coldest, wettest, and most-forested region in Spain. It's also the new standard-bearer for Spanish white wines.

The shrine of Santiago de Compostela, which is said to contain the remains of Saint James, is here. It was a major pilgrimage destination during the Middle Ages.

The west coast of Galicia features several fjord-like inlets called "rías" just north of the Portuguese border. This is where the most notable vineyards are located.

As you move inland, the climate changes from cool to hot and from humid to dry. The most favored vineyard sites are near the cool coast.

Spain's Principal White Wines

- Airen (Spain's most widely planted white grape)

- Albariño (Rías Baixas)

- Godello (Galicia)

- Verdejo (Rueda, Valladolid)

- Viura/Macabeo (Rioja, Penedés, and many other regions)

A Typical Galician Vineyard in Rías Baixas

- Rías Baixas is the only wine-growing region in Spain that experiences high humidity on a regular basis. Its soils are largely granite and chalk.

- The preferred trellising system used here is the pergola system, which keeps the grape clusters high off the ground.

- Often vine shoots are trained upward on stone or cement pillars attached to the pergola to maximize ventilation and help prevent disease. Vines are usually widely spaced for ventilation, unlike most modern vineyards, which prefer close vine spacing to inhibit vine vigor.

Until 1986, when Spain joined the EU, Galicia produced no export-quality wine. But with fresh infusions of investment capital and the discovery of the potential of Galicia's signature white grape, Albariño, quality began to rise.

Galicia has three main wine regions (DO): Rías Baixas, Ribeiro, and Valdeorras. Of these, Rías Baixas (lower inlets) is by far the most important. It consists of three small separated regions, two of which are on the Miño River that forms the boundary with Portugal. The Rías Baixas is complemented by the Rías Altas, or "northern inlets," which are not a significant wine-growing area. Galician winemakers have so far resisted the temptation to experiment with international varieties, choosing to focus on the indigenous varieties of the region. Albariño is always made as a single varietal wine, never blended, because its structure and flavor profile are complete. Most other Galician wines are blends.

Mencía is the most-promising red grape of Galicia. It is grown in Rebeiro and Valdeorras.

Blended white wines and some reds are exported from the Ribeiro DO, but few from Valdeorras.

A Galician Albariño

- Albariño is not only the signature wine of Galicia but also is Spain's finest white wine. The wine reputation of Galicia rests largely upon the success of this variety.

- Albariño evokes aromatic aromas and flavors of peach, melon, and minerals.

- Formerly restricted to Spanish Galicia, Albariño has been introduced to Oregon, Virginia, and California's Santa Barbara County, where it is expected to flourish.

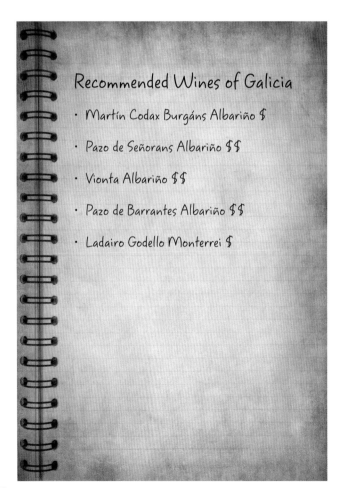

Recommended Wines of Galicia

- Martín Codax Burgáns Albariño $
- Pazo de Señorans Albariño $$
- Vionta Albariño $$
- Pazo de Barrantes Albariño $$
- Ladairo Godello Monterrei $

LA RIOJA: SPAIN'S CLASSIC REGION
Spain's most famous, versatile blended red wine is grown here

The Rioja produces Spain's best-known wine, a Tempranillo-based blend that is one of the world's finest wines to pair with savory foods.

Most of the Rioja region lies on the banks of the Ebro River at an elevation of around 1,500 feet. The climate is continental—warm and dry during the growing season.

La Rioja was the first Spanish wine-growing region to receive the prestigious Denominación de Origen Calificada (DOCa) in 1991.

The term rioja reflects the nature of the soils, which are red from a high concentration of chalk and iron.

There are three delimited Rioja regions reflecting their elevation: Rioja Baja, Rioja Alavesa, and Rioja Alta. Wines from the Rioja Alta reflect the older styles and are leaner. Rioja Baja

Village of Laguardia

- Laguardia is a medieval walled village in La Rioja, built in the thirteenth century. Very little has changed since that time.

- During the Middle Ages residents of Laguardia dug deep cellars and tunnels under the city for food storage in La Rioja's hot climate.

- As the surrounding countryside developed into a wine region, cellars and tunnels provided a perfect place for making and aging wine.

- Many wine tours of the La Rioja region begin in this fascinating village.

A Vineyard in La Rioja

- La Rioja's climate is continental, with little maritime influence. It is hot and windy throughout the growing season.

- The Cantabrian Mountains to the north offer a measure of protection from the fierce winds that characterize this region.

- There are many old-vine vineyards in the Rioja Alavesa. These produce smaller berries with concentrated flavors.

- The classic Rioja blend consists of 80 percent Tempranillo, 15 percent Mazuelo, and 5 percent Graciano.

wines ripen much more easily and are often used to provide strength to the leaner wines.

Red Rioja wines are Tempranillo blends. A typical blend will consist of approximately 60 percent Tempranillo and up to 20 percent Garnacha and smaller proportions of Mazuelo and Graciano. They are the Spanish counterparts to the Italian Chianti and can be used interchangeably.

Bodega Rioja Santiago developed the first bottled version of the pop wine Sangría back in the 1960s using Rioja wine and exhibited it at the 1964 New York World's Fair. An import subsidiary of Pepsi Cola purchased the rights to the wine and marketed it worldwide.

In 2008 the Regulatory Council for La Rioja Denomination of Origin created a new logo to go on all bottles of Rioja. In an attempt to appeal to younger wine lovers, the former logo has been replaced with a brighter, more modern logo. The aim is to reflect the new, modern aspects of wine growing in La Rioja. The new logo represents a Tempranillo vine symbolizing "heritage, creativity, and dynamism."

A Rioja Wine Label

- Spanish wine labels are required to show several specific items. Additional information may be added.

- The producer's name is always given, along with the date when the winery was founded.

- The best Spanish wines will carry a DO classification. Exceptional wine regions may qualify for DOCa (Calificada).

- Other facts include vintage winery location, quality classification, and the Consejo Regulador sticker, usually found on the back label.

Spanish Wine Quality Classifications

- Crianza: The wine was aged in the winery (bodega) for two years prior to release, minimum of twelve months in oak.

- Reserva: The wine was aged for at least three years: twelve months in oak and twenty-four months in bottle. Whites and rosados spend six months in oak and one and one-half years in bottle.

- Gran Reserva: The wine was aged for five years: two years in oak and three years in bottle.

RIBERO DEL DUERO
Explore the home of Spain's most-expensive luxury red wines

The Ribero del Duero region lies southwest of La Rioja. The name means "banks of the Duero River." Do not confuse the Ribero del Duero with the Ribeiro district in Galicia. This is the headwaters of Portugal's Douro River, where the great Porto wines are made. The river's name changes to Douro at the border.

The region enjoys a more temperate climate than La Rioja, with hot summer days but cool nights. At 2,300–2,790 feet above sea level, the Ribero del Duero is Spain's highest wine-growing region.

Although wine had been made here for centuries, Ribero's rise to international acclaim began in the late nineteenth century when Don Elroy Lecanda Chaves opened a winery on the south bank of the river. He named his winery "Vega-Sicilia"

Castle of Peñafiel

- The castle of Peñafiel, with its keep and eight turrets, was built in the eleventh century. It is now surrounded by some of Spain's most-precious vineyard land.

- The village of Peñafiel is the center of Ribero's wine industry and a tourist destination.

- The vineyards here are in three designated locations: the campinas along the riverbank featuring alluvial, sandy soils; the laderas or slopes above the river, which have chalky limestone soils; and the cuestas—hillsides too steep for practical viticulture.

Vega Sicilia—Spain's Preeminent Red Wine

- For more than a hundred years Vega-Sicilia has been Spain's most-celebrated and most-expensive wine. The top-of-the-line wine is called "Unico."

- The original Vega-Sicilia vineyard, in the western end of the Ribero del Duero, was planted to a particular strain of Tempranillo as well as French varieties.

- Vega-Sicilia was the first Spanish wine to blend native Tempranillo with Cabernet and Merlot. Spanish DO rules permit French varieties to be planted only where they have been previously grown.

162

and planted a strain of Tempranillo, along with Cabernet Sauvignon and Merlot. In the ensuing years Vega-Sicilia became Spain's most sought-after wine. Even the king of Spain had to be put on a waiting list to receive his allotment.

Vega-Sicilia ruled the roost for decades with little or no competition until the arrival of Alejandro Fernández in the 1970s. Fernández planted the strain of Tempranillo known locally as "Tinto Fino." He offered a splendid wine made from 100 percent Tempranillo that many consider the best example of that grape in all of Spain. He called his wine "Pesquera."

Pesquera—Spain's Superstar Tempranillo

- Pesquera was the first challenger to legendary Vega Sicilia.

- Its creator, Alejandro Fernández, has been an evangelist for the supremacy of the Tempranillo grape in Spain and has contended that it needs no blending companions.

- Pesquera, a 100 percent Tempranillo wine, is an affordable alternative to Spain's luxury wines.

- Other excellent wines by Fernández include Condado de Haza, Dehesa la Granja, and El Vinculo.

Traditional versus Modern Styles

- Spanish winemakers wrestle with the choice to stick to their indigenous varieties or to blend with international varieties.

- The indigenous varieties yield wines that reflect their Spanish origins and are unique in an international market dominated by international blends that closely resemble each other.

CATALONIA/CATALUNYA

You'll find a full range from sparkling CAVA to muscular reds

After centuries of political turmoil, Catalonia became one of Spain's nineteen autonomous regions in 1977 with Barcelona as its capital. Like Alsace, its population is bicultural and bilingual. Native Catalans prefer to speak in their own Catalan language.

Catalonia's largest and most important DO region is Penedés, south of Barcelona. It was here that José Raventós opened a winery specializing in traditional method sparkling Cava in 1898. He called it "Cordoniú." His winery eventually became one of Spain's largest. Cordoniú makes most of the Cava consumed in Spain today. The firm Freixenet followed suit in the early years of the twentieth century. These two wineries supply most of the world's Cava wines.

So successful were these two megawineries that the

"Riddling" of Cava

- Unlike Italy's Prosecco, which undergoes its secondary fermentation in pressurized stainless steel tanks, Spain's Cava is made by the traditional methods used in Champagne.

- Finished wine is bottled with added yeast and sugar, corked, and cellared for a minimum of nine months. The bottles are stored almost upside down so the sediments can settle on the cork. Riddling is the process of turning the bottles over a thirty-day period to collect all the sediment. The bottle neck is frozen, and the cork and sediment are removed. The wine is then recorked.

A Village in Priorat

- Priorat is named for the Carthusian priory that was established here in the twelfth century.

- Rising to 2,600 feet, it is Spain's highest-elevation DO region after Ribero del Duero.

- The vineyards are planted on terraces cut from steep, stony slopes. Olive and almond trees often share vineyard space.

- Great Priorat vineyards include Clos Mogador, Clos de l'Obac, Costers del Siurana, and Clos Figueres.

entire region of Penedés became identified with Cava and little else until 1961, when Miguel Torres returned from his winemaking studies in France. Torres almost single-handedly revolutionized the wine industry in Penedés by focusing on international varieties and blends. Torres's Gran Coronas Cabernet Sauvignon is one of Spain's best red wines and the flagship wine of what has grown to be one of the world's largest wine empires, with wineries in California and Chile as well as in Penedés.

The rising star in Catalonia is the tiny region of Priorat, which received DO status in 1954 and DOCa (Denominación de Origen Calificada) status in 2000, making it the third DOCa region in all of Spain, after La Rioja and Ribero del Duero.

Priorat is one of Europe's most-scenic wine regions. Vines are planted on steep slopes below craggy peaks west of Tarragona. Garnacha is the main grape, and the Garnachas of Priorat are among the finest and most-expensive in the world. Thick, aromatic, and plush with flavor, these wines are the product of an unusual soil called "llicorella," consisting of slate, quartz, and heat-retaining mica fragments.

A Cava Winery

- The wineries of Penedés produce over 200 million bottles of Cava annually. Most of the production is from Cordoniú and Freixenet.

- Cava is sold ready to drink. It will deteriorate, not improve, with age.

- Cava is made in seven degrees of sweetness: Brut Nature (no added sugar), Extra Brut, Brut, Extra Seco, Seco, Semi-seco, and Dulce (sweet). Sweeter Cavas are rarely seen outside of Spain.

Costers del Siurana Clos de l'Obac

- Clos de l'Obac is the flagship wine of Priorat's distinguished winery Costers del Siurana. It was first released in 1989.

- The blend used for this magnificent wine is 35 percent Garnacha, 35 percent Cabernet Sauvignon, and 10 percent each of Syrah, Merlot, and Carignan. It is one of Spain's finest red wines.

- The *Wine Spectator* recently described this wine as "Like a chocolate-covered cherry, this red is sweet and fresh at once, with lively fruit, round tannins and enough acidity to keep it lively."

SHERRY/JEREZ
World-famous fortified wines come from southern Spain

The word Sherry is an English corruption of the Moorish *ceris,* which is what the Moors called the modern city of Jerez when they occupied southern Spain. The wines produced here are among the most unusual and complicated wines in the world. Although extremely popular in former times, especially in England, Sherry has fallen out of fashion with the rise and availability of quality red and white wines.

Consequently, today's Sherry represents some of the greatest value in wine.

Sherry begins its career as a bland dry wine made from the Palomino grape. Most modern Sherries are fermented in stainless steel tanks before they are transferred to aged oak barrels. Winemakers then decide which style of Sherry they intend to produce. If they add grape brandy to fortify the

Important Sherry Regions

• San Lucar de Barrameda: coastal fishing village and second-largest Sherry-producing area. Proximity to the sea provides greater humidity for the flor. The bone-dry Sherry of San Lucar is called "Manzanilla."

• El Puerto de Santa Maria: seaside town and location of many Sherry bodegas, including Osborne.

• Jerez de la Frontera: The main Palomino vineyards are here. Some bodegas are here also, but fruit is sold to bodegas all over the region.

Albarizo Soils of Jerez

• The finest Palomino vineyards are planted on white Albarizo soils containing 60–80 percent chalk.

• The chalk soaks up and stores winter rains, providing moisture for the vines during the hot summer.

• Exposure to the hot sun causes the Albarizo soils to crust over during the summer months, preventing the moisture underneath from evaporating.

• A similar soil type, known as "linne calodo," is found in California's Central Coast region.

wine to around 15 percent, a film or cap of yeast cells called "flor" will form to protect the wine from oxygen and impart its special flavor characteristic. The thickness of the flor cap is determined by the humidity present and will not form in dry environments. The flor can live as long as six years if there is adequate oxygen in the barrel and the wine is continually refreshed with newer vintages. The system of introducing new wines into older wines is called the "solera system." Some soleras are more than a century old.

Fino and Manzanilla Sherries are made using the flor and solera system. The other major Sherry style is called "Oloroso." Oloroso Sherries are dark, caramely, and nutty. Fortifying the original wine to a higher degree of alcohol, typically around 18 percent, prevents the flor from forming. This wine is placed in its own solera and allowed to gently oxidize over time.

All Sherries are bone dry unless a sweetening agent is added. Grape juice, grape concentrate, and sweet wine are all used to make Cream Sherry and sweet Olorosos.

Four Styles of Sherry

- Fino is bone dry and makes a perfect accompaniment to Spanish tapas. Finos from San Lucar, called "Manzanilla" Sherries, are the lightest and driest.

- True Amontillado Sherries are Finos that have lost their flor and are allowed to oxidize to a medium golden brown color. Oloroso Sherries are dark, rich, and nutty with caramel overtones. They possess higher alcohol levels and were not influenced by the flor. Pedro Ximenez (PX) is a sweet grape grown in outlying areas. It makes a delicious stand-alone wine, but is used to sweeten dry Sherries.

A Spanish Solera

- The solera system is used throughout the Sherry-producing region. It is a fundamental part of Sherry production. It consists of stacks of neutral oak barrels called "butts."

- Butts of wines from successive vintages are stacked on top of each other. A portion of wine is drawn from the oldest barrel for bottling.

- The partly empty barrel is filled with wine from the next-oldest barrel, which in turn receives younger wine. The oldest barrel is never emptied completely. New oak is never used in Spanish soleras.

LA MANCHA: CENTRAL SPAIN

Spain's largest wine-growing region is the source of half the country's wine

The region of Castilla—La Mancha, south of Madrid—is the largest wine-growing region in the world. At last count it consisted of nearly a million acres under vine and produced 53 million gallons of wine annually.

The term La Mancha is derived from the Moorish term *al-Manshah,* meaning "parched earth," and water is the principal factor in determining which grape varieties grow here. Some sources report that 90 percent of La Mancha is planted to the indigenous white grape Airén. Airén is well suited to this desolate region because of its thick skin and heavy leaf canopy. The wines it yields are not yet suitable for export but find their way into export-quality reds as blending components.

KNACK WINE BASICS

The Five Most Widely Planted Wine Grapes Worldwide

- Cabernet Sauvignon (614,800 acres worldwide)

- Merlot (598,000)

- Airén (572,000)

- Grenache/Garnacha (572,000)

- Chardonnay (171,200)

A Vineyard in Valdepeñas

- Vineyards in La Mancha and Valdepeñas use ultrawide vine spacing because of drought conditions in the summer. The number of vines per acre here is one-eighth of that in Bordeaux, Burgundy, and Champagne.

- Vines in La Mancha are bush pruned to allow the canopy to shade the grape clusters from the intense sun and heat.

- La Mancha's vineyards must be hand harvested because mechanical harvesters require rows and trellises.

- Vineyard workers are often imported from Morocco.

Airén was the world's most widely planted wine grape until 2000. It's still the most widely planted white grape. It supplies the Spanish populace with cheap, quaffable white wine as well as copious amounts of grape brandy.

The vast, semiarid, wind-swept region consists of flat land and undulating hills. It is almost treeless and sparsely populated. But the vineyards stretch out to the horizon in all directions. The two main DO areas are La Mancha proper and Valdepeñas in the south. Only around 10 percent of La Mancha wine satisfies the DO requirements, but experimental vineyards in Valdepeñas are growing more-distinguished varieties. La Mancha is a wine region that is slowly realizing its potential, but there are no fine wines yet to appear under the "La Mancha" DO appellation. Stainless steel tanks are beginning to dot the region—a sign that proper temperature control will raise the quality of La Mancha's wines. To the southwest of La Mancha lie several smaller appellations stretching out to Valencia on the Mediterranean. Yecla and Jumilla are the rising stars. El Nido, a Cabernet-Mourvedre blend, is now one of Spain's highest-rated wines.

Monastrell

- Monastrell is the Spanish word for Mourvedre. In Portugal and the New World it is known as "Mataró."

- Monastrell is a thick-skinned red grape that yields a deeply colored tannic wine.

- It ripens best in locations near large bodies of water, such as the Mediterranean Sea.

- In Jumilla it produces world-class wines with ratings approaching one hundred points on the one-hundred-point scale.

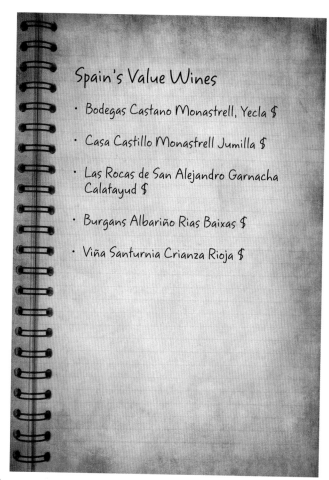

Spain's Value Wines

- Bodegas Castano Monastrell, Yecla $
- Casa Castillo Monastrell Jumilla $
- Las Rocas de San Alejandro Garnacha Calatayud $
- Burgans Albariño Rias Baixas $
- Viña Santurnia Crianza Rioja $

PORTUGAL

A sleepy Old World wine region embraces modern technology

While France, Italy, Germany, and California were sucking up international wine notoriety, the winemakers of Portugal largely stuck to their old-fashioned ways, and the nation's unfortified wines were rarely found outside the country.

Almost 50 percent of Portugal's land is delimited for wine growing. A confusing myriad of indigenous grapes with nearly unpronounceable names is grown on small farms.

Historically the growers sold their grapes to large cooperatives that provided a sea of low-quality wine for local consumption.

Portugal's wine industry turned a corner with the nation's entrance into the EU. Recognizing the country's enormous potential for fine unfortified wine, many of the small growers opted out of the cooperative system and established private

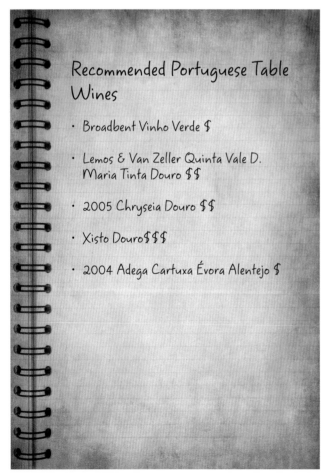

Recommended Portuguese Table Wines

- Broadbent Vinho Verde $

- Lemos & Van Zeller Quinta Vale D. Maria Tinta Douro $$

- 2005 Chryseia Douro $$

- Xisto Douro $$$

- 2004 Adega Cartuxa Évora Alentejo $

A Traditional Trellis in Vinho Verde

- Modern vineyards in the Vinho Verde region require supporting structures different from those in any other region.

- The pergola system of traditional trellising is widely used. The vines form overhead arbors, which encourage ventilation in the humid climate of Vinho Verde.

- Another common practice in Vinho Verde is to allow grapevines to climb up into tall trees. The term vinho verde (green wine) refers to the directive to drink it young, or "green." Local Vinho Verde wines may be white or red.

wine estates called "quintas." Typical mixed-variety vineyards were purged of lower-quality varieties and replanted with better, such as Touriga Nacional. Portugal's best table wines come from these small private estates, but quality is very spotty, and few enjoy export. The products of the cooperatives are improving and are more consistent.

Recently wineries in the Setúbal Peninsula southeast of Lisbon have imported winemakers from Australia and California who are raising the bar by planting international varieties alongside the best Portuguese grapes.

The most-promising table wine regions at present are Vinho Verde in the far north, Douro (which is delimited for table wine as well as port), Dão south of Douro, Alentejo in the southeast, and Setùbal. The other regions are still works in progress. The only Portuguese white wine widely exported is Vinho Verde. Export Vinho Verde is a light, slightly fizzy wine, slightly sweetened to accommodate international tastes. Thick, plush reds from Douro, Dão, and Alentejo are beginning to become available in the United Kingdom, Canada, and United States. These wines are priced very attractively.

Portuguese Reds

- Most Portuguese red wines are simple, pleasant, and ordinary. These are inexpensive and offer good value.

- The past decade has seen a huge effort to raise the quality of Portugal's red table wines to compete with the great blended red wines of Spain and Italy.

- Portugal's best red wines are all blends because this region does not produce single-variety, stand-alone red wines.

- The best reds come from the upper Douro Valley. They receive outstanding ratings in reviews and are priced attractively.

Portugal's Traditional Grapes

- Alvarinho: white. Same as Spain's Albariño.

- Touriga Nacional: red. Main grape of Port and red Douro.

- Tinta Roriz: red. Same as Tempranillo. Grown in Alentejo.

- Baga: red. High in acid and tannin. Used as a base for Mateus Rosé.

171

PORT & MADEIRA
Portugal's incomparable dessert wines

Contrary to popular opinion, the English did not create the wine we call "Port." The sons of a Liverpool wine merchant discovered it in 1678. The earliest Port wine on record was made in a monastery in the Douro Valley by an abbot who arrested the fermentation of red wine by adding brandy. The resulting wine was sweet and alcoholic. The sweet, fortified red wine traveled well, and the English loved it. Most of the

modern Port houses are owned by English firms and carry English names: "Dow," "Graham's," "Warre," "Osborne," and "Taylor-Fladgate," to name a few.

Madeira is a fortified white wine from the Portuguese island of Madeira, 435 miles off the north African coast. Its history goes back to the Age of Exploration when Madeira was a port of call on the east-west trading routes. White wines were

The Douro River Valley

- The Douro DOC begins 50 miles upstream from Oporto, Portugal's second-largest city and location of the export houses. The DOC region runs to the Spanish border. The vineyards lie on steep terraces, largely held in place by stone retaining walls. Often only a single row or two of vines occupy

a terrace, making mechanization impossible.

- The English Port houses have shipped Port wine from the Douro for over three hundred years. All the great Port wines of the world originate here. At its best, vintage Port has no peers.

Graham's Twenty-year-old Tawny Port

- Tawny Port's style is different from other Port styles. It is the only style that is matured in barrels for long periods of time.

- With age, tawny Ports are transformed from a rich, deep, ruby color to a golden red-orange, or "tawny" color. Tawny

Ports are lighter and more elegant on the palate than other Port styles except very old vintage Ports.

- Tawny Ports are bottled after wood aging, and the bottling year is always listed on the label. They are not intended for further cellaring.

fortified with a little brandy to preserve them on their long voyages. The heat, humidity, and sloshing around for weeks or months gave the wine a desirable nutty quality, and the producers back on the island developed methods of obtaining the effect by cooking the wine in barrels around fires.

Madeira is now made using more modern techniques. The traditional grapes are Verdelho, Malvasia, Bual, and Sercial.

ZOOM

Styles of Port
Ruby: young, inexpensive, does not improve with age
Late-bottled Vintage (LBV): intermediate-grade Port intended for early drinking
Colheita: vintage Port from an undeclared year
Vintage: designed to mature in the bottle over many years

Blandy's Fifteen-year-old Bual Madeira

- Madeira is the world's most-resilient and longest-living wine. Vintage Madeiras can age gracefully in barrel or bottle for a century or more.

- Inexpensive Madeiras are made in concrete tanks with heating elements that hold the wine at 122° F for three months. Higher-quality

Madeiras are "cooked" more slowly, the best in wooden barrels outside the winery. These can remain in place for twenty years before bottling.

- Most modern Madeira is made from Tinta Negra Mole, rather than the traditional varieties.

Styles of Madeira

- Sercial: driest style with notes of almond

- Bual: dark, raisiny, medium-rich, sweet

- Malmsey: the sweetest and finest of all Madeiras. These are the most age-worthy.

SOUTH EAST AUSTRALIA
An unlikely location produces uncommon wines

The appellation "south east Australia" (SEA) encompasses all the wine-growing regions of Australia except for Queensland and Western Australia. It's a catch-all term that wines produced in the southeastern states are entitled to use.

Wine growing came to Australia late compared with other regions of the world. There was no indigenous grapevine, no culture of wine, and it was settled by the British—a people not known for their wine-growing expertise. This turned out to be to Australia's advantage: There were no precedents. No revered terroirs. No established procedures. And no regulations.

This is an unlikely region for wine production, with voluminous sunshine but very little water. The only suitable areas are on the fringes of the southeast coast, a tiny microclimate

Wine Regions of South East Australia

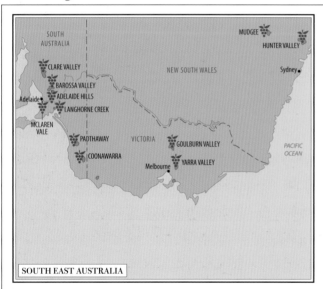

Penfold's Winery in Adelaide

- Australia's most-productive wine regions lie in the states of South Australia, Victoria, and New South Wales.

- Star subregions are Barossa Valley (Shiraz), Eden Valley (Shiraz), Clare (Cabernet, Shiraz), Coonawarra (Cabernet), Padthaway (Cabernet), Yarra Valley (Pinot Noir), and Hunter Valley (Cabernet, Shiraz). Cool-climate grapes are grown in Tasmania. These wines have a distinctly leaner character than those of the mainland. Fifty-two Tasmanian wineries welcome visitors. Chardonnay is grown everywhere, and Sémillon is becoming an Aussie specialty.

- Several very large conglomerates dominate Australian exports.

- Giant Southcorp merged with Fosters to create the Fosters Group, the second-largest wine empire in the world after U.S. Constellation Brands.

- The Fosters Group owns the Penfold's, Rosemount, Wolf Blass, and Lindemans brands as well as other brands in California and Italy.

- The United Kingdom is the largest export market for Aussie wine; the United States is slightly behind, and Canada is third.

in Queensland, and the Hunter River Valley north of Sydney.

England provided the primary market for cheap Australian wine until a breakthrough occurred at the Penfold's winery in Adelaide in 1951. Penfold's winemaker, Max Schubert, sought out the best available grapes in the country to create a Shiraz-based blend that was destined to become one of the world's greatest red wines, Grange. Grange is unlike any of the other great red blends; the blend changes to reflect the finest possible grapes available, but Shiraz remains the base.

Shiraz is Australia's finest red grape. It's the same grape as France's Syrah, but where the great Syrahs of the northern Rhône are lean and minerally, Aussie Shiraz is plush and mouth-filling with rich flavors of black cherry, blueberry, cedar, and vanilla. The best stand alongside the best Syrahs in the world. Outstanding producers are Eden Valley's Henschke and Barossa Valley's Two Hands.

Australia produces a full range of white wine, but the clear frontrunners are Chardonnay and late-harvest dessert wines, both red and white. Late-harvest Muscat from the Rutherglen appellation is an inexpensive luxury.

Hardy's Cabernet Sauvignon

- Thomas Hardy & Son began as a family operation in 1850. By 1894 it was Australia's largest wine producer.

- Through a program of continual acquisitions Hardy's maintained its preeminent place until 1990, when giant Southcorp overtook it.

- Hardy's is Australia's second-largest producer today and has been acquired by Constellation Brands (U.S.), the world's largest wine conglomerate.

- Hardy's offers a large portfolio from sound, inexpensive wines to premium Cabernet Sauvignon and Shiraz.

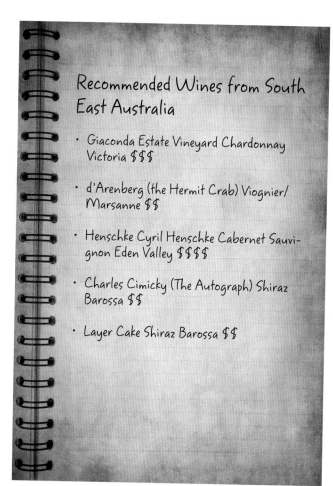

Recommended Wines from South East Australia

- Giaconda Estate Vineyard Chardonnay Victoria $$$

- d'Arenberg (the Hermit Crab) Viognier/Marsanne $$

- Henschke Cyril Henschke Cabernet Sauvignon Eden Valley $$$$

- Charles Cimicky (The Autograph) Shiraz Barossa $$

- Layer Cake Shiraz Barossa $$

WESTERN AUSTRALIA

This area produces well-structured wines in the European style

One of the world's hottest wine-growing regions is found in Western Australia from the city of Perth south and around Australia's southwest corner. Summer temperatures rise to 114° F.

The grapevine was introduced to this unlikely region soon after the region became settled in the nineteenth century. For almost a century a single wine dominated the Western

Australian scene—a white Burgundy made in a thick, viscous, overripe style from Chenin Blanc and Muscadelle from the Houghton Winery, founded in 1859 and now owned by Hardy's/Constellation Brands.

Western Australia remained a backwater while the wine industry in southeastern Australia found its footing. A visit from the University of California at Davis's Professor Harold

Western Australia Wine Regions

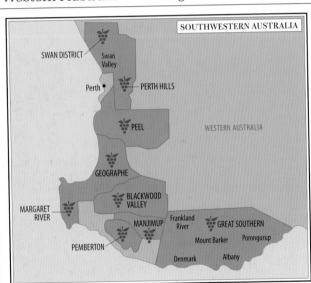

- In contrast to the wine regions of the Northern Hemisphere, the north is hotter and the south is cooler.

- The Swan Valley is the hottest wine-growing region in Australia.

- Coastal regions enjoy a maritime climate, particularly Perth Hills and the Southwest Coastal Plain.

- The Margaret River region is remarkably similar to Bordeaux's Médoc, and Bordeaux varieties do well here. Margaret River Chardonnay is particularly fine.

A Margaret River Vineyard

- Margaret River is a premium area for wine of export quality. A large percentage of Western Australia's best wineries is located here.

- The vineyards of Margaret River experience a unique climate as a result of the confluence of two oceans.

- Vineyards here are planted on low rolling hills at elevations below 150 feet.

- Vineyards in Margaret River are planted as close as 2 miles from the sea and run east for around 30 miles.

Olmo in 1956 sparked development in the more-viable regions, especially Margaret River and Great Southern. Quality rose to heights never before imagined, and by the 1990s Western Australia became competitive in the international marketplace.

The uniqueness of this region stems from the cool influence of the Southern Ocean and the warmer influence of the Indian Ocean. Add to that some vineyard locations at elevations up to 1,150 feet and a wide variety of soil types. Everything imaginable is grown here, from Riesling to Zinfandel.

ZOOM

Top Producers in Western Australia
Cape Mentelle
Evans & Tate
Leeuwin Estate
Howard Park
Moss Wood
Plantagenet
Vasse Felix

Howard Park Cellar Door

- Howard Park is one of Australia's most modern wineries. It's located at the northern "gateway" to the Margaret River region, about a three-hour drive south from Perth.

- Cellar Door is the Aussie equivalent of a tasting room. Over twenty Western Australia wineries welcome visitors.

- Howard Park's Cellar Door was nominated as one of the best architectural buildings in Australia.

- Howard Park's primary focus is on ultrapremium Bordeaux varieties.

Bouverie Chardonnay

- Bouverie is one of the fine wineries found in Western Australia's Great Southern region.

- The Great Southern wine region includes Albany, Denmark, Frankland, Mount Barker, and the Porongurup Foothills. It's Western Australia's coolest area for wine growing.

- Great Southern Bordeaux varieties are among the highest-rated wines in Western Australia.

- Great Southern wines bear little resemblance to the wines of southeastern Australia.

NEW ZEALAND: NORTH ISLAND

New Zealand finds its stride with Chardonnay and Bordeaux varieties in Hawke's Bay

New Zealand is one of the most recent important wine regions to be developed. After decades of Prohibition, restrictive alcohol consumption, and wine-growing failures, New Zealand's wine industry has achieved remarkable success with the world's best-loved grape varieties.

New Zealand's North and South islands occupy a 1,000-mile-long territory, roughly the distance from Morocco to Paris. The prevailing climate runs from cool in the north to cold in the south. The main factors affecting viticulture are western rains, eastern cyclones, and overly fertile soils.

Although there are wine-growing regions all over North Island, the premier area is Hawke's Bay on the southeast

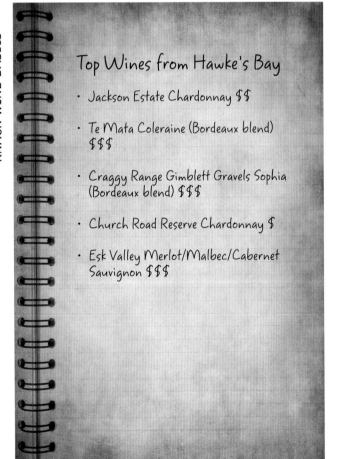

Top Wines from Hawke's Bay

- Jackson Estate Chardonnay $$

- Te Mata Coleraine (Bordeaux blend) $$$

- Craggy Range Gimblett Gravels Sophia (Bordeaux blend) $$$

- Church Road Reserve Chardonnay $

- Esk Valley Merlot/Malbec/Cabernet Sauvignon $$$

A Hawke's Bay Vineyard

- An overwhelming majority of North Island's export wine comes from Hawke's Bay.

- Almost all Hawke's Bay vineyards are on flat land, although the best vineyard locations, yet to be planted, are probably on the slopes that rim the area.

- Hawke's Bay wineries export New Zealand's finest Chardonnays, Cabernet Sauvignons, and Bordeaux blends.

- Hawke's Bay Sauvignon Blanc is rounder and less intense than the more-famous Sauvignons of South Island.

coast. Some soils here are deep, pure gravel and are often compared with the soils of Margaux in Bordeaux.

Hawke's Bay is the sunniest region in all of New Zealand, and it's the only region where Bordeaux red varieties can be satisfactorily ripened. The western mountains rise to over 5,000 feet and soak up most of the rain while providing ample water for irrigation in eastern-draining rivers. Only 10 percent of Hawke's Bay vineyards are irrigated. Those planted on the gravelly soils need not only irrigation but also added nutrients, a practice unheard of elsewhere on the island.

The most successful North Island variety is Chardonnay. Hawke's Bay Chardonnays are pure and full of varietal and mineral character, unlike many Aussie Chardonnays that are overly rich and plush. They occupy a middle ground between flinty Chablis and oaky New World styles. Cabernet Sauvignon and Bordeaux-style blends from this region are amazingly complex, with enough herbal and mineral notes to convince you that they are not from California or Australia.

Morton Estate Chardonnay

- Morton Estate Chardonnay is typical of Hawke's Bay Chardonnays and is widely exported.

- Despite their attractive price, Morton Estate Chardonnays are barrel-fermented and matured in French oak. Importing French oak barrels to New Zealand is extremely costly; Australian barrels could be obtained for a fraction of the price.

- Unlike the typically fat and buttery Chardonnays of southeastern Australia, quality Hawke's Bay Chardonnays improve when cellared for two to five years.

New Zealand's Certified Origin System

- Certified origin: The law guarantees that 85 percent of the grapes used come from the geographic area, vintage, and variety stated.

- Geographical denomination: The broadest appellation is "New Zealand," followed by "North Island" or "South Island." The finest wines will carry regional designations, such as "Hawke's Bay," "Marlborough," and "Otago."

NEW ZEALAND: SOUTH ISLAND

A new style of Sauvignon Blanc emerges from the world's newest major wine region

South Island's meteoric rise to prominence began in 1973 when the first vine was planted in Marlborough, a flat, nondescript region on South Island's northeast corner. Because of its cool climate, it seemed to be a suitable region for German varieties. But vintners hit paydirt when they planted Sauvignon Blanc, an unlikely variety for this region.

The breakthrough occurred with the first release of Cloudy Bay Sauvignon Blanc in 1985. Marlborough was elevated by wine writers to a position equal to, if different from, Sancerre and Bordeaux. Some praised it as the best region for Sauvignon Blanc in the world. And Cloudy Bay still bests all others in the area with gorgeously balanced examples.

Wine Regions of South Island

- Nelson: forty-one wineries, cool climate varieties

- Marlborough: world-class Sauvignon Blanc

- Canterbury: Pinot Gris, Chardonnay, sparkling wine

- Otago: Pinot Noir

South Island Vineyard near Canterbury

- Marlborough and Canterbury vineyards enjoy a protected environment with Pacific maritime influence.

- Marlborough is best known for its exciting Sauvignon Blanc from producers such as Cloudy Bay.

- Marlborough vineyards

are largely on flat land. Canterbury vineyards enjoy a rolling hill terrain well suited to viticulture.

- An old red Loire grape, Enigma, is cultivated in Canterbury. It is used to make a rosé with raspberry and strawberry flavors.

The Sauvignons of Marlborough are unlike all others. You love them or hate them, depending on your taste. Unlike the elegant Sauvignons of Bordeaux and the bright, citrusy Sauvignons of Sancerre, these are aggressive with strong herbal and gooseberry flavors, substantial body, and racy acidity.

Marlborough isn't the only important wine region on South Island. Just down the coast is Canterbury. All varieties ripen slowly here, developing their flavors in pace with their sugars, creating well-balanced wines. The best wines are Pinot Gris and Riesling. If Marlborough is the superstar with its world-class Sauvignon, Otago is the supporting actor. This is the most southerly wine region in the world, and its class act is Pinot Noir. Nestled in the southern Alps, Otago produces resplendent Pinots. Today there are around one hundred wineries offering everything from Sauvignon Blanc to Pinot Noir. But the major export wine is Pinot Noir made in a style somewhat reminiscent of Oregon, which lies at the same latitude north—45 degrees.

Lowburn Ferry Pinot Noir Central Otago

A Vineyard in Central Otago

- Lowburn Ferry Pinot Noir was a gold medalist in the very prestigious AWC Vienna International Wine Challenge in 2006. Over five thousand wines were evaluated in this competition, the second-largest in the world.

- Lowburn Ferry Pinot Noir is priced very attractively, similar to comparable Pinots from Oregon and California.

- These outstanding New Zealand Pinot Noirs are exported to the United States, United Kingdom, and Canada.

- Central Otago, the world's most southerly wine region, is a land of extreme climates that locals say are ideal for quality wine growing and lead to distinctive wines.

- More than twenty-five wineries and more than seventy vineyards are found here.

- Sixty percent of the plantings are of Pinot Noir, which thrives here and yields wines that equal or surpass all other Southern Hemisphere Pinot Noirs.

- Central Otago is the fastest-growing wine region in New Zealand.

SOUTH AFRICA
After a century of missed opportunities, South Africa rises to prominence

The winelands of South Africa lie at 34 degrees south latitude, comparable to southern California. The region experiences a similar climate with hot summers and mild winters. Many South African winemakers have lamented that South Africa doesn't extend farther south, mimicking the cooler wine regions of France. But South Africa's hot summer climate is

tempered by the icy Benguela current that flows north from Antarctica, which brings cooling breezes to the vineyards during the day and fog and moisture during the night. With conditions like these, South Africa's winelands could rival the best in the world.

South Africa's wine history is older than that of any other

KNACK WINE BASICS

South Africa Wine Regions

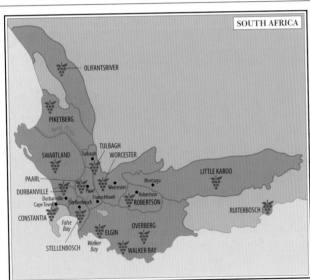

Constantia Valley

- Constantia was the first wine region to be developed in South Africa. It remains a center of wine tourism.

- Most quality table wine is produced in Paarl, Stellenbosch, and Franschoek.

- Malmesbury is home to

the Swartland Wine Route, consisting of eighteen wineries of various sizes that welcome visitors.

- Klein Karoo is known for its fortified wines and brandy production. Muscadel, made in both red and white versions, is South Africa's answer to Port.

- Constantia is the peninsula south of Cape Town. It is one of South Africa's prettiest wine regions.

- Constantia was named after the granddaughter of a Dutch East India official by the cape's first governor, Simon van der Stel.

- The luxury dessert wines of Constantia disappeared at the end of the nineteenth century, when the vineyards were devastated first by powdery mildew and then by phylloxera.

- Wineries in this region are small and called "wine farms."

New World area, discounting the failed efforts of the earliest Americans. The first South African wine was made by the Dutch in 1659, shortly after their arrival. The vineyard area was located near False Bay southeast of Cape Town in a region called "Constantia." These early wines were blends of Chenin Blanc and Muscat.

Throughout the eighteenth century the dessert wines of Constantia were highly prized in Europe and affordable only by the aristocracy. Only Hungarian Tokaji Aszú commanded a higher price. But the market for quality dry table wine didn't keep pace with the rest of the Western world; local consumers remained happy with their cheap and simple Steen (Chenin Blanc) made from highly overcropped vineyards. Even today, half of the South African harvest is used for brandy and grape concentrate. The wine revolution of the 1990s is still running its course. Better varieties and better clones replace old vines, and more small quality-oriented wine farms appear. South Africa was slow to join the international wine community, but everything is now in place for South Africa to gain its rightful place as one of the world's premier wine regions.

KWV: South Africa's Largest Wine Cooperative

- The KWV was established in 1918 as a giant wine cooperative. It now has 4,600 grower-members and is South Africa's largest producer of alcohol-related products.

- The KWV conducts research and vine propagation, makes wine under its own label, and administers South Africa's Wine of Origin system.

- The KWV is the nation's largest producer of Steen, South African Chenin Blanc. It's the country's most widely consumed white wine.

South Africa's Major Grape Varieties

- Chenin Blanc (18.7 percent)
- Cabernet Sauvignon (13.1 percent)
- French Colombard (11.4 percent)
- Syrah/Shiraz (9.6 percent)
- Sauvignon Blanc (8.2 percent)
- Chardonnay (8 percent)
- Pinotage (6.2 percent)

183

SOUTH AFRICA: STELLENBOSCH
South Africa's "Napa Valley" is home to its finest producers

Every major wine-growing area in the world has its "sweet spots": Australia's Eden Valley, Germany's Mosel, Oregon's Willamette, and France's Burgundy. In South Africa, it's Stellenbosch and the adjacent valleys of Paarl and Franschoek.

Stellenbosch is the center of the South African wine industry. The giant KWV company is based in Paarl, and most of South Africa's ultrapremium wine producers are here as well.

Like all the world's best vineyard locations, Stellenbosch enjoys a unique geo-climatic situation. Although it lies at 34 degrees south latitude—like most of the world's hottest wine-growing regions—it is open at its southern end to False Bay, without which Stellenbosch would be like South Africa's interior wine regions. The heat of the interior valleys sucks strong and chilly winds of the Southern Ocean inland,

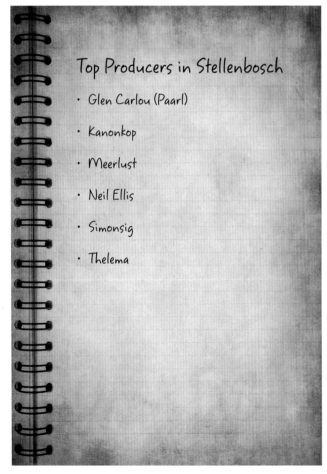

Top Producers in Stellenbosch

- Glen Carlou (Paarl)
- Kanonkop
- Meerlust
- Neil Ellis
- Simonsig
- Thelema

A Stellenbosch Vineyard

- The Stellenbosch and Paarl Valleys are flanked on the east by spectacular mountains that provide decomposed granite soils well suited to viticulture.

- The vineyards of Stellenbosch begin about 1 mile from False Bay. As in California's Napa Valley, the entire valley system becomes progressively hotter as one travels away from the bay.

- All Stellenbosch vineyards are irrigated. Those planted on the mountain slopes rise as high as 1,900 feet. Soils here are less fertile and receive more rainfall.

cooling the vines while not preventing the abundant sunshine to ripen the fruit.

Most of the Stellenbosch vineyards are on the valley floor, but each passing year brings a steady climb upward into the mountains, where the finest vineyard sites are undoubtedly to be found. The potential of this region is still in its infancy.

The principal grape varieties grown here are Chardonnay, Sauvignon Blanc, Sémillon, Chenin Blanc, Bordeaux varieties, Pinot Noir, and Pinotage.

ZOOM

South Africa's Wine of Origin system was finalized in 1993. Wine labels reflect the grape variety rather than the vineyard. Varietally labeled wines for export must contain 85 percent of the named variety. To qualify as an "estate" wine, all the grapes must be produced from grapes grown on the producer's own property or adjacent vineyards cultivated in the same manner.

Pinotage—a South African Creation

- Pinotage is a grape variety that was created in 1925 by Abraham Izak Perold, the first professor of viticulture at Stellenbosch University.

- It's a cross of Pinot Noir and Cinsault that bears little resemblance to either parent.

- Pinotage is a thick, almost opaque red. Drinking it is like biting into a very ripe plum. South Africa is the only major supplier, but two California wineries have offered it. Pinotage has a worldwide following, and there is a South Africa–based Pinotage Association.

Kanonkop Pinotage

- If South Africa is compared to Bordeaux, Kanonkop Wine Estate would be considered one of a handful of Première Grand Cru wineries.

- Kanonkop is one of South Africa's most awarded wineries. Platter's Guide to wines and wineries of South Africa named it its 2009 Winery of the Year. Kanonkop's winemaker, Abrie Beeslaar, was voted International Winemaker of the Year at London's 2008 International Wine & Spirits Competition.

- Kanonkop was one of the first wineries to establish Pinotage as a commercial crop and that variety has become a specialty of the winery.

OTHER REGIONS

ISRAEL
Stunning red wines are made in a lean European style from a warm region

Many Christians and Jews consider Israel to be the birthplace of wine. According to the book of Genesis, Noah planted the first vineyard. And there are 168 references to vines and vineyards in the Old Testament. Wine figured prominently in Israel until the Muslim conquest in 636 AD.

Winemaking lay fallow in Israel until 1870, when Baron Edmond de Rothschild (son of James de Rothschild, who purchased Bordeaux's Château Lafite) restarted Israel's wine industry with an infusion of 60 million gold francs, many times more than his father had paid for Ch. Lafite. His winery was called "Rishon Le Zion" and still operates as Israel's largest winery, exporting wines under the "Carmel" label.

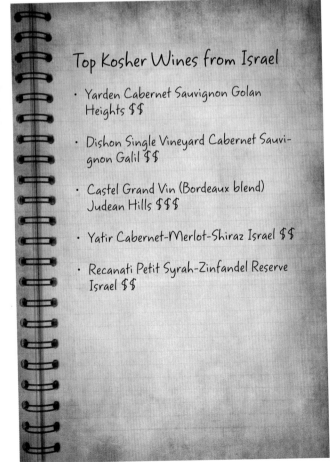

Top Kosher Wines from Israel

- Yarden Cabernet Sauvignon Golan Heights $$
- Dishon Single Vineyard Cabernet Sauvignon Galil $$
- Castel Grand Vin (Bordeaux blend) Judean Hills $$$
- Yatir Cabernet-Merlot-Shiraz Israel $$
- Recanati Petit Syrah-Zinfandel Reserve Israel $$

Israeli Vineyard

- The coolest Israeli wine-growing areas are the Golan Heights and Upper Galilee. Golan soils are volcanic and elevated (3,500 feet); Galilee soils are iron-rich Terra Rosa. Both terroirs yield splendid Cabernet Sauvignon.

- Heavy clay soils are found in the coastal plain region of Shomron. These soils are detrimental to viticulture in regions receiving adequate rainfall. In central Israel they are a blessing.

- The Judean Hills surrounding Jerusalem are the fastest-growing wine region in Israel.

186

It would take another hundred years before creditable wine would flow from Israel. The spark that ignited the modern Israeli wine industry was the acquisition of Syria's Golan Heights, the only relatively cool wine-growing region in the country. At elevations around 3,500 feet, the Golan Heights possessed excellent volcanic soils perfectly suited to viticulture. And by the late 1980s superior Cabernet Sauvignon from Israel found its place in the export market.

Today wineries dot the entire country from Galilee in the north to the Negev Desert in the south.

ZOOM

The major wine-growing regions in Israel (north to south) are Galilee (Galil), including Golan Heights; Samaria (Shomron), on the coast south of Haifa; Samson (Shimshon), in the hills south of Tel Aviv; Judean Hills (Harey Yehuda), between Jerusalem and the Dead Sea; and Negev, south of the Dead Sea.

An Israeli Wine Bar

- Over the past decade, Israel has embraced a wine culture second to none in the world.

- The first of Israel's wine bars opened in Jaffa just a few years ago. Now they are in all of Israel's major cities.

- Israel patterned its wine bars after Spain's tapas bars. Finger foods and small plates are offered along with wines by the glass or bottle.

- Wines sold in Israeli wine bars reflect only a very modest markup, so the bars become social gathering places much like England's pubs.

Yarden Cabernet Sauvignon

- Yarden Cabernet Sauvignon ($$) was the wine that catapulted Israeli wine into the international spotlight.

- It was the first Israeli wine to appear in the *Wine Spectator's* top one hundred wines of the world.

- Yarden (Jordan) is the top brand of the Golan Heights Winery. Other brands are Gamla and Golan.

- The Golan Heights Winery produces around 6 million bottles annually, 30 percent of which is exported.

GREECE
Ancient vines grow amid a modern wine revolution

The story of Greek wine might be compared with the course of Western civilization. A golden age of science and philosophy became lost and devastated by the Dark Ages, after which a rebirth of art and science refashioned the course of events for future generations.

The Greeks certainly didn't invent winemaking. That honor probably should be reserved for the Georgians. But a vast number of indigenous wine grapes are found all over Greece, many with ancient pedigrees. Over three hundred varieties have been catalogued so far—more than any other country except Italy.

Winemaking in classical Greece was certainly crude, and additives were commonly used to tame the bitter tannins. The most common of these were pine pitch and seawater.

KNACK WINE BASICS

Greece's Top Wine Grapes

- Assyrtiko: dry, refreshing white from Santorini

- Muscat: aromatic white grape of Samos, Patra, Rhodes, and Cephalonia

- Moschofilero: major aromatic and flowery white grape of the Peloponnese

- Agiorghitiko: Greece's noblest red grape

- Xinomavro: distinctive red grape of Macedonia and Thrace

- Mavrodaphne: common blending red grape of the Peloponnese

A Greek Vineyard

- Greek vineyards occupy a 450-mile swath of longitude from the mountains of Macedonia to Crete. Vineyard elevations rise from sea level to 2,600 feet.

- Most Greek vineyards are planted on rocky limestone soils of low to medium fertility.

- The overwhelming majority of Greek vineyards are very small parcels of land, giving rise to the cooperatives.

- Traditional Greek varieties are usually bush pruned or allowed to grow into trees. Imported varieties are usually trained on trellises.

Greece's most significant contribution to the world of wine was its export of vine stock to southern Italy, where it found a happier environment than anywhere in the homeland. Ancient Greek varieties such as Greco and Malvasia formed a foundation upon which the southern Italian wine industry was founded.

Greek winemaking collapsed in the late fifteenth century with the conquest by the Ottoman Turks. Winemaking did not resume on any scale until Greek independence in 1913 but was slow in developing. The modern Greek wine industry did not flower until the 1990s and is just now finding its footing.

The best Greek table wines so far are blends of Greek and international varieties, but a strong movement is afoot to deny appellation labeling to any wine with more than 50 percent "foreign" grapes.

Greece's most-exciting wines are the products of small wineries. Most exports are products of four cooperatives, established in the late nineteenth century: Achaia Clauss, Boutari and its subsidiary Cambas, Tsantalis, and Kourtakis.

Retsina—Greece's Traditional Wine

- Retsina reflects ancient winemaking practices used throughout the eastern Mediterranean.

- In classical and preclassical times when wine was fragile and subject to rapid oxidation, many wines were resinated. Typical large amphoras, holding up to 50 gallons, were lined with pine pitch as a sealer, and pieces of pine pitch were added to the grape must during fermentation.

- Modern export Retsina is a white wine with strong turpentine notes that many find offensive. Others consider it an acquired taste.

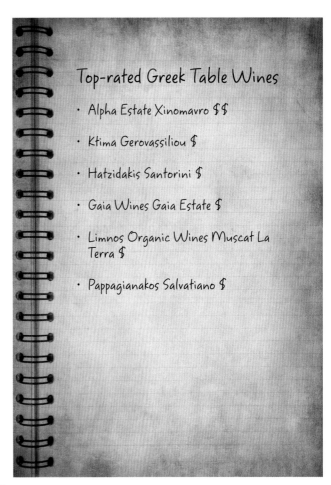

Top-rated Greek Table Wines

- Alpha Estate Xinomavro $$
- Ktima Gerovassiliou $
- Hatzidakis Santorini $
- Gaia Wines Gaia Estate $
- Limnos Organic Wines Muscat La Terra $
- Pappagianakos Salvatiano $

HUNGARY
New wines rival New Zealand Sauvignon Blanc, French Sauternes, and Alsatian Pinot Gris

Hungary is poised to surpass its former glory after a generation of lethargy initiated by a set of regulations and procedures put in place under Soviet domination. The historic wines of Hungary were among the world's most treasured. In the seventeenth and eighteenth centuries the wines of Tokaji were the most expensive and cherished wines in the world, coveted by the czars of Russia.

A flash-in-the-pan occurred in the 1960s when an attempt to reestablish the quality of Hungarian table wines was made, but Hungary's most-famous red wine, Egri Bikavér, had been so emasculated that the entire industry's reputation suffered.

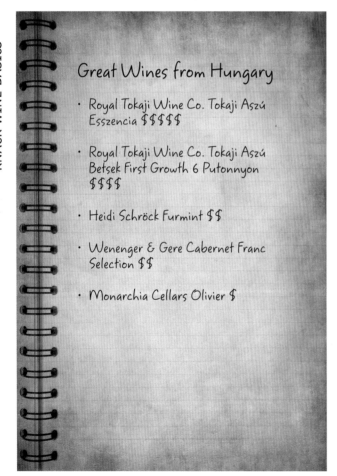

Great Wines from Hungary

- Royal Tokaji Wine Co. Tokaji Aszú Esszencia $$$$$

- Royal Tokaji Wine Co. Tokaji Aszú Betsek First Growth 6 Putonnyon $$$$

- Heidi Schröck Furmint $$

- Wenenger & Gere Cabernet Franc Selection $$

- Monarchia Cellars Olivier $

A Winery near Lake Balaton

- The modern wine industry of Hungary is dominated by hundreds of small vineyard owners, many of whom make excellent wines for local consumption.

- Because the Hungarian wine industry is still recovering from the doldrums of the past, there are very few quality exports except for Tokaji Aszú. Hungary's traditional fine red variety, Kadarka, has fallen into decline with the growth of international varieties. The current export market for Hungarian wines is largely based on international varieties made by itinerant winemakers.

A renaissance of viticulture and winemaking is now under way and rapidly gaining momentum as modern methods and international varieties are adopted. Chardonnay and Sauvignon Blanc are enjoying particular success. But Hungary's native grapes are playing a role, too. Furmint, the great grape of Tokaji, is now offered in a dry style that is exciting the modern market. It's been compared with the best Vouvrays from the Loire. Dry Hungarian white wines will assume a greater presence in international markets as their quality becomes better known.

The star of Hungarian wine has always been Tokaji Aszú. Tokaji Aszú is made in a way unlike all other dessert wines. A mixture of grapes is used, Furmint being prominent. It's made in a range of quality levels, and the highest-quality examples can cost as much as $1,000 per liter.

Tokaji Aszú is characterized by flavors of honey, apricots, butterscotch, and citrus. Its exquisite acid balance keeps the sweetness in check. Often enjoyed alone, it pairs well with foie gras, fruit tarts, and blue cheeses.

Egri Bikavér

- This is Hungary's best-known exported table wine. The name means "bull's blood of Eger."

- Eger is a region near Tokaji in northeast Hungary. In former days its wines were highly prized. They are blends of three or more native varieties.

- After the Soviet occupation, Egri Bikavér became a blend of the best and worst wines of the region. Those wines are still in commerce. Quality Egri Bikavér is rarely seen in American and British markets.

Tokaji Aszú—King of Wines

- Tokaji Aszú is made in a unique way. The free-run juice is separated and fermented. It takes over a decade to complete fermentation. This is Esszencia, the most prized Tokaji.

- The remaining must (skins and pips) is made into a paste and introduced into a dry base wine for re-fermentation. The amount of paste used is measured in puttonyos. Six is the maximum, except for Esszencia, which receives up to eight.

- After a long fermentation, the solids are removed, and the resulting nectar becomes Tokaji Aszú.

191

ARGENTINA
Spurned in its land of origin, Malbec finds its true home in the New World

Argentina's wine region is a land of extreme contrasts. Of all the world's major wine-producing countries, it's one of the hottest (up to 107° F) and driest (10 inches per year). It's also one of the highest, with vineyard elevations topping 6,000 feet. At 42 degrees south latitude, it's also the southernmost vineyard area in the Americas, almost as far south as New Zealand's Otago region. Mendoza, Argentina's most prominent wine region, lies at the same latitude as New Zealand's Hawke's Bay.

Argentina's wine-growing areas lie close to the eastern escarpment of the perennially snow-covered Andes Mountains, which provide a thrilling backdrop and an inexhaustible

Principal Wine Regions of Chile and Argentina

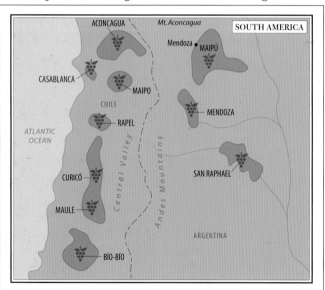

- The wine regions of Chile occupy a longitude of about 600 miles in contrast to Argentina's 1,200 miles.

- The Andes Mountains separate the two wine-growing regions and provide stunningly different growing conditions.

- The Chilean Central Valley enjoys some maritime influence as a result of a series of east-west valleys that punctuates the low-lying coast range.

- The Andes cause a rain shadow on the Argentinean side, providing a hot, dry climate.

A Mendoza Vineyard

- Argentinean vineyards are among the most picturesque and unpolluted in the world. Mendoza vineyards lie at elevations from 2,000–3,600 feet.

- Soils here are well-drained sandy alluvium with some clay.

- In the past twenty years plantings of premium varieties increased from 36 percent to more than 61 percent.

- The Mendoza region accounts for about 70 percent of Argentina's total wine production.

supply of water to the vineyards through an elaborate system of canals and irrigation furrows.

Argentina is the fifth-largest wine-producing country in the world, but only around 10 percent has been of export quality. Approximately 50 percent of the area under vine is planted to high-yielding nondescript varieties to supply a historically unappreciative, if thirsty, population. Argentina's undistinguished Criolla Chica grape is widely believed to be the progenitor of California's Mission grape.

If the Cinderella story were told in viticultural terms, the star would be Malbec, a Bordeaux variety sometimes used to add color to the Bordeaux blends. In spite of the variety's French origins, no region in France possesses ideal conditions for Malbec to perform at its best. Malbec requires sun, heat, and a large diurnal temperature swing to reveal its true nature.

Malbec is now the most widely planted quality variety in Argentina and accounts for the majority of its export wines.

The second signature wine of Argentina will almost certainly be Torrontés, which yields pleasant, soft, grapey white wines reminiscent of Pinot Grigio.

Torrontés—Argentina's Flagship White Wine

- Torrontés is a native Argentinean white variety that yields soft, flowery dry wines. It yields Argentina's signature white wine and its only indigenous grape variety.

- Most of the export Torrontés is unexceptional but pleasant. Fine examples are just beginning to appear in the United States, Canada, and the United Kingdom.

- The best examples of Torrontés display Pinot Grigio–like characteristics of peach, almond, flowers, and orange peel.

A Mendoza Malbec

- Malbec is Argentina's unique contribution to the world of wine. Although some fine examples are made elsewhere, Argentina is to Malbec what Burgundy is to Pinot Noir.

- Argentine Malbecs are deep inky reds with juicy flavors of plum and soft tannins.

- Argentine Malbecs are usually offered as stand-alone wines but are sometimes blended with Cabernet Sauvignon.

- Top Argentine Malbecs are priced over $100, but extraordinary examples can be found for less than half that price.

CHILE

Enjoy affordable everyday wines and world-class Cabernet Sauvignon

Chile is unique among the major wine-producing nations of the world. It's the only country that has never experienced the ravages of the phylloxera louse. The vast majority of grapevines worldwide are grafted onto phylloxera-resistant rootstock. And more than one Chilean viticulturist has trumpeted the reminder that nothing destroys the ability of a grapevine to express its terroir more than foreign rootstocks. Chilean vines are almost all planted on their own roots.

Chile's dilemma is that there is no middle market. It flooded the export market with excellent inexpensive wines, which framed the country's reputation as a source of cheap and drinkable wines. But Chile's high-end wines rank with the best

Main Wine Regions in Chile (North to South)

- Aconcagua: This is the hottest region.

- Casablanca: This is the coolest region. Ninety percent is planted to Chardonnay.

- Maipo: just south of Santiago. Superb reds.

- Rapel: great Cabernet Sauvignon. Casa Lapostolle is here.

- Curicó: Sauvignon Blanc and Pinot Noir. Torres, Montes, and Echeverria are here.

- Maule: fruity, intense red wines

Casablanca Valley Vineyard

- The Casablanca Valley, east of Valparaiso, is Chile's premier cool wine-growing region.

- Open to the sea, morning fogs cool the valley. The valley is often compared with California's Carneros region, which is a prime location for Chardonnay and Pinot Noir.

- Most, but not all, of Chile's Chardonnay comes from the Casablanca Valley. Wines made exclusively from Casablanca fruit will carry the "Casablanca" appellation on the label. If this appellation is not listed, the wine probably originates from southern Chile in less-desirable locations.

in the world. They cost much less than comparable wines from Europe and America. But there's little in between.

Chile's wine-growing region consists of an almost contiguous strip running north and south between two mountain ranges, the Andes and the coast ranges. Rivers draining the Andes flow to the sea, providing ample irrigation for the vineyards.

Most of Chile's export wines are products of Concha y Toro, Santa Rita, and Santa Carolina, all based in Santiago. These companies offer a range of qualities from sound and simple wines to luxury brands. Although these exporters dominate the wines seen in the United Kingdom, Canada, and the United States, they represent only 20 percent of bottled Chilean wine.

Eighty percent of Chilean wine is made by small- and medium-sized wineries. Some private estates are large enough to enjoy international distribution. These include Montes, Cousiño Macul, Los Vascos, Santa Monica, and Santa Inés.

The rise to prominence of high-end Chilean wine is credited to foreign investment in the 1980s.

Carménère—Chile's Signature Red Wine

- Chile's Carménère, like Argentina's Malbec, is a Bordeaux blending variety that has found a more suitable home in the New World.

- Originally thought to be Merlot, Carménère was only recently correctly identified. Many Chilean Merlots, particularly the inexpen-

sive ones, are actually Carménère.

- Carménère features a profound smoky sensibility and structure with dark blackberry notes.

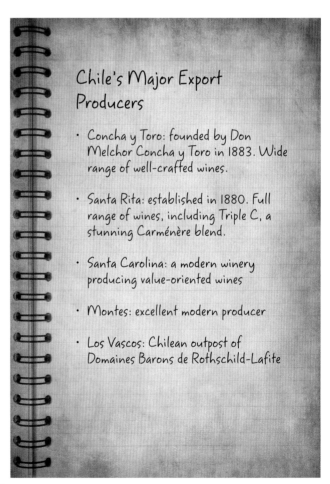

Chile's Major Export Producers

- Concha y Toro: founded by Don Melchor Concha y Toro in 1883. Wide range of well-crafted wines.

- Santa Rita: established in 1880. Full range of wines, including Triple C, a stunning Carménère blend.

- Santa Carolina: a modern winery producing value-oriented wines

- Montes: excellent modern producer

- Los Vascos: Chilean outpost of Domaines Barons de Rothschild-Lafite

CHILE: CENTRAL VALLEY
Clos Apalta and Don Melchor are two of the finest Cabernet Sauvignon-based wines in the New World

Chile and California share a similar climate. Both have a central valley around 600 miles long framed by a coast range in the west and high mountains in the east. Both valleys are major viticultural regions irrigated by rivers flowing down from the snow-capped mountains. But there the similarity ends.

California's Central Valley is the state's least-celebrated wine region, so much so that there is no Central Valley AVA. Wineries that source their fruit from that region use the broader "California" appellation.

Chile is understandably proud of its Central Valley because it is the source of Chile's best wines—and its least. The "Central Valley" or "Valle Central" appellation appears on many

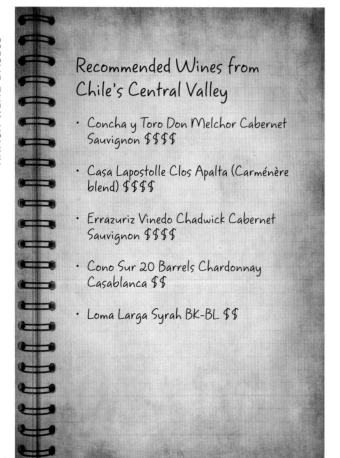

Recommended Wines from Chile's Central Valley

- Concha y Toro Don Melchor Cabernet Sauvignon $$$$

- Casa Lapostolle Clos Apalta (Carménère blend) $$$$

- Errazuriz Vinedo Chadwick Cabernet Sauvignon $$$$

- Cono Sur 20 Barrels Chardonnay Casablanca $$

- Loma Larga Syrah BK-BL $$

A Central Valley Vineyard

- Central Valley vineyards are planted on deep volcanic alluvium.

- Most Central Valley grapevines are planted on their own roots because phylloxera has not posed a problem here. Newly planted vineyards are using American phylloxera-resistant rootstock as an insurance measure.

- Rainfall in the Central Valley is approximately one and one-half times that of Argentina's Mendoza Province on the other side of the Andes.

inexpensive Chilean wines. It carries no more meaning than the ubiquitous "California" appellation. Chile's fine wines use a more narrowly defined appellation such as "Maipo" or "Rapel."

Viticulturally, Chile's Central Valley extends from Santiago south to Maule and is composed of four large appellations: "Maipo," "Rapel," "Curicó," and "Maule." The regions of Itata and Bio Bio lie south of Maule and are planted largely to Pais (Argentina's Criolla Chica and California's Mission) and Muscat to be distilled into Pisco, the nation's most-popular spirit. Inexpensive Bio Bio wines from Sauvignon Blanc, Gewürztraminer,

and Pinot Noir appear in the United Kingdom.

Unlike neighboring Argentina, whose wine reputation rests almost entirely on its Malbec, Chile produces a full range of superior wines, all from international varieties. Chile has no native grape varieties.

Chile's Central Valley wine industry was formed in the 1980s when skilled winemakers from France, Spain, and California formed partnerships to explore the region's potential. Modern equipment and techniques have replaced the old ways, and Chile's finest wines now compete with the world's best.

Concha y Toro's Don Melchor

Viña Carmen Cave

- Both the *Wine Spectator* and Robert M. Parker Jr. hailed Don Melchor as the best Cabernet Sauvignon from Chile.

- This wine was named after the founder of the company, Don Melchor de Concha y Toro.

- It's a product of a single vineyard, Puente Alto in the Maipo Valley, and consistently rates as outstanding by major reviewers.

- Don Melchor is the flagship wine of the large firm Concha y Toro, which offers everything from Pais in boxes to elegant reserve wines.

- Founded in 1850, Viña Carmen is one of Chile's largest exporters. Its modern winemaking facility was built in 1992.

- Viña Carmen offers a full range of Chilean wines from Casablanca Chardonnay to award-winning Cabernet blends. All Carmen wines

are solidly made and attractively priced.

- Viña Carmen exports 94 percent of its production to fifty countries.

- The Carménère grape was first identified in one of Viña Carmen's vineyards.

APÉRITIF & PARTY WINES
Classic starters won't dull your taste buds for the foods that follow

Entertaining with wine is easy if you keep a few simple rules in mind. When you are uncertain about the preferences of your guests, serve wines that are not too assertive. Avoid racy Sauvignon Blancs, very dry Muscadets, sweet wines, and full-bodied red wines.

Although Chardonnay is America's favorite white wine, many are made in an overly sweet style with strong notes of

vanilla and tropical fruit. Such wines dull the palate. American Chenin Blanc may also be too rich and sweet for stimulating appetites.

You can't go wrong with Champagne or other sparkling wines. These wines always add a festive note and prepare the palate for foods and wines to follow. Dry rosé wines are also an excellent choice that has wide appeal. If your preference

Cold Appetizers

- Softer whites like Pinot Grigio work well with crudités, but more-acidic white wines like Sauvignon Blanc and Muscadet cut through richer appetizers like salmon.

- Like all sauced foods, the wine should be chosen to complement the sauce. The

richer the dip, the more bodied the wine should be. Gainey Sauvignon Blanc offers a classic example of oak-finished Central Coast Sauvignons. Oregon Pinot Gris such as the Chehalem Pinot Gris pictured here complements a wide range of appetizers.

Sparkling Rosé and Dry White Wine

- Champagne is perfect here. Serve in a flute, not a coupe. The flute showcases the texture of the bubbles. The coupe causes bubbles to dissipate, and the wine is easily spilled.

- Although Champagne and sparkling white wines properly accompany a broad

range of foods, dry rosé sparkling wines are more versatile. Sparkling roses are not limited to expensive pink Champagne. Affordable pink *crémants* such as Bailly-Lapierre fill the bill nicely. Grüner Veltliners from Austria such as the Hugl pictured above are crisp and refreshing choices.

is for a dry white wine, choose one that's light in body, very dry, and not sweet, such as Pinot Gris/Grigio, Albariño, or a dry Riesling. If you choose a red wine for your apéritif wine, choose a light dry one that's not overly fruit driven. A good choice would be Beaujolais.

Consider choosing a dry Sherry for your apéritif wine. Dry Sherry makes an excellent accompaniment to many hors d'oeuvres, especially Spanish tapas. Be sure to choose a Fino, Cocktail Sherry, or Manzanilla. All other types are too sweet and will mask the flavors of most appetizers.

ZOOM

Classic Kir Cocktail
The classic Kir consists of a glass of Aligoté (any full-bodied dry white wine will do) with a dollop of crème de cassis. Use the best crème de cassis you can find. The best comes from Dijon. The liqueur may be mixed into the wine or allowed to settle in the bottom of the glass for visual effect. A Kir Royale substitutes Champagne for the Aligoté.

Hot Appetizers

- Hot appetizers are good with sparkling white and rosé wines but are even better paired with rounder, full-bodied whites.

- Choose a dry, unoaked Chardonnay, French Chablis, Pinot Blanc, dry Riesling, or Pinot Gris/Grigio for a good accompaniment to most savory appetizers. Alsatian Pino Gris such as offered by firms like Trimbach are more substantial wines and good choices for meaty appetizers. Cru Beaujolais such as the example by Labouré-Roi are among the more versatile red wines.

Dry Sherry

- Kir is the classic wine cocktail from Burgundy. There are dozens of cocktails that substitute various liqueurs or fruit syrups for the crème de cassis.

- Always choose a dry Sherry, such as Lustau Fino, Manzanilla, or Cocktail Sherry for apértifs. Sherry is traditionally served in small stemware that is filled to the top because Sherry is not swirled. In Spain it's served in a 10-ounce tulip-shaped stem called a *"copita."*

199

WINES FOR SOUP & SALAD COURSES
Useful wine pairings for difficult food courses

Pairing wines with soup and salad courses can be very tricky, so some people choose to forgo serving wine entirely with these courses. Others carry over the apéritif wine into the soup or salad course.

There are some established traditions: Clear soups are often paired with fortified wines such as dry Sherry or dry Madeira. Madeira makes a perfect complement to consommé. The fullness and high alcohol of fortified wines provide an interesting contrast and textural element. Avoid overly sweet fortified wines with these courses.

Cream soups also pair well with dry fortified wines, and richly flavored soups can work well with medium-dry fortified wines such as Amontillado Sherry and Rainwater Madeira.

Seafood soups call for dry wines. If the base is creamy, as

Consommé with Garnish

- Clear soups are best paired with fortified wines such as dry Sherry, dry Portuguese Moscatel, or Madeira like the delicious Rainwater from Broadbent.

- Champagne and sparkling wines can work well, but choose one with a touch of sweetness, such as an extra dry or sparkling Vouvray. Avoid "Natural" and Brut sparkling wines.

- For clear chicken broth–based soups, off-dry white wines such as a Kabinett Riesling can be paired.

Cream Soup

- Chowders and creamy seafood bisques call for a light, unoaked white wine with medium body, such as Albariño, Gruner Veltliner, or dry Riesling.

- Avoid bone-dry wines with racy acidity such as Muscadet, Viura, Trebbiano, or very dry Sauvignon Blanc.

- These wines will cleanse the palate but provide little complement to the soup.

- Delicate cream soups based on vegetable purees are best paired with very light, dry, unoaked wines such as Fulget Albariño or the Silver Chardonnay pictured above.

in a chowder or bisque, choose a full-bodied white such as Pinot Blanc or dry Chenin Blanc. A hint of sweetness in the wine can provide an excellent complement. Kabinett Rieslings would be a good choice also.

For tomato-based seafood soups such as bouillabaisse and ioppino, choose a medium-bodied red wine such as Beaujolais, Valpolicella, Barbera, or a light Pinot Noir.

Salads present a special problem because they are usually dressed with a vinegar or lemon-based dressing. The sharpness of the vinegar ruins the taste of most wines—but not all.

Try a bone-dry rosé or Brut Champagne with vinegar-based salads. Neutralize the acidity of your salad by adding nuts, cheese, or olives.

Salads consisting of meats and vegetables, such as an Italian antipasto or Cobb salad, are complemented by Beaujolais, a light Grenache, Aglianico, or Barbera. Salads with very sharp flavors, such as niçoise, can be served with an equally bright wine such as Sauvignon Blanc. Choose one with herbal and gooseberry flavors such as those from New Zealand. Choose tank-fermented Sauvignons rather than oak-influenced ones.

Cobb Salad

- Mixed salads are easier to pair with wine than simple vinaigrette-dressed salads because they contain a spectrum of rich flavors.

- For mixed salads such as antipasto, choose a crisp, white Sauvignon or Italian Trebbiano.

- For salads consisting of meat, vegetables, and cheese, choose a light red such as Bardolino, an inexpensive Italian red that is often served lightly chilled. Dry rosé wines, still or sparkling, complement all salad courses. A Blanc de Noirs such as Chandon is an excellent choice.

Cold Artichoke

- Artichokes and asparagus are not as difficult to pair with wine as many people believe.

- There is an acidic substance in artichokes and asparagus that reacts with other flavors in the mouth, so a complex, flavorful wine may turn bitter and lose

much of its appeal. Bonny Donn's Vin Gris de Cigare is one of California's first Rhône-styled rosés. It's very dry and makes a good complement to artichokes, asparagus, and green bean dishes. Dry Creek Chenin Blanc, one of California's outstanding Chenins, has just the right acid balance.

201

WINES FOR MEAT COURSES
Choose delicate wines for delicate foods, robust wines for richer dishes

Meat courses call for special wines that not only provide a suitable complement but also offer a marriage of flavors that results in a culinary delight that exceeds the pleasure of the meat and the wine enjoyed separately. There are many well-known marriages, most involving meats and cheeses.

The old adage "red wines with red meat, white wines with fish and fowl" is much too simple to lead you to the best matches.

Prime rib, a red meat, is good with a range of medium-bodied red wines if it's cooked rare to medium. If it is cooked past medium, you're better off with a full-bodied white. Add horseradish and choose a spicy dry Gewürztraminer.

Roast Chicken

- Recommended white wines are white Burgundy, New World Chardonnay, Chenin Blanc, Riesling (Kabinett or Spätlese), Pinot Gris/Grigio, Albariño, Grüner Veltliner, Roussanne, and Marsanne.

- Recommended red wines are Rioja, Chianti, Valpolicella, Pinot Noir, Beaujolais,

Tempranillo, Sangiovese, and light-styled Grenache. Maculan Pino & Toi is a blend of three Italian white varieties. It has an excellent balance between ripeness, acidity, and structure. Yangarra Old Vine Grenache from Australia works well with more fully flavored chicken dishes.

Roast Rack of Lamb

- Lamb and Merlot is a classic match. Leonetti's is one of the richest and finest Merlots from Washington State. Equally delicious is Yangarra's Old Vine Grenache from Australia.

- With fruit-based sauces these wines are recommended: medium-bodied

Zinfandel, Australian Shiraz, New World Syrah, Spanish or Australian Grenache, and Pinot Noir. Very dry red wines such as most Italian and French wines fight with sweet fruit sauces, so choose a fruity, rich red from the United States or Australia. White wines are never the best choice for lamb.

Poached chicken responds best to a light white wine. Roasted chicken needs a more-substantial wine such as Chardonnay. Grilled or barbecued chicken pairs well with Chardonnay. Thanksgiving turkey is especially problematic because the breast meat pairs best with a soft white such as Soave or Vernaccia, the dark meat with a light red. Serving two wines solves the problem. Or compromise by serving a dry rosé.

The first rule of food and wine pairing: *The wine and food must complement each other, neither one overpowering the other.* Before you open a buttery California Chardonnay or a Cabernet Sauvignon or Zinfandel, be sure you have foods that can stand up to them. Grilled and barbecued meats are good choices for those wines. The second rule: *If your meat is sauced, pair the wine to the sauce.* Poached salmon is nicely paired with a soft, delicate white, but cover it with Hollandaise sauce, and you will be better advised to choose a full-bodied white or a light red. Some classic pairings include duck with Pinot Noir; grilled salmon with Pinot Noir; grilled steaks with Merlot or Cabernet Sauvignon; meat with Chianti or Rioja.

Italian Stuffed Pork Roast

- Try to match ethnic and regional cuisines with wines from the same region.

- Meat dishes with complex flavors are best served with medium-bodied, very dry red wines.

- Recommended wines for complex meat dishes are Chianti, Valpolicella, Primitivo, Salice Salentino, Rioja, Tempranillo, and Sangiovese.

- For meat dishes fully cooked, full-bodied white wines can be chosen: un-oaked Chardonnay, Alsatian Pinot Blanc, dry Riesling, and Chenin Blanc.

Prime Rib of Beef

- Prime rib calls for lighter wines than grilled steaks because the surface of the meat is less caramelized.

- Wines for prime rib must be chosen with regard to the doneness of the meat. Choose medium-bodied dry reds for rare to medium; full-bodied whites for medium-well to well done.

- Marshall Cellars' highly-rated Juliet Peery is a Cabernet-based proprietary blend from two of Napa Valley's most distinguished vineyards. For a rich and seductive choice, consider a top Châteauneuf-du-Pape from Château La Nerthe.

WINES FOR SPICY & ETHNIC FOODS

Beer may be the beverage of choice for these foods, but wonderful wine alternatives exist

Wine is not often associated with the cuisines of Asia, India, the Middle East, and Mexico, even though wine is produced in all those regions.

The cuisines of most of the non-European world developed with other beverages in mind, mostly beer and ale. Those are usually considered beverages of choice for ethnic and spicy foods. But today wine is becoming increasingly popular worldwide simply because every food can be complemented with wine.

A principal issue is the Third World's dependence on capsicum, or chili peppers. Chile adds depth of flavor to many foods but also heat that makes wine pairing difficult.

Chinese Stir-fry

- For delicately seasoned vegetable or chicken-based dishes, choose a crisp white wine such as a French or California Sauvignon Blanc. New Zealand Sauvignons may be too overpowering. If ginger is prominent, consider a dry Gewürztraminer.

- A dry Kabinett Riesling such as Selbach-Oster's from Germany's Mosel Valley provides an excellent pairing for many stir-fried dishes. If the dish is on the spicy side, try a Zinfandel such as St. Amant's Old Vine Zinfandel from Lodi, California.

Thai Curry

- Intensely flavored curries require more assertive wines than do delicate stir-fries.

- Because Thai curries are sweet, avoid high-acid wines. They will not complement this cuisine.

- Rombauer Chardonnay

from California's Carneros region has a complex minerality and slight sweetness that marries well with many Thai dishes. Fuller-bodied Thai dishes work nicely with Grenache. The Tres Picos Grenache from Spain's Borsao region is deep and sweet.

Rich spice and heat are mitigated and complemented by sweetness. So wines such as Gewürztraminer, sweeter Rieslings, and Zinfandel often pair well with these foods.

Sake, a rice wine, is thought to be the ideal wine for many Oriental foods, but other wines work very well, too. Ethnic foods with delicate flavors such as sushi, sashimi, tempura, and mild stir-fries are beautifully matched with complex, dry, white wines such as Viognier. Another good choice is a bone-dry Chenin Blanc such as Savennieres. Muscadet would also be appropriate.

Indian Curry

- Choose the wine according to the intensity and heat of the dish.

- Most Indian curries served in restaurants are moderately spiced, but the wine must not overpower the delicacy of the spices.

- Choose a soft, off-dry white such as Albariño, Soave, Vernaccia, Kabinett Riesling, Malvasia Bianca, or Tocai Friulano. Zinfandel pairs well with richly spiced Indian dishes. Ravenswood offers an extensive lineup. A dry Riesling such a Chateau Ste.-Michelle is a good choice for vegetarian Indian dishes.

Tex-Mex Chili

- Choose a full-bodied, bold, fruity red wine. Avoid overly complex wines because spicy food always takes center stage.

- The spiciness of these chilies overpower any delicate wine. You want a powerful red wine with forward fruit and a note of sweetness.

- A full-bodied Zinfandel like Neyers is a great match for the meaty, spicy flavors of chili. A Petite Sirah from Rosenblum provides even more body and darker fruit flavors.

CLASSIC PAIRINGS

WINES FOR DESSERT COURSES

Dessert wines should be slightly less sweet than the foods they accompany

Pairing wine with desserts can be difficult because you need to balance the sweetness of the food with the sweetness of the wine.

Coffee or tea is always an option, but some wines can be surprisingly good with sweet desserts.

Wines with greater apparent sweetness do not comple-

ment foods that appear less sweet. But if the wine is not sweet enough, the sweetness of the food will make the wine taste more acidic than it really is.

The key is balance. Dessert wines must appear to be just slightly less sweet than the foods they accompany. Good candidates might be Auslese Rieslings, Alsatian Gewürztraminers,

Fruit Tart

- Fruit tarts are easy desserts to pair with wine because fruit and wine have a natural affinity.

- The flavors are not intense, so choose a light, medium-sweet white wine such as Muscat Canelli, Spätlese

Riesling, or Gewürztraminer. A Missouri dry Vignoles would work well, too.

- A sweet Riesling like Karls-müle Spätlese is an ideal choice for a fruit tart or any fruit dessert that isn't too acidic.

Crème Brulée

- Sweet, creamy textures call for a wine with fuller body and greater sweetness.

- A California–style rich Chardonnay might work well or a New World Chenin Blanc.

- The creaminess and caramelized sugar would allow even sweeter wines to pair.

Try a Tokaji Aszú, Quarts de Chaumes, Canadian or German Ice Wine, or Sauternes. Pine Ridge offers a splendid complexe blend of Chardonnay and Viognier that offsets the sweetness of crème brulée. Mission Hill's Ice Wine from Canada's Okanagan Valley offers flavors of apricots, honey, and raisins.

or sweet Vouvrays. A quality Asti Spumante works well with many desserts. An excellent choice for most desserts is a sweet Champagne or sparkling wine. These are labeled *"Doux."* Most wines listed as dessert wines are really desserts in themselves. Sauternes—a great sweet wine—pairs better with organ meats than with apple pie. It and others like it complement fruit very well but not cakes and pies. Late-harvest wines make difficult matches with foods and should be avoided for most dessert courses except for late-harvest red wines. They pair exquisitely with chocolate desserts.

Fruit Bowl

- Dress up a fruit bowl by pouring wine over the fruit. Suggested wines are French or American hybrids such as dry Vignoles, Seyval, and Vidal. Spätlese Rieslings, California Chenin Blanc, and Muscat Canelli work well here also.

- Choose sweet white wines with good body. Delicate wines taste watered down. Martin & Weyrich's Moscato Allegro is a popular sweet wine that pairs especially nicely with fresh fruit. Sparkling wine is always appropriate with fruit. We suggest one with a slightly sweet edge, like Chateau Ste.-Michelle's Extra Dry.

Flourless Chocolate Cake

- Cabernet Sauvignon is the wine of choice for chocolate and Mettler's from Lodi, California, is an example that has garnered double gold metals. Vintage Port, such as Churchill's 2003, matches the sweetness of chocolate desserts.

- The combination of sweet or bittersweet chocolate with dry red wine is surprisingly successful. Port and late-harvest red wines complement chocolate well also. Ruby, Reserve, LBV, and Vintage Ports work best. Other red wines that complement chocolate desserts are Australian Shiraz, Syrah, and Zinfandel.

CLASSIC PAIRINGS

WINES FOR CHEESE COURSES
The optimum choices might surprise you

It's easy to choose appropriate wines to complement your cheese course if you try to balance the delicacy of the cheese with similar characteristics in the wine. But made-in-heaven marriages require more care. Because of variations within cheeses of the same type, different wines are sometimes called for. Those who know cheese best will advise Stilton to be paired with Port or Madeira but

Roquefort, a saltier cheese of the same type, with Sauternes. What's useful in this case is to note the generalities: Both cheeses are blue veined, and both wines are extremely sweet. So we can say that very sharp, strong cheeses call for very sweet wines.

A small selection of wines covering a spectrum of styles will facilitate excellent matches for any cheese you serve. In

Goat Cheeses

- Mild goat cheeses are well paired with very light, dry whites. Try Champagne, Muscadet, or Sauvignon Blanc.

- Light goat cheeses are best complemented by a crisp, light Sauvignon Blanc, such

as Girard from Napa Valley.

- If strongly flavored or soft-ripened, like Humboldt Fog, choose a rich Chardonnay. Chalk Hill Chardonnays are always a fine choice.

Cheddar Cheeses

- Cheddar is one of the few cheeses that is best served with a full-bodied red wine. Try Cabernet Sauvignon, red Bordeaux, or Syrah.

- Cheddar is also excellent with Alsatian Gewürztraminer and Auslese Riesling.

- Both Brut Champagne and Oloroso Sherry make fine, if very different, complements. Sharp, ripe Cheddar cheeses work well with red Bordeaux. Ch. Tour St Bonnet is an inexpensive wine that will fit the bill. Sweet Sherry is a perfect choice. Choose an Oloroso or Pedro Ximenez from Lustau.

the case of a formal cheese course where samples of several cheeses are served together, a selection of wines should always be offered.

Full-bodied red wines such as Cabernet Sauvignon, Merlot, Syrah, and Zinfandel work well with a few strong cheeses, but in general, lighter reds work better over a wider range of cheeses.

White wines with a touch of sweetness, such as New World Chardonnay, work surprisingly well with many semisoft cheeses such as Swiss and other alpine cheeses.

ZOOM

The most-versatile wines for cheese courses include Champagne, Chardonnay, Beaujolais, Sauternes, Oloroso Sherry, and Port. These wines work better over a large spectrum of cheeses than do most dry red wines.

Soft-Ripened Cheeses

- Soft-ripened cheeses range from mild to stinky strong.

- For very mild soft-ripened cheese, Albariños from Rias Baixas are dependable choices.

- Stronger soft-ripening cheeses like Reblochon and Pont l'Eveque pair very well

with Beaujolais, particularly Beaujolais Villages and Cru Beaujolais.

- Very strong soft-ripening cheeses work well with Alsatian Gewürztraminer and Auslese Riesling.

Blue-veined Cheeses

- Blue-veined cheeses include Roquefort, Stilton, Gorgonzola, Danish Blue, and a large number of artisanal cheeses.

- Their sharp flavors and saltiness pair best with sweet dessert wines such as Sauternes, Madeira, and Port.

- Red wine combinations include Beaujolais, Zinfandel, Australian Shiraz, and Italian Amarone.

- White pairings include a sweet Alsatian Pinot Gris, Gewürztraminer, and Italian Moscato.

WHITE WINES FOR COOKING
Choose a great all-purpose white wine for cooking

Television chefs frequently include wine in their recipes but almost never tell you what it is. The usual admonition is "don't cook with any wine you wouldn't drink." That's little help because you might choose to drink wines whose flavors don't properly complement your food.

Avoid all wines that are labeled "cooking wine." These are poor-quality wines that have been salted, making them unpalatable for either drinking or cooking.

For general purposes choose a dry white wine with medium to full body. Unoaked Chardonnay has full body and none of the oaky sweetness found in most New World Chardonnays. Don't choose wines with a lot of distinct flavors, such as Gewürztraminer, Muscat, Viognier, or New Zealand Sauvignon Blanc. They will impact your food in unexpected ways.

Pork and Linguini in Chili Cream

Ingredients

- 2 or 3 green onions, chopped

- 1 large jalapeño pepper or 2 small serrano chilies, minced

- 2 cloves garlic, minced

- 4 thin pork chops

- 1 cup white wine

- 1/2 cup heavy cream

- 1/2 pound linguini or other pasta

- 1/2 cup Parmesan or Romano cheese, grated

- Butter the bottom of a cold large skillet; strew green onions peppers (of chilies), and garlic on top. Arrange pork chops on top and season. Pour wine over, bring to a boil, cover, and simmer until pork is tender, 15 minutes.

- Remove pork. Cover and keep warm. Meanwhile, strain poaching liquid and reduce it to around 1/2 cup. Add cream and continue to reduce until slightly thickened, about 5 minutes.

- Cook linguini and toss with the sauce. Place pork chops on top, cover with more sauce, and top with cheese.

Don't use wines with high acidity and delicate flavors such as Sauvignon Blanc and Muscadet. They contribute little flavor. The main factors in choosing a white for cooking are (1) round, unassertive flavors, (2) sufficient alcohol (12–18 percent), and (3) price. Table wine does not possess sufficient alcohol to ignite, so no need to remove the pan from the cooktop. Recommended wines for cooking are Albariño, Marsanne, unoaked Chardonnay, Pinot Gris, and Soave.

· · · · · · · · · · GREEN ● LIGHT · · · · · · · · · · ·

Most Useful White Wines for Cooking
White Vermouth
Unoaked Chardonnay
Dry Sherry
Marsala

Pouring Wine

- The herbal flavor of Vermouth complements most foods. Inexpensive wines are completely satisfactory for this purpose.

- Its high alcohol content (18 percent) is useful for deglazing pans.

- White Vermouth was the choice of Julia Child. She recommended decreasing the amount of wine called for by 25 percent because Vermouth is strongly flavored.

- Vermouth is inexpensive compared with all alternatives and keeps well unrefrigerated because of its high alcohol content.

Tossing Linguini

- Use about half the sauce to toss with the pasta. Reserve the rest to pour over the pork.

- Finish this dish with a sprinkling of freshly grated Parmesan cheese on both the pork and the linguini. A sprinkling of toasted pine nuts on the linguini would provide a nice embellishment.

- Preparation time for this delicious, easy dish is about 30 minutes from start to finish. It serves four people.

- The only item needed to complete this entrée is a vegetable or salad.

RED WINES FOR COOKING
Choose very dry red wines for savory dishes

Red wines are used for a wide spectrum of foods ranging from the classic French *coq au vin* to *boeuf bourguinnone*. Sometimes specific wines are called for. These dishes are named after the wine and showcase its special flavors. More often a good generic red wine fills the bill quite well.

Never use a sweet red wine for cooking unless you want the sweetness in your food. Red Vermouth can substitute for Marsala when making dishes such as veal scaloppini.

Red wines of choice for cooking can be high in alcohol, but with the higher alcohol will come intensity of flavor and often a sweet aspect. This is prevalent in Zinfandel, so that variety is best avoided unless you want a lot of sweet fruit flavors. A Zinfandel pan sauce or reduction is very good with duck and lamb, but you would choose a drier red for most dishes.

Ingredients

- 4 lamb shanks

- 2 large onions, sliced

- 1 each: large carrot and celery stalk, finely chopped

- 2 whole garlic cloves, peeled

- herbs to taste (rosemary, oregano, bay leaf)

- 12 ounces Chianti, Salice Salentino, or other dry red wine

- 2 cups chicken stock

- 1 24-ounce can whole tomatoes, crushed or cut in the can

Italian Braised Lamb Shanks

- This rich and hearty dish is an Italian version of comfort food. Preparation time: 40 minutes. The long, slow oven braising is largely unattended. Four servings. Brown the lamb over medium high heat in a Dutch oven and remove from pan. Cover to keep warm.

- Reduce heat to medium low and caramelize onions, about 20 minutes. Raise heat to medium high and add vegetables and garlic. Cook about 5 minutes, stirring occasionally. The caramelized onions and sautéed vegetables provide for a richer sauce.

The best all-purpose red cooking wines are European. French, Italian, and Spanish red wines are leaner and drier than typical American, South American, and Australian wines.

Don't use great wines for cooking unless the dish showcases the specific qualities of the wine. Don't use cheap generic reds because they will not contribute interesting flavors to your food.

Adding Wine

- When the vegetables are aromatic, return the lamb shanks to the pan, along with the herbs.

- Pour the wine over the meat, scraping the bottom of the pan to thoroughly deglaze it. Reduce the volume of the wine by one-half, about 10 minutes.

- Add the chicken stock and tomatoes to the pot along with their juice.

- Bring to a simmer. Meanwhile, preheat oven to 275° F.

Level of Liquid

- The level of the liquid should be three-quarters the height of the meat. Adjust accordingly by adding more wine or stock.

- Place the pot in the preheated oven and cook, covered, for about 3 hours, or until the meat is very tender.

- Greek or Italian black olives may be added after the meat has finished cooking.

- Just before serving, prepare a pasta of your choice to be served alongside. The meat is served separately from the sauce, which is tossed with the pasta.

FORTIFIED WINES FOR COOKING

Dry, medium-sweet, or sweet fortified wines add depth of flavor to many dishes

Fortified wines are wines to which grape brandy has been added to bring the alcohol level up to 18–20 percent. Classic examples are Sherry, Port, Madeira, and Marsala. Fino and Manzanilla are dry versions of Sherry, but the others have varying degrees of sweetness.

If you have only two wines reserved for cooking, they should be white Vermouth and dry Sherry.

Madeira and Marsala have similar flavor and sweetness profiles and can be used interchangeably. Madeira is an essential ingredient in certain classic French sauces, such as *Sauce Périgord*, and Marsala is traditionally used to make a pan sauce for veal scaloppini and veal Marsala. Both Madeira and

Ingredients

- 2 boneless chicken breasts pounded thin, or 2 veal scaloppini pounded thin

- Seasoned flour for dredging meat

- 2 tablespoons olive oil

- 2 tablespoon butter

- 8 ounces fresh mushrooms, sliced

- 1/2 cup Marsala wine

- 1 tablespoon balsamic vinegar

- 1/2 cup chicken stock

- 2 tablespoons cold butter

Classic Veal or Chicken Marsala

- This is a classic Italian dish using the sweet, nutty wine of Sicily. The same recipe can be made with real scaloppini or chicken breasts, pounded thin. This easy and flavorful dish can be made in fifteen minutes, start to finish, and serves two people.

- Dredge chicken or veal in seasoned flour and shake off excess. Heat a sauté pan over medium high heat. Sauté meat in a mixture of butter and olive oil until lightly browned on both sides. Do not overcook. Remove and reserve.

Marsala bring a rich, roasted nut note to sauces.

A dry Sherry is the wine of choice for all Chinese dishes that require wine and provides the best substitute for sake in Japanese dishes.

Dry Sherry is also the wine of choice for enriching soups and consommés, although sweeter Sherries can work well also. Formal dinners sometimes include 1- or 2-ounce vials of Sherry to be added to the soup at the table. Port wines are used in sauces only when the flavor of the wine is to dominate, as in Cumberland Sauce.

YELLOW LIGHT

The high alcohol content and aggressive flavors of fortified wines can easily become dominant in soups and foods. Use a delicate hand.

Adding Wine

- Add mushrooms and cook until they render their juices. It will take several minutes for the mushroom liquor to evaporate.

- Add the wine, vinegar, and stock. Cook until reduced by about one-half, about 5 minutes. During this time the flavors of the separate ingredients will combine to make a delicious sauce.

- Off heat, stir in the cold butter to enrich and thicken the sauce.

- Return meat to the pan to coat. Check seasoning and serve immediately.

Plating Dish

- This classic dish can be made using Sercial or Rainwater Madeira to an equally good effect, but Marsala is traditional. Dry Sherry or Amontillado can also be substituted but will result in a very different flavor.

- Veal or chicken Marsala is traditionally served with saffron risotto and peas. Any rice dish can be substituted.

- Chianti or a robust Italian red wine such as Italian Primitivo or Nero-d'Avola makes an excellent accompaniment.

THREE WINE REDUCTION SAUCES
Easy sauces elevate simple foods to extraordinary heights

Wine is a component in most sauces intended to accompany meat dishes. Simple pan sauces use it to deglaze the pan in which meat or fish has been cooked. Pan sauces can be made in two or three minutes by this method: Remove the sautéed meat or fish, pour one-quarter cup of wine into the pan—either white or red—and turn up the heat, scraping the pan to dissolve the browned bits created by the initial

cooking. Reduce the wine to about half or until the sauce will coat a spoon. Off heat, swirl in a pat of butter and serve immediately. Pan sauces are useful for most meats, chicken, pork, veal, and fish.

More elegant sauces are made by cooking wine with flavoring ingredients until the flavors become intense and the texture thickens. Don't confuse these sauces with simple pan

Classic Beurre Blanc/White Pan Sauce

- Cube 12 ounces cold unsalted butter and set aside.

- In a nonreactive sauce pan combine 4 ounces dry white wine, 2 tablespoons white wine vinegar or tarragon vinegar, a few peppercorns, and one or two chopped shallots. Cook over medium

high heat until reduced to half its original volume. Strain out solid ingredients.

- On very low heat incorporate the cold butter a little at a time, whisking constantly. Check for seasoning.

- Serve with poached or sautéed fish.

Madeira Sauce

- Bring 1 liter of veal stock or consommé to a boil. Add 1 stalk of celery, finely chopped, along with 2 fresh tomatoes, peeled, seeded, and chopped.

- Cook until liquid reduces by half. Add 1 tablespoon tomato paste. Reduce heat to a simmer; cook

10 minutes. When sauce is thick enough to coat a spoon, add Madeira; cook slowly until sauce regains its consistency.

- Strain sauce. Add chopped black truffles. The sauce is then called "sauce Périgord." Serve with roasted game or tournedos of beef sauces. They are wine reduction sauces.

Pan sauces are associated with simply prepared dishes like sautéed fish, veal, or pork chops; wine reduction sauces are common accompaniments to the most elegant of food preparations.

Those that include vinegar or fruit are called *"gastriques."*

Wine reductions that do not include cream or butter can be frozen and kept up to three months.

Classic Sauce Bordelaise

- Roast 5 pounds beef marrow bones along with a few carrots, an unpeeled yellow onion cut into quarters, and celery sticks 2 hours at 400 degrees. Add beef, veal, or chicken stock and an equal amount of water to cover. Simmer uncovered until it thickens slightly, 2 hours.

- Remove marrow from bones and dice. In a smaller saucepan sauté 4 ounces sliced mushrooms with 3 ounces minced onion. Add 1 cup each of red wine and stock. Simmer until sauce thickens. Add diced marrow; correct for seasoning. Serve with grilled or roasted meats.

Blackberries in Zinfandel Gastrique

- Boil 1 bottle Zinfandel down to 1/2 cup. Use a tall saucepan because the wine will spatter.

- Add 1/2 cup white sugar; continue to cook over medium heat until sauce reaches the desired consistency.

- Add 1 cup of fresh blackberries, raspberries, or strawberries, remove from heat, and allow to cool. Refrigerate. May be made a day in advance, but don't freeze it after fruit has been added Serve over vanilla ice cream.

- Serve sauce cold over desserts or warm over pork.

WINE WEB SITES
Recommended Retail Wine Merchants

Shipping Note: All the U.S. merchants listed below ship wine at retail prices to customers whose state laws allow them to receive alcoholic beverages through the mail. State laws vary greatly. Most states that permit postal delivery also allow wine shipments directly from individual wineries. The majority of small wineries sell most or all their products through their Web sites or to their mailing lists.

Canada allows wine shipping only within the country. Provincial laws vary greatly.

Wine can be shipped by U. K. merchants to customers anywhere in the U. K.

California: HiTime Wine
www.hitimewine.net
Large selection of hard-to-find, rare, and obscure wines; ships nationwide in the U.S.

California: K and L Wines
www.klwines.com
One of the "10 Top Online Shops" —*Food and Wine* "Great Value and Selection"–*Time*

California: Wine.com
www.wine.com
Outstanding selection of domestic and international wines; very attractive shipping options; based in Napa Valley.

California: Wine Exchange
www.winex.com
Thousands of wines, domestic and international, at attractive prices. Ships nationwide in the U.S.

California: Wine Expo
www.wineexpo.com
Largest selection of Italian wines and Champagne in the U.S.; shi nationwide in the U.S.

California: Wally's
www.wallywine.com
"The #1 wine store in Los Angeles" —*Zagat Survey*

California: Woodland Hills Wine Co.
www.whwineco
Large selection; fast shipping; outstanding customer service.

Illinois: Binny's Beverage Depot
www.binnys.com
Huge inventory of domestic and international wines; Web site easy navigate; ships worldwide.

Illinois: Sam's Wines & Spirits
www.samswine.com
Extensive selection of domestic and international wines; shi internationally.

New York: Bedford Wine Merchants
www.bedfordwines.com
Large selection of domestic and international wines; ships natio wide in the U.S.

Oregon: Oregon Wine Merchants
www.orwines.com
Largest selection of Oregon wines online.

Washington D. C.: Schneider's of Capitol Hill

www.cellar.com

Outstanding selection of domestic and international wines; 160 different grape varieties stocked; ships internationally.

Canada: Winery to Home.com

www.winerytohome.com

Canada's largest online wine retailer; very reasonable shipping charges; ships only to Ontario.

United Kingdom: Berry Bros & Rudd

www.bbr.com

Very fine selection of wines from every wine producing region. Free shipping within the U.K. on orders over £100.

United Kingdom: Laithwaites Wine

www.laithwaites.co.uk

Very large inventory of European and Australian wines; good South American selection. Ships to all parts of the U.K. except for the Channel Islands and remote parts of the Scottish highlands.

INFORMATIONAL WINE WEB SITES

There are many informative wine Web sites that do not require paid subscriptions. The sites listed below have operated successfully for many years and enjoy a wide readership. Some sites offer wine reviews by professional staffers.

About.com: Wine
http://wine.about.com/cs/a.htm
Rich resource of articles covering a broad range of wine subjects; international focus.

Appellation America
http://wine.appellationamerica.com
Sharply focussed source of current information on all major (and many minor) grape varieties grown in U.S. appellations; articles by well-known wine writers, buying guide, and recommended wines from each appellation.

Robin Garr's Wine Lovers Page
www.wineloverspage.com
The oldest, largest, and most popular independent wine-appreciation site on the World Wide Web.

Suite101.com/New World Wine
http://newworldwine.suite101.com
Feature articles and reviews by the present author and contributing authors; international in scope.

Wine Anorak
www.wineanorak.com
The U.K.'s premier online wine magazine; hosted by wine scientist Jamie Goode.

Winegeeks.com
http://winegeeks.com
Extensive site offering articles and many wine resources; extensive listing of major wineries worldwide with links and contact information; discussion forum and member reviews.

Wine Spectator
www.winespectator.com
Feature articles and up-to-date wine information; wine reviews require a membership fee.

The World Wide Wine
www.theworldwidewine.com
Very extensive source of worldwide wine reportage; folksy writing style, hundreds of informative articles; focus is on value wines.

221

WINE MAGAZINES

Periodical publications provide feature articles, current information, wine reviews and graded purchase recommendations. *Wine Spectator* popularized the 100-point rating system now in use by most reviewers. These are the numbers seen in wine displays in supermarkets and wine shops. These numbers reflect the opinions of a small number of experienced tasters whose preferences may or may not coincide with yours. They strongly influence the retail price of wine. A wine rated at 89 points in a major publication will often be priced considerably lower than one rated at 90, even though the quality of the two would probably be indistinguishable to most consumers. Wines that appear on highly recommended lists such as the *Spectator*'s "Top 100 Wines of the Year" often find their retail prices double overnight.

The most widely acclaimed wine reviews are published in the periodicals listed here:

Wine Spectator
Monthly
America's best-selling wine publication. Each issue contains a buyer's guide. WS92 refers to a *Wine Spectator* rating of 92 points.

Wine Enthusiast
Monthly
Twenty-year-old periodical focusses on fine living, travel, food and wine; has over 700,000 subscribers.

Food & Wine
Monthly
International focus on food, recipes, travel, and wine. Published by Time, Inc.

The Wine Advocate
Bi-monthly
Expensive, no-frills presentation of wine ratings by Robert M. Parker, Jr. Considered by many to be the Bible of wine reviews. RP92 refers to a Robert Parker rating of 92 points as published in *The Wine Advocate*.

Stephen Tanzer's *International Wine Cellar*
Bi-monthly
Expensive 56-page periodical containing 1,000-1,500 wine reviews by Stephen Tanzer in each issue. Web version is also available by subscription. ST92 refers to a Stephen Tanzer rating of 92 points.

223

FURTHER READING

Wine books fall into five categories: wine books with a travel focus; purchasing guides; technical books on the science of winemaking; encyclopedias; and books devoted to specific varieties or regions. Buying guides lose currency with each new vintage and are not listed here. Of the hundreds of books currently available, we believe the following to be among the most useful.

Ancient Wine: The Search for the Origins of Viniculture, by Patrick E. McGovern.
A fascinating and scholarly discourse on the origins of wine.

Biodynamic Wine, Demystified, by Nicolas Joly.
An explanation of biodynamic winegrowing by one of the world's leading practitioners.

The Geography of Wine: How Landscapes, Cultures, Terroir, and the Weather Make a Good Drop, by Brian J. Sommers.
An illuminating discussion about the influence of geography and culture on the development of the wine industry worldwide.

Great Wine Terroirs, by Jacques Fanet.
A soil scientist explains the role of geology in winegrowing. The book has a strong French focus, but deals with important terroirs worldwide.

A History of Wine in America, by Thomas Pinney.
2 vols. The definitive reference on the history of American wine from the first attempts in the late sixteenth century to the present day.

Napa Wine, by Charles L. Sullivan.
The definitive history of the wine industry in California's Napa Valley.

North American Pinot Noir, by John Winthrop Haeger.
The most comprehensive treatment of American Pinot Noir in print.

The Oxford Companion to Wine, by Jancis Robinson.
The standard encyclopedic wine reference book.

The Oxford Companion to the Wines of North America, by Bruce C and Jancis Robinson.
A useful wine encyclopedia focussing on North American wine.

The Science of Wine: From Vine to Glass, by Jamie Goode.
Viticulture, terroir, and winemaking as seen through the eyes c scientist.

The University Wine Course, by Marian W. Baldy, Ph.D.
A wine appreciation course and self tutorial.

Vino Italiano: a Regional Guide to the Wines of Italy, by Jose Bastianich.
A must-read book for anyone planning a wine tour of Italy.

The Wine Bible, by Karen MacNeil.
Comprehensive, casually written book on grape varieties, wine-grow regions, and practical information for wine lovers.

Zin: The History and Mystery of Zinfandel, by David Darlington.
Informative and easy-reading discussion on the history of Zinfan in California.

Zinfandel: A History of a Grape and Its Wine, by Charles L. Sullivan.
The authoritative reference on the fascinating history of Zinfandel

KNACK WINE BASICS

NORTH AMERICAN WINE REGIONS

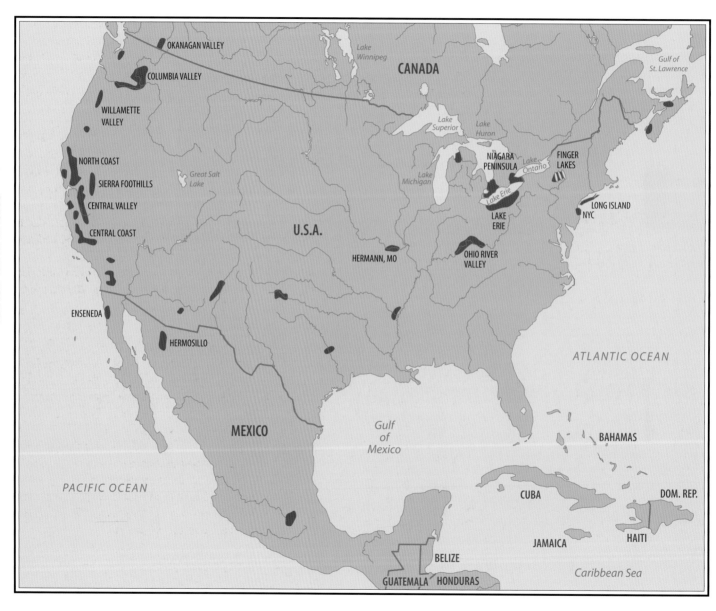

226

No region in the world has challenged traditional notions of quality wine production more than North America. And the road to success has been more tortuous here than anywhere else in the world. Early efforts were concentrated in the Atlantic seaboard states, focusing on native varieties. Tried-and-true European varieties were uniformly unsuccessful in this inhospitable environment and the native varieties produced unpalatable wine.

Eastern U.S. Wine-Growing Areas

Pockets of promise turned up in the mid-Atlantic states in the nineteenth century with Scuppernong in the southeast, Concord in Massachusetts, and Norton in Virginia. The Norton grape is the mainstay of red wine production in western Missouri. Today a felicitous combination of clone selection and microclimate discovery has allowed successful viniculture based on European varieties in the eastern U.S.

The most successful wine-growing areas in the eastern U.S. are in New York State, particularly Long Island and the Finger Lakes district; and in Virginia. Lake Erie is one of the nation's largest viticultural areas, largely devoted to the Concord grape.

California Wine-Growing Areas

Concurrent with the development of the wine industry in the eastern U.S. was the introduction of the Mission grape to the southwest by the padres who founded the missions in California, Northern Mexico, and in the Rio Grande Valley of New Mexico.

The great leap forward occurred in California during the mid-nineteenth century when pioneer winegrowers found a climate that closely resembled many European terroirs. The great experiment spread from Sonoma Valley to nearby Napa Valley and ultimately to Mendocino County. These three counties comprise the North Coast appellation.

Concurrent with the rise of viniculture in the North County was a rapidly developing industry in Los Angeles County, particularly in the Cucamonga area. This industry still exists, although profoundly downsized. South of Cucamonga, the Temecula AVA is a recent development and is now the most promising wine-growing region in southern California.

The Sierra Foothills of California enjoys a tradition rising from Gold Rush days, but its rise to prominence didn't occur until the past quarter century. Nevertheless, some of the original nineteenth century Zinfandel vines are still in production. The Sierra Foothills is home to California's oldest continuously producing vineyard—Grandpere in Amador County.

California's Central Coast is the principal rival to the North Coast. Splendid Chardonnay, Pinot Noir, Syrah, and Zinfandel hail from Monterey, San Luis Obispo, and Santa Barbara Counties.

The bulk of America's inexpensive "jug wine" hails from California's hot Central Valley, but there are pockets of high quality sites in the north, such as Lodi and Clarksburg.

Western U.S. & Beyond

Washington State was catapulted into prominence when the Baron Philippe de Rothchild declared the Columbia Valley ideally suited to Merlot production. Superb wines now flow from this region.

Oregon's Willamette Valley produces superb Pinot Noir which some consider equal to the world's finest.

Canada's modern wine industry developed within the past forty years. Ontario produces world-class ice wine; British Columbia's Okanagan Valley produces a spectrum of wines.

Mexico's wine industry is still in its infancy, although several major European houses have set up shop in Ensenada. Wine from Hermosillo is largely restricted to local consumption.

EUROPE'S WINE-GROWING REGIONS

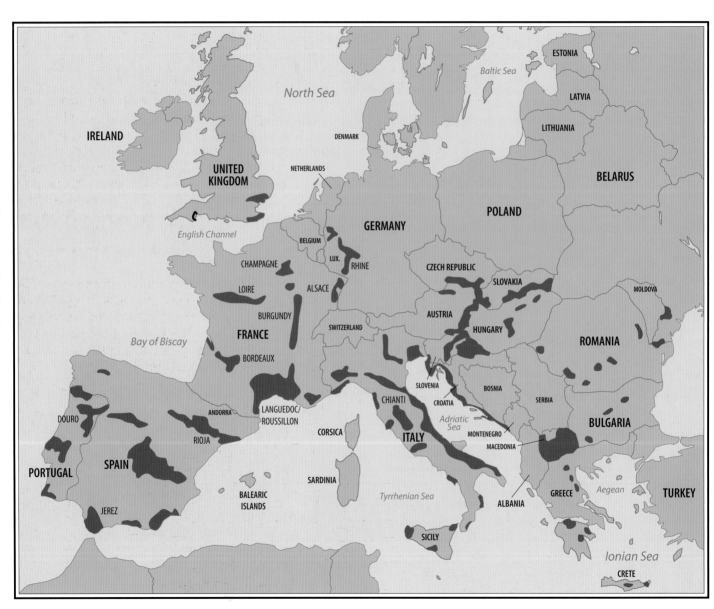

Although it is widely believed that viticulture originated in the Caucasus region, it was perfected in Europe. The Romans were great admirers of the fruit of the vine and brought cuttings to France's Rhône Valley in the early years of the Common Era. These Roman grapes ultimately mutated into some of France's classic noble varieties: Syrah, Pinot Noir, Pinot Blanc, and Chardonnay.

While thousands of indigenous wine grapes sprang up throughout southern Europe, only four distinguished varieties appeared outside France: Tempranillo (Spain), Sangiovese (Italy), Nebbiolo (Italy), and Riesling (Germany).

The latitude of the Loire Valley in France is the approximate northern limit of European winegrowing based on traditional varieties. But important microclimates exist in northern river valleys such as Germany's Mosel and Rhine drainage, Alsace's Rhine, and Austria's Danube.

The Champagne District

The Champagne district is unique. Its climate is continental and ill-suited to traditional winemaking. But Champagne is made from unripe grapes and the three varieties used for Champagne (Chardonnay, Pinot Meunier, and Pinot Noir) thrive there, but do not ripen enough for the production of palatable still wine. The still wine from which Champagne is made is called "clairette," and is not intended for drinking before it is transformed into the world's greatest sparkling wine.

The Old, the New & the Booming Wine-Growing Areas

Two of the world's largest wine-growing areas are the La Mancha region of Spain and the Languedoc-Roussillon region in southern France. These two regions provide most of the quaffable wines for those countries and are sources of inexpensive exports.

Winegrowing in England and Wales has a spotty history. At the time of Henry VIII (sixteenth century), there were 139 sizeable vineyards recorded. That number sharply diminished with the dissolution of the monasteries and again with the advent of the "little ice age." After several false starts commercial winegrowing completely ceased for a quarter century between the two World Wars. The recent success of south coastal vineyards is fueling a new, vibrant wine industry. There are now more than 400 English vineyards. It should be noted that "English" wine must be made in England from English grapes; "British" wine is made from imported grape concentrate.

Italy is the most vine-saturated country in Europe, with extensive vineyard acreage in every province. The Veneto in the northeast and Puglia in the southeast supply most of the wine destined for local consumption. Sicily has risen to prominence as a producer of fine wine in recent years.

A growing commercial export wine industry is developing in Bulgaria and Macedonia.

North Africa lies on the same latitude as southern California. Burgundy corresponds to Washington's Columbia Valley. The vineyards of British Columbia correspond to those of southern England. California's cool Napa Valley corresponds to Spain's hot La Mancha region. Varying climates and terroirs account for the vast differences between the wines of these corresponding regions.

MAJOR WINE-GROWING REGIONS OF THE WORLD

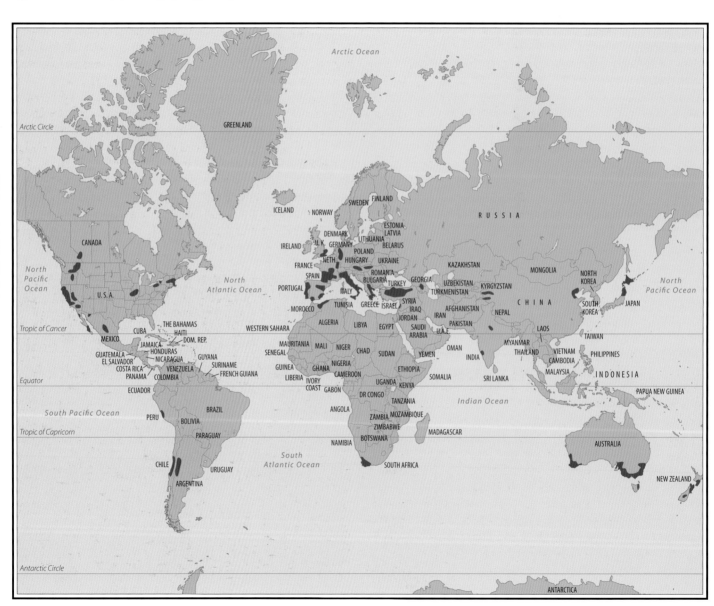

All the world's major wine-growing areas lie between 30° and 45° north and south latitude. Wine grapes will not ripen in colder climates and vine diseases prevent successful grape growing in hot, humid tropical climates.

Prior to the twentieth century almost all commercial wine production was concentrated in Europe, mostly in France, Italy, and Germany. But efforts to establish a wine industry were made as early as the seventeenth century in South Africa and the eighteenth century in Australia. South Africa quickly became a favored source of dessert wines, but Australians didn't become enamored with wine until the last decades of the twentieth century.

Except for South Africa's dessert wine, no country outside Europe was able to compete with the refined products that were a culmination of more than a thousand years of viticulture.

Reshaping the Wine World

In the mid-twentieth century, viticultural studies at Geisenheim, Germany, and the University of California ushered in a scientific approach to grape growing and winemaking that reshaped the world of wine forever. New viticultural areas sprang up in regions previously thought unsuitable for winegrowing: New Zealand, Canada, China, and even Japan. Countries that grew wine grapes for local consumption quickly learned techniques and procedures that elevated their rustic wines to international standards. Chile became one of the largest wine exporters in the world. Argentina, once the fourth largest wine producer in the world (mostly for local consumption), now offers the world's finest examples of Malbec. Western Australia, whose wine industry began in the 1830s, was unable to establish a successful export market outside the country until the final decades of the twentieth century.

The quality of wine worldwide has risen to the point where it is difficult to find poor wine in the export market. There is now so much creditable wine available that competition forces out inferior products. And the taste for wine has filtered down to the middle classes. No longer considered a luxury product, wine is now found on more dining tables than ever before. And prices have fallen to the level of everyday affordability. Decent wine can now be found at the price of bottled water. Cultures previously not associated with wine drinking are now warmly embracing it. Wine consumption is rapidly growing in China, Japan, Russia and the Ukraine. India now has more than thirty wineries.

Fine wine is rapidly becoming one of Israel's most important exports. As Muslim countries embrace modernity and developed countries look to renewable energy sources, wine could replace oil as a fundamental regional export. Great wine exists in Lebanon today; there is a small wine industry established in Egypt; Turkey has an enormous acreage under vine, mostly for table grapes; and Syria possesses some of the finest vineyard sites in the Middle East.

While the world wine map still shows a strong concentration of vineyard acreage in Europe, there remain vast untapped regions suitable for viticulture worldwide.

GLOSSARY

Appellation: The delimited region where the grapes were grown and the wine produced. See introduction.

AC: Appellation Contrôlée (France). Controlled appellation of origin. DOC in Italy, DO in Spain.

Acid: A necessary and desirable component of wine. The primary acid in wine is tartaric acid, from which Cream of Tartar is derived.

ATF: U.S. Bureau of Alcohol, Tobacco, and Firearms. Formerly BATF. The bureau oversees the AVA system and grants appellation status. A new government agency, the Alcohol and Tobacco Tax and Trade Bureau (TTB), has been created to oversee alcohol-related issues.

AVA: American Viticultural Area. Replaces the older appellation of origin system used in the U.S.

Balance: A wine is balanced when the levels of acid, body, and ta nin complement each other.

Central Coast: A large appellation including the California coun of Santa Cruz, Monterey, San Luis Obispo, and Santa Barbara.

Clone, clonal selection: A genetically uniform group of indiv als derived originally from a single individual by asexual propagat (cuttings, grafting, etc.). Cloned varieties are usually heat treatec insure that they are virus-free.

Cru: French term for growth. The finest wines are classified as gr cru (or grand cru classé in Bordeaux).

Cuvée: A blend resulting from the mixing of wines.

Dry: Lacking sweetness. The sugars in fermenting grape juice t into alcohol, but some fermentations are stopped short of total ness. The resulting wines are said to be off-dry.

Eiswein: Sweet wine made from healthy grapes that have frozer the vine. Also called ice wine and icewine.

EU: European Union.

Hybrid Grapes: New grape varieties resulting from natura induced crossings of native and vinifera grapes, e.g., Norton, Se Blanc.

International Variety: A grape variety of *vitis vinifera* associa with Europe. These are the most common and successful of w grape varieties, e.g., Cabernet Sauvignon, Chardonnay, Syrah.

Native Variety: An indigenous grape variety that grows natu in a region or country, e.g., *vitis labrusca*, a U.S. native used for gr juice and grape flavoring.

Noble Grapes: Members of the species *vitis vinifera* that have historically yielded the highest quality wines.

North Coast: California counties of Napa, Sonoma, Marin, and Mendocino.

NV: Non-vintage. The wine is a blend of two or more vintages.

Old Vine: Unregulated term used to describe vines planted prior to the 1960s. Many "old vine" vineyards are more than a century old. As a vine grows old its yield decreases and the flavor components become more concentrated.

Phenolics: Chemicals in wine that are responsible for color, flavor, and tannin.

Prohibition: A period during which the consumption of alcoholic beverages was forbidden. In the U.S. it was from 1920 to 1933. Prohibition occurred at various times in Canada, Scandinavia, Russia, and Australia, as well.

South Coast: California counties of Ventura, Los Angeles, Riverside, and San Diego.

Tannin: An astringent phenolic compound present in red wine and tea that puckers the mouth and makes it feel dry. Tannins are said to be "soft" or "hard."

Terroir: The combination of soil, aspect, and climate that distinguishes a particular vineyard location from others.

Variety: A particular grape cultivar. Some older sources use the term "varietal."

Vineyard Selection: A grapevine grown from a cutting from an especially desirable vineyard. Similar to clones, but not subjected to the rigors of laboratory propagation.

Viniculture: The science and practice of growing grapes for wine.

Viticulture: The science and practice of growing grapes.

Winegrowing: The science and practice of growing grapes for wine.

RESOURCES

Total Wine & More
www.totalwine.com

Paul's Wine & Spirits
5205 Wisconsin Ave. NW
Washington, DC 20015
202.537.1900
www.paulsdc.com
Rick Bellman

Addy Bassin's MacArthur Beverages
4877 MacArthur Blvd. NW
Washington, DC 20007
202.338.1433
www.bassins.com
Phil Berstein

Private Wine Collectors:
Steve Borko
Marty Block

Prop Stylist:
Audrey Weppler
www.audreyweppler.com

Prop Credits:
Sur La Table
5211 Wisconsin Ave. NW
Washington, DC 20015
202.237.0375
www.surlatable.com

Becky Percynski
Lana Papjnik
Richard Hoppe
Philip Fought

Bloomingdales
www.bloomingdales.com
Heather Guay

Kathy Hegwood
Kate McConnell

Ravenscroft Crystal
Zork Pty Ltd

Food Stylist:
Lisa Cherkasky
www.lisacherkasky.com

Assistants:
Suzie St. Pierre
Naz Freidouni
Todd Parola
Dov Block

Café Bonaparte
1522 Wisconsin Ave NW
Washington, DC 20007
202.333.8830
www.cafebonaparte.com
Fatima Popal

Ella's Wood-Fired Pizza
901 F Street NW
Washington, DC 20004
202.638.3434
www.ellaspizza.com

Ed Hanson

PHOTOGRAPHER CREDITS

interior photos by Renée Comet with the exception of: p. 22 (right): © silkova | Dreamstime.com; p. 23 (right): © shutterstock; p. 24 (right): © silkova | Dreamstime.com; p. 26 (right): © Cool(r) | Dreamstime.com; p. 29 (left): © Ene | Dreamstime.com; p. 30 (right): © Tom Higgins/shutterstock; p. 32 (right): © Tom Maack; p. 36 (right): © Sherri R. Camp/shutterstock; p. (right): Wikipedia/public domain; p. 40 (right): © 2007 Jason Tinacci; p. (right): © Peter Griffith, www.sonomacountry.com; p. 43 (right): © Alan Behmer; p. 44 (right): © Jim McCarty/Rural Missouri Magazine; p. 48 (left): Wikipedia/public domain; p. 50 (right): Courtesy L'Aventure Winery; p. 52 (left): © Rachell | Dreamstime.com; p. 54 (right): © Soundsnaps | Dreamstime.com; p. 63 (left): Courtesy of Dr. Konstantin Frank Vinifera Wine Cellars; p. 72 (right), p. 73 (left): Courtesy of Anderson Valley Winegrowers Assoc; p. 74 (right): © Natalia Bratslavsky/shutterstock; p. 75 (left): Courtesy Ferrari-Carano/Vintners Inn/John Ash & Co.; p. 75 (right): Courtesy Ascentia Wine Estates; p. 76 (right): Courtesy Napa Valley Winery; p. 77 (left): © Light | Dreamstime.com; p. 77 (right): Courtesy of Stone Hill Winery © 2007 Jason Tinacci; p. 78 (left): Wikipedia/creative commons; p. 78 (right): Dwight Smith/shutterstock; p. 79 (left): Courtesy A Taste of Monterey; p. 80 (left): Courtesy Paso Robles Wine Country; p. 80 (right): © Chiyacat | Dreamstime.com; p. 81 (left): Courtesy Baileyana Winery © Marya Figueroa; p. 81 (right): Courtesy Laetitia Vineyard & Winery; p. 82 (left): © Dinala | Dreamstime.com; p. 82 (right): Courtesy Cambria Winery; p. 83 (left): © Alan Boehmer; p. (right): Courtesy Brander Vineyard; p. 84 (right): Dcbhs05 | Dreamstime.com; p. 85 (left): Courtesy Thornton Winery; p. 86 (right): © shutterstock; p. 88 (left): © Sparky2000 | Dreamstime.com; p. 88 (right): Harris Shiffman/shutterstock; p. 89 (left): © istockphoto; p. 89 (right): © Jim Feliciano/shutterstock; p. 90 (left): © jeff shanes/shutterstock; p. 90 (right): Wikipedia/creative commons; p. 91 (left): © Alexanderd | Dreamstime.com; p. 92 (left): Courtesy The Bainbridge Vineyards; p. 92 (right): © Zts | Dreamstime.com; p. 93 (left): Courtesy Quilceda Creek Winery; p. 94 (right): Courtesy L'Ecole p. 41; p. 95 (left): Wikipedia/creative commons; p. 96 (right): Courtesy Lake Chelan Chamber of Commerce; p. 98 (left): Courtesy Phelps Creek Vineyards; p. 98 (right): Courtesy Cathedral Ridge Winery; p. 99 (left): Photo by Robert Lorkowski; p. 100 (right): © 2007 Jason Tinacci; p. 101 (left): Courtesy Argyle Winery © Jason Tomczak; p. 102 (right): Courtesy Valley View Winery; p. 103 (left): Courtesy Weisinger's Vineyard-Winery; p. 104 (right): © Ted Crane/tedcrane.com Seneca; p. 105 (left): Courtesy Belhurst; p. 106 (right): Courtesy Broadley Vineyards; p. 107 (left): Courtesy Castello di Borghese Vineyard & Winery; p. 108 (right): © Tom Ligamari; p. 110 (right): Courtesy Jefferson Vineyards; p. 111 (left): Courtesy Barboursville Vineyards; p. 112 (right): Wikipedia/creative commons; p. 113 (left): Courtesy Gruet Winery; p. 114 (right): Courtesy Fall Creek Vineyards; p. 115 (left):© 2007 Jason Tinacci; p. 115 (right): © Michael R. Page; p. 116 (right) and p. 117 (left): Courtesy Stone Hill Winery; p. 118 (right): © Treephoto | Dreamstime.com; p. 120 (right): © Fotokate/Dreamstime.com; p. 121 (left): © Jorisvo | Dreamstime.com; p. 122 (right): Wikipedia/creative commons; p. 124 (left): © Bogdan | Dreamstime.com; p. 124 (right): Wikipedia/creative commons; p. 126 (left): © Akarelias | Dreamstime.com; p. 126 (right): Courtesy Georges DUBOEUF; p. 128 (right): Courtesy E. Guigal; p. 129 (left), p. 129 (right), p. 130 (right),; p. 131 (right), p. 132 (right), p. 134 (left), p. 135 (left), p. 136 (right): Wikipedia/creative commons; p. 139 (left): Courtesy Mezzacorona Winery - Trentino, Italy; p. 140 (right): Wikipedia/creative commons; p. 142 (right): © Agaribaldi | Dreamstime.com; p. 144 (right): Wikipedia/creative commons; p. 146 (right): Gianluca Figliola Fantini/shutterstock; p. 147 (left): Courtesy Vermentino di Gallura; p. 148 (right): Courtesy Librandi Winery; p. 150 (right), p. 152 (right), p. 154 (right), p. 156 (right), p. 158 (right): Wikipedia/creative commons; p. 160 (left): © Breathtaking | Dreamstime.com; p. 160 (right): © Csp | Dreamstime.com; p. 162 (right), p. 164 (left), p. 164 (right): Wikipedia/creative commons; p. 165 (left): Courtesy of Codorniu Winery; p. 165 (right): Courtesy Clos de l'Obac; p. 166 (right), p. 167 (right): Wikipedia/creative commons; p. 168 (right): © istockphoto; p. 170 (right): Courtesy Alto Adige Wines; p. 172 (left): © Jason Tinacci; p. 174 (right): Courtesy of Penfold's; p. 176 (right): © istockphoto; p. 177 (left): © Christian Fletcher Photography; p. 178 (right): Wikipedia/creative commons; p. 179 (left): Courtesy of Morton Estate Wines; p. 180 (right): Courtesy Daniel Schuster Vineyards; p. 181 (left): Courtesy Lowburn Ferry; p. 181 (right): Wikipedia/creative commons; p. 182 (right): Courtesy South Africa Tourism Library; p. 183 (left): Courtesy KWV Steen; p. 184 (right): Wikipedia/creative commons; p. 186 (right): © Effip/Dreamstime.com; p. 187 (left): © Sebcz | Dreamstime.com; p. 188 (right): Andrey Kudinov/shutterstock; p. 190 (right): © Tompi | Dreamstime.com; p. 192 (right): © The Vines of Mendoza Private Vineyard Estates; p. 194 (right): Wikipedia/creative commons; p. 196 (right): © Sparky2000 | Dreamstime.com; p. 197 (left): Courtersy Concha Y Toro; p. 197 (right): © Filip Fuxa/shutterstock

235

INDEX

INDEX

INDEX